Rendering in SketchUp

Rendering in SketchUp

From Modeling to Presentation for Architecture, Landscape
Architecture, and Interior Design

Daniel Tal

WILEY

Library of Congress Cataloging-in-Publication Data:

Tal, Daniel, 1971-
  Rendering in SketchUp: from modeling to presentation for architecture, landscape architecture and interior design/Daniel Tal.
  1 online resource.
  Includes index.
  Description based on print version record and CIP data provided by publisher; resource not viewed.
  ISBN 978-1-118-33277-1 (pdf)—ISBN 978-1-118-33001-2 (epub) — ISBN 978-1-118-33445-4 (mobi) — ISBN 978-0-470-64219-1 (pbk.) (print) 1. Architectural design--Data processing. 2. Landscape architectural drawing—Data processing. 3. Interior decoration—Computer-aided design. 4. SketchUp. I. Title.
  NA2728
  720.28'4025668—dc23
                    2012028296

Printed in the United States of America

10 9 8 7 6 5 4 3 2 1

Contents

Acknowledgments

In my previous book, *SketchUp for Site Design*, the acknowledgments page was inadvertently omitted, so these acknowledgments are intended as a thank you for both books!

First, to my wife, Jennifer Seidman Tal, who helped cowrite both of these books, I dedicate both these manuscripts to you. Thank you for teaching me how to write and for supporting me through the process.

Dedicated to Jenn Seidman

To my family, Nissim, Ruth, Amanda, Eliza, Josh and Jake, Orly, Dave, Karen and Steve, Shara and Carlo, Sue, Joel and Carl, thank you for your support.

Thank you to John Palmer whose definitions, patience, and deep concepts on the nature of rendering, light, modeling, and life (in general) helped shape this book's approach, concepts and, conveyance. John Palmer contributed some of his modeling talent to this book. It would not be the same without him.

A special thank you goes to John Pacyga, who helped review and contribute to the books content and approach. His help was invaluable.

Thanks to Avraham Zhoari, who turned 13 in April 2012 and who is a SketchUp master in his own right. Even at such a young age, he can model with the best of them.

Thank you to my brother, Ryder Cauley, whose teachings, inspiration, and artistic vision grace all the works I have ever done and who was an integral part of bringing this book to life.

Thanks to the SketchUp team for their continued support and friendship: Nancy Trigg, Aidan Chopra, Tyler Millar, Chris Dizon, John Baccus, Chris Kronin, Shara Rice, Tasha Danko, and the rest.

To Michael Brightman, SketchUp and Layout master extraordinaire—always remember the REI Starbucks! Thank you to Mark Carvalho for educating and helping me with complex models and organization. Mark, an architect by trade, was one of the six original developers of the SketchUp program when it was @Last. Many of Mark's building models are included in this book.

Where's Waldo? (rendering by John Palmer)

Thank you to my professors at Colorado State University: Merlyn Paulson, Brad Goetz, and Jeff Lakey.

Jeff Lakey deserves a double thank you for his continuing mentorship!

A thank you goes to the team at ArtVPS: Kate Marshal, Martin Cox, Grahm Wiley, Richard Mead, and others.

A thanks goes to David Wayne from SU Podium for the support he provided.

Thank you to Shane Fletcher (and Chris) from Twilight Render for his endless patience and help.

Thanks to Mark Kosmos, who helped start this fun!

To Jared Green and Terry Poltrick from ASLA, you will recognize many of the images in these books as being from the projects we worked on for the sustainable sites animations. Thank you for the opportunity and chance to exercise a creative agenda.

Thanks to the 3D artists who helped contribute to this book (you can see them in Chapter 5): Rashad Al-Ahmadi, Ryan Knope, Aikio Akabe, Kala Letts, Matea Soltec, Anna Cawrse, Victor Perex Amado, Duane Kemp, and Sid Porobic.

Coen Nannick, thank you for your friendship over the years.

Thanks to SketchUcation (Mike Lucy), Smustard (Todd Burch), and the general SketchUp community. Special mention goes to Chris Fulmer for his Ruby Scripts and being a fellow LA promoting 3D.

Building models by Avraham Zhoari, age thirteen

To the unsung Ruby Script writers, I bow down to your efforts, brilliance, and diligence. You make SketchUp functional. To Fredo6, ThomThom, Dale Martens, TIG, tak2hata, Chuck Vali, Jim Foltz, Rick Wilson, C Philips, and more, thank you!

Thanks to my publisher, Margaret at Wiley, for being supportive and never providing anything but solid advice.

Thanks to my friends and colleagues at RNL: Andrew Irvine, Marc Stutzman, Brian Nicholson, Trent Cito, and Scott Anderson.

Thank you to Diego Matho, whose organization and suggestions made both books possible. He is my unsung hero and deserves a huge thank you!

Thank you to Edson Mahfuz for your friendship, support, and advice.

To Mitchel Stangl, thank you for Christmas dinners and the assurance of SketchUp Apocalypse.

Thanks to Dennis Rubba, who helped me start this path and encouraged me to take risks.

Thank you to Jim Leggitt, whose passion and energy makes anything seem possible.

Thank you, Len Horydk and DynaSCAPE, for the work and exploration I have gotten to enjoy over the past year, which contributed to this book's content.

Thanks to Fred Abler and FormFonts, whose products and business provide the SketchUp community with excellent models. To Alan and Gabriel (and others who have contributed models to FormFonts), thank you. Your models grace the pages of this book. You do amazing work!

Thank you to Land8Lounge and Andrew Spiering for supporting my work and listening to endless conversations about the possible ways to make social networking work for landscape architects.

Thank you to the University of Maryland and Jack Sullivan, FASLA, for his support and enthusiasm in letting me lecture to his students.

To my friends in Hawaii ASLA (Chris, Dacus, Brian Wolf, Drew Braley, Robert James), thank you for allowing me to teach and visit paradise.

Last, a thank you to the Divine Presence of life for the gifts and blessings. My gratitude is eternal.

Overview and Concepts

Introduction to Rendering in SketchUp

This book is designed to teach SketchUp users how to generate photorealistic images using integrated rendering programs (IRPs). It will teach you how to prepare models to be rendered, and it will show you how to use integrated rendering programs to create graphic images (Fig. 1.1 and Fig. 1.2).

Fig. 1.1: A SketchUp model

Fig. 1.2: SketchUp model rendered using Twilight Render

The step-by-step process you'll learn includes five main areas:

- ▶ Placing texture images on model surfaces that appear like real-world materials
- ▶ Adding relevant detail to a SketchUp model to create more realistic renderings
- ▶ Setting up SketchUp to establish the lighting environment for the rendering
- ▶ Fine-tuning the Integrated Rendering Program settings to generate the desired photo-realistic images
- ▶ Altering images in a photo-editing program to enhance renderings during the post-production process

In addition, you'll learn how rendering programs generate an image and learn about the computer specifications those programs require.

Integrated Rendering Programs

Integrated rendering programs (IRPs) are third-party plug-ins that are installed and work within SketchUp (Fig. 1.3, Fig. 1.4, Fig. 1.5). They provide enhanced features that offer big advantages to users generating photorealistic images. First, IRPs use a limited number of menus and settings that are all accessible within SketchUp's interface. Second, they allow you to use SketchUp's features and settings, eliminating the need to learn a lot of new tools and methods. The combination of these two advantages provides an effortless learning curve, which means you'll be producing photorealistic images quickly.

Fig. 1.3: Shaderlight IRP menu in SketchUp   Fig. 1.4: Twilight Render IRP menu in SketchUp

Fig. 1.5: SU Podium IRP menu in SketchUp

Studio Rendering Programs

Most professional rendering artists and offices use studio rendering programs (SRPs) to generate images (Fig. 1.6). SRPs are third-party programs that cannot be directly integrated into SketchUp. To use them, the SketchUp model must be exported into the studio application. Although SRPs offer more features and in some cases better rendering quality for images, they tend to be expensive and significantly harder to learn and master, particularly for those new to rendering. When used correctly, IRPs can yield excellent results on par or better than many SRPs.

Learning to use an IRP is an excellent stepping stone to using advanced studio rendering programs. In this book, you'll learn the fundamentals necessary for using both IRPs and the more advanced and complex rendering programs.

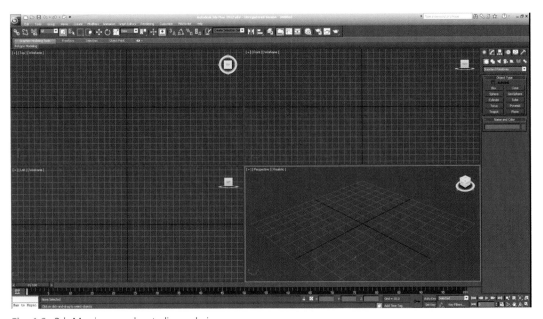

Fig. 1.6: 3ds Max is a popular studio rendering program.

Digital Rendering and Photorealism

The term *photorealism* originally described a genre of oil painting in which the painter proceeds from a photograph rather than from direct observation and then produces a meticulously painted image that appears "photographic" in its realistic depiction of detail.

Computer rendering is the act of simulating the play of light on a 3D model. Virtual light reflects from the model surfaces, allowing them to take on the appearance of real-world objects and materials. The goal is to create images that look like photographs (Fig. 1.7 and Fig. 1.8).

Fig. 1.7: SketchUp model of cover image

Fig. 1.8: Rendering of cover model

This book will teach you how to create renderings with photorealistic qualities. By applying the methods taught here, you will be able to generate images that appear richer and more realistic than non-rendered images exported directly from SketchUp. Don't expect expert results immediately, though. Most users have to work through a learning curve, and their first attempts can range from non-photorealistic to photorealistic (Fig. 1.9 and Fig. 1.10). To generate more realistic images, you'll need to practice the concepts outlined in this book with diligence and repetition. The more effort you put in, the better your results and the faster you will advance, steadily increasing the level of realism in your renderings (Fig. 1.11).

Fig. 1.9: Non-photorealistic rendering

Fig. 1.10: Photorealistic rendering (Shaderlight)

Fig. 1.11: Rendering with hyper-realistic qualities

Computer rendering is a huge and endless topic. It is not possible to cover every nuance and method of rendering in a single book. Similarly, there are multiple ways to accomplish some of the processes outlined in this book. This book is simply intended to be an introductory to intermediate guide for people approaching rendering for the first time.

Using This Book

This book is ideal for many levels of SketchUp users. People who have been using SketchUp to generate models for specific goals or projects will benefit from this book. Intermediate and advanced users can shine with this book, leveraging what they already know to build quick models and generate renderings.

However, if you are brand new to SketchUp, this book is not for you. The book does not offer basic SketchUp instruction nor does it give detailed step-by-step modeling guides. If you are interested in learning SketchUp basics, *SketchUp for Dummies* by Aidan Chopra is an excellent resource.

Professionals and Hobbyists

If you are an architect (Fig. 1.12), landscape architect (Fig. 1.13), interior designer (Fig. 1.14), set and stage designer, woodworker, product engineer, or SketchUp hobbyist, you will be able to use this book to render your models. The process and concepts directly translate to any SketchUp model.

Rendering Terms

The professional rendering community uses many common and technical terms. These terms (*specularity,* for example) can be complex and hard to understand as they relate to the underlying computer science of how renderings are created.

Most integrated rendering programs avoid using or referencing these terms, making it easier for users new to the process or not versed in computer terminology to work with these programs.

This book takes the same approach, not defining or using these terms and explaining the rendering process and methods in straightforward, layperson language. If you are interested in the more technical vocabulary, check out the following link: **ftp://ftp.futurenet.co.uk/pub/arts/Glossary.pdf.**

Fig. 1.12: Clarum Homes rendering (SU Podium) of Green/LEED certified architecture (model by Mark Carvalho and Daniel Tal)

Fig. 1.13: Interior render of school kitchen (Shaderlight)

Fig. 1.14: Brownfield Redevelopment render (SU Podium)

The Software

SketchUp is the core program used for modeling and preparing your model for rendering. There are many different IRPs. This book references most often Shaderlight by ArtVPS. The accompanying online chapters review versions of SU Podium and Twilight Render.

SketchUp

All of the modeling and rendering work for this book has been done in SketchUp 8. If you are using SketchUp 7 or an older version, it is strongly recommended that you download SketchUp 8 or the most current SketchUp version. You can use either the Free or Pro version, but Pro is recommended, as it includes some key tools (such as Solar North, which helps establish lighting) and enhanced import/export options that make preparing the model easier.

If you are using a version of SketchUp beyond SketchUp 8 (for example, SketchUp 2013) the book's content is still relevant and viable. In addition, any of your models or components created in SketchUp 8 or older versions are fully compatible with all newer SketchUp releases.

The IRPs

Many integrated rendering programs are available for use with SketchUp. (The complete list can be found on SketchUp's official website). This book and the supplemental online chapters use three of them: SU Podium by SU Plug-ins (Fig. 1.15), Shaderlight by ArtVPS (Fig. 1.16), and Twilight Render (Fig. 1.17).

Fig. 1.15: Campus building render (SU Podium), part of ASLA Sustainable Sites Animations

Fig. 1.16: Riverwalk render (Shaderlight), part of ASLA Sustainable Sites Animations

Fig. 1.17: Rapid City Plaza concept render (Twilight Render)

The processes described in this book will work with almost any integrated rendering program, including:

Shaderlight, (www.artvps.com)

SU Podium (www.suplugins.com)

Twilight Render (www.twilightrender.com)

RenderPlus/RendernXt (http://www.renderplus.com)

Light Up (http://www.light-up.co.uk/)

LumenRT (http://www.lumenrt.com/)

Maxwell for SketchUp (http://www.maxwellrender.com/#)

Render[in] (http://www.renderin.com/)

Renditioner (http://www.idx-design.com/)

VRay (http://www.vray.com/vray_for_sketchup/)

The processes will also work, to some extent, with many studio rendering programs. A list of such programs compatible with SketchUp can be found on the SketchUp website (www.sketchup.com).

This book focuses on three IRPs to emphasize the universal nature of the book's rendering processes, to expose readers to multiple IRPs, and to provide readers with options in terms of which IRP to use. While the book and online chapters describe some unique features of each IRP, they do not address every tool and function that the IRPs offer. Instead, they emphasize getting immediate rendering results and learning to use the base functions of each program.

Chapters discussing Shaderlight are included in Part 6. Downloadable chapters on Twilight Render are available at the author's official website (www.ambit-3d.com). Chapters on other rendering programs will be available in the future at www.ambit-3d.com. Chapters are being made available online instead of here in print to ensure that the content addresses the most current version of each software program. Please note that the author has no association with any of the featured IRPs and does not receive any compensation for featuring them here.

The modeling and rendering process is more important than the specific IRP used. Which IRP to use from the three reviewed will come down to personal preference. Each is useful regardless of your profession and goals.

Photoshop

When you're first learning to render, photo-editing software is not necessary. However, it plays an important role when you want to adjust the texture images applied to model surfaces prior to rendering—and it's important when you're tweaking completed renderings during postprocessing (Fig. 1.18). The examples in this book reference Adobe Photoshop for postproduction processing; however, other photo-editing programs (such as Gimp) can be used instead.

Fig. 1.18: Rendered image before postproduction (top) and after postproduction in Photoshop (bottom)

Contents and Extended Features

*R*endering *in SketchUp* is designed to provide a straightforward method for rendering. Although some books are designed so that you can skip around as you read, this one is not. You should progress through it in a linear manner because each part and chapter builds on the previous sections. As you follow along, keep in mind the following topics.

Companion IRP Chapters

Software can change very quickly, given updates, patches, and new releases. SketchUp is established software; even with new version releases, the software at its core remains the same. Its tools, menus, and methods have not changed dramatically.

However, IRPs can and will change with new releases and updates. The specifics of each IRP can quickly become outdated.

To accommodate this changing landscape, companion chapters to this book are available online for your use. These review the settings and tools for other integrated rendering programs, and they are kept up-to-date. You should go to www.ambit-3d.com and download these chapters before you continue with the remainder of the book (Fig. 2.1, Fig. 2.2).

Part 6 provides detailed settings and instructions for using Shaderlight by ArtVPS. The online chapters follow the same format used in Part 6. As of the initial release of this book, the online chapters review Twilight Render.

Fig. 2.1: Download the accompanying chapters at www.ambit-3d.com.

Fig. 2.2: Website where chapters can be downloaded

Fig. 2.3: Twilight Render chapters (Part 9) can be downloaded.

Fig. 2.4: Example of Twilight Render.

This book makes many references to these programs and to the rendered images in the supplemental chapters and IRPs. By utilizing the online chapters, you ensure that the book's content and process work in tandem with current versions of the IRPs. And the core content of the book remains relevant, because it can be applied to existing versions of IRPs.

IRP Versions

Each IRP has a free demo version and full version that you can purchase. The chapters covering the specific IRPs (Part 6 in the book; and Part 9 which is online) are geared toward the full versions of the software. The demo versions are not full featured—that is, they have some features turned off (for example, limited resolution options). (See Fig. 2.5, Fig. 2.6, and Fig. 2.7.)

The Macintosh Chapters

The difference between SketchUp on a PC and on a Mac is subtle. Generally, a tool might be located in a different menu or location, but it will work the same. However, there is one major exception: the Paint Bucket tool, which figures prominently in preparing a model for rendering.

The Paint Bucket tool and related functions are reviewed in Chapter 8, "SketchUp Texture Tools." However, the focus there is the PC version of the tool. If you are a Mac user, download the online accompanying chapter "Texture Tools for Macs" from the website (**www.ambit-3d .com**) instead of using Chapter 8 in this book.

Fig. 2.5: The ArtVPS website

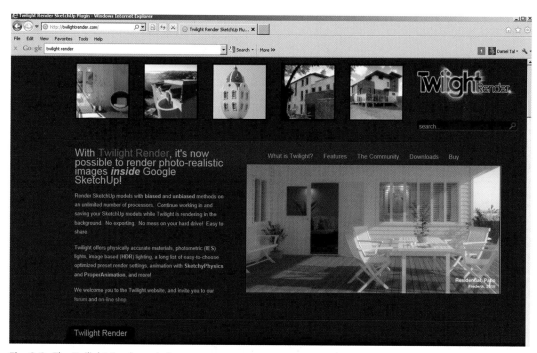

Fig. 2.6: The Twilight Render website

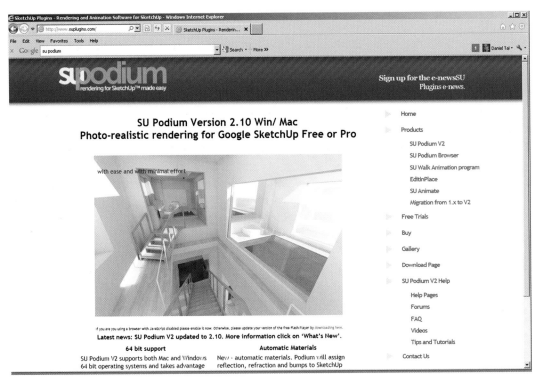

Fig. 2.7: The SU Podium website

Additional Resources

The website www.ambit-3d.com, the author's official online site, contains many other links and resources to use in tandem with this book. The goal is to help you easily find and download the various tools and materials outlined here. It is strongly recommended that you view these resources before continuing with the remainder of the book.

Method and Reference Guide

This book describes specific methods and can be used as a reference guide. The linear progression describes the rendering process. Some chapters provide specific settings for texture values and list exact modeling components useful for detailing and precise rendering settings.

Both the process and reference aspects of the book are intended to be read more than once; they should be reread and referenced while working on your models.

The Modeling Process

The methods and applications in this book have two universal aspects that allow great versatility and easy learning. The method for preparing your model for rendering is the same regardless of which IRP you use. This is true for IRPs not reviewed in this book and for future IRPs that will surely be developed.

You will be working in SketchUp to generate the model geometry, apply textures, and set up lighting using the SketchUp Shadow menu. The IRPs all reference the same factors and settings to generate renderings. This allows you to pick and choose which IRP you want to use and easily experiment with different IRPs.

Similarly, the book's modeling process is useful when working with studio rendering programs (applications that require you to export your SketchUp model). Although more complex to use, these applications reference the same information (more or less) from the SketchUp model.

Because of the uniformity, a good portion of this book focuses on how to add appropriate detail, organize, and richly texture SketchUp models (Fig. 2.8). Parts 2 through 4 focus on SketchUp and the universal process that can be leveraged across all these applications. (See Fig. 2.8.)

Figure 2.8: Interior model in SketchUp. The process for creating and processing a model for rendering is universal. This allows users to leverage their models to be used with almost any IRP.

IRP Similarities

The three IRPs covered in this book, while utilizing different interfaces, all function in a similar way. Each relies on four or five menus and applies values to the model textures and lighting in a parallel fashion. These parallels make it easier to jump between and experiment with the three applications. Part 5 explores the universal aspects of working with these IRPs, and Part 6 delves into IRP specifics (Fig. 2.9, Fig. 2.10, Fig. 2.11).

Fig. 2.9: Interior model rendered in Shaderlight

Fig. 2.10: Interior model rendered in Twilight Render

Fig. 2.11: Interior model rendered in SU Podium

Book Images and Graphics

This book uses many diagrams and illustrations. If an image is identified as a SketchUp graphic, that means it is not rendered. Rendered images will be noted and will include the rendering program used to create the image: Shaderlight, SU Podium, or Twilight Render. All images and models were created by the author unless otherwise noted.

Book Parts and Progression

Rendering in SketchUp is partitioned into ten parts ordered in a linear progression, presenting the entire rendering methodology. Many chapters are short and, as stated, some are reference guides that list specific resources or are designed to help you set up your renderings. Parts 9 and 10, which cover Twilight Render and SU Podium, are available online.

Part 1: Overview and Concepts

Part 1 offers an introduction to concepts, introduces integrated rendering programs and the rendering process, and reviews computer specifications and requirements. The chapters are quick reads filled with important information.

Part 2: Textures

Part 2 provides detailed instructions on how to obtain, place, and edit the texture images that are applied to models. All chapters in Part 2 should be reviewed and mastered. Textures are the key to creating good renderings.

Part 3: Modeling Detail

Having sufficient detail, with the right components, is crucial for rendering. Part 3 provides instructions on how to insert and arrange components to create richly detailed and composed models. The chapters review how to use layers, scenes, and the component browser to efficiently dress up models and specific rendering views. Part 3 includes a detailed catalogue of exterior and interior plant components that will help you build a Component Library for rendering. Part 3 also reviews the essential steps of using layers to work with large models and maintain computer performance.

Part 4: Setting Light with Shadows

Setting the exterior and some interior lighting environments for rendering is accomplished by using the SketchUp Shadow Menu. The many integrated rendering programs reference the SketchUp Shadow menu. Part 4 reviews how the Shadow menu works and demonstrates strategies for composing lighting for exterior and interior scenes.

Part 5: The Iterative Rendering Process

The chapters in this section provide both general and specific instructions on the rendering process. The information in these chapters is crucial regardless of which IRP is being used. You will learn how exterior and artificial lighting works and how to set up output resolution. You will also learn the similarities and differences between the three IRPs and the iterative process that is part of rendering.

Part 6: Shaderlight by ArtVPS

Part 6 delves into the specific use of Shaderlight by ArtVPS. It includes overviews and tables of specific settings for texture values, draft and final renderings, and lighting options. Part 6 references tables and instructions, allowing you to set up your models for renderings without having to guess at the needed settings.

Part 7: The Photoshop Postproduction Process

By focusing on Adobe Photoshop, you will learn how to tweak color, adjust contrast, add filters, and overlay layers to enhance the quality of outputted renderings. Part 7 includes a crucial chapter that provides easy-to-apply adjustments to increase an image's realism.

Part 8: Anatomy of a Rendering

Part 8 deserves special attention. The chapters in Part 8 provide a case study of the entire process outlined in this book. The example focuses on a single model that combines architecture, site, and interior design aspects. The chapters in Part 8 correspond to the previous parts and chapters in the book.

The contents of Part 8 were placed at the end of the book to ensure that the tools and processes it demonstrates were described first. However, you should flip through Part 8 (it's mostly images with captions) while reading the various other parts of the book.

The Rendering Process

This chapter provides an overview of the entire rendering process. To fully utilize the information in this book, make sure you read this chapter. Subsequent chapters flesh out the steps outlined here.

The rendering process is divided into three general steps (Fig. 3.1):

1. Create the SketchUp model, and then add texture, detail, and set lighting.

2. Provide render values to the model using the IRP's menus.

3. Use external photo-editing software to enhance the generated image.

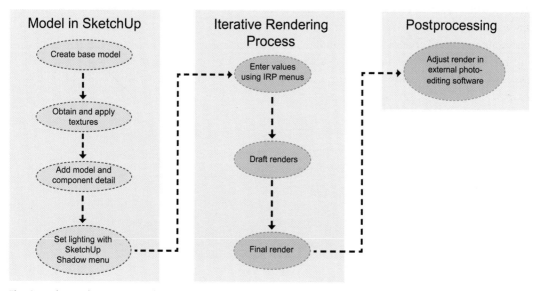

Fig. 3.1: The rendering process flowchart

Create the SketchUp Model

Rendering can be summed up by a simple formula composed of three elements (Fig. 3.2):

Textures + Model Detail + Light = Rendering

These elements are arranged in the SketchUp model and represent the bulk of the work needed to produce a rendering. The beauty of it is that these typical steps can be completed in many SketchUp models regardless of whether the model will be rendered. What's important is optimizing the elements for rendering.

The initial base model is the general model form and intent (Fig. 3.3). During the first step, textures are added to the surfaces concurrently, as the model is being constructed (Fig. 3.4).

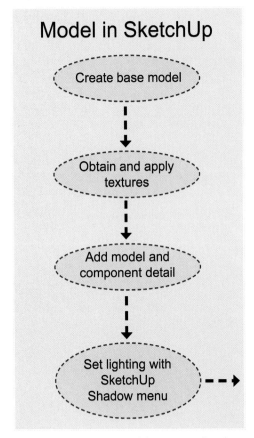

Fig. 3.2: The SketchUp modeling process flowchart

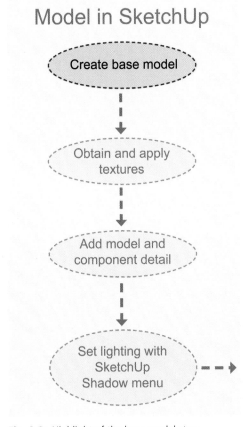

Fig. 3.3: Highlight of the base model step

Fig. 3.4: A base model in SketchUp

Textures

Textures are images that represent materials such as brick, concrete, granite, lawn, carpet, fabric, siding, tiles, metals, and more. Textures are applied to model surfaces using the Paint Bucket tool (Fig. 3.5). Arguably, they are the most important aspect needed for rendering. The quality, type, scale, and appearance of the texture will dictate the quality of the rendering (Fig. 3.6). Part 2 delves into how to obtain, arrange, and edit textures in a SketchUp model.

Throughout this book, textures are referred to with various terms, including *textures, materials, texture images,* and *material images.*

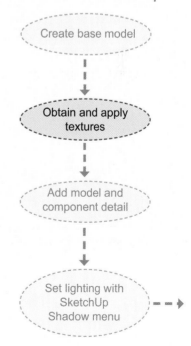

Fig. 3.5: Highlight of the texture step

Fig. 3.6: A textured SketchUp model

Model Detail

Model *detail* refers to additional objects, geometry, and context usually added by employing premade components (Fig. 3.7, Fig. 3.8). The more detailed a model is, the more realistic it appears. Part 3 provides instructions for adding comprehensive component and model detail.

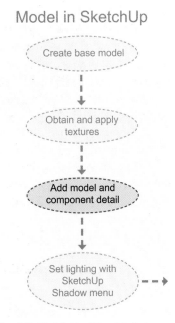

Model in SketchUp

Create base model

Obtain and apply textures

Add model and component detail

Set lighting with SketchUp Shadow menu

Fig. 3.7: Highlight of the detailed modeling step

Fig. 3.8: Detail added to the model

Light

Lighting controls the shadows, time of day, and cast of light in a rendering. All three IRPs rely on the SketchUp Shadow menu to establish lighting for exterior and, in some cases, interior renderings (Fig. 3.9, Fig. 3.10). Part 4 describes how to work with SketchUp shadows and save your camera views for rendering.

SketchUp shadows, visible in the model, are used to set the lighting for the rendering. Simulated lighting in a rendering (not shown in the figures) comes from artificial light sources such as a bulb, fixture, or lamp. These settings are set by each IRP, and they vary depending on the application.

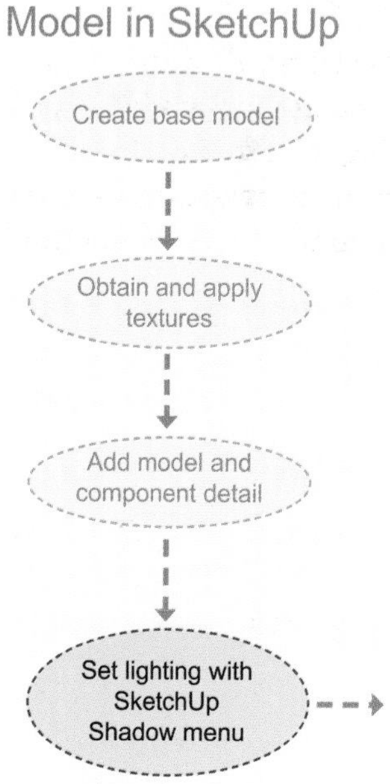

Model in SketchUp

Create base model

Obtain and apply textures

Add model and component detail

Set lighting with SketchUp Shadow menu

Fig. 3.9: Highlight of the lighting step

Fig. 3.10: SketchUp shadows, visible in the model, are used to set lighting for the rendering.

The Iterative Rendering Process

During this step (Fig. 3.11), the various IRP menus (in SketchUp) are used to assign values to textures, fine-tune the lighting, set the image output resolution, and generate the image. This step includes the draft-to-final render process, which encompasses creating a series of draft images, assessing them, and adjusting the previously mentioned values. This leads to the final rendered graphic.

Texture Values

For textures to render with real-world character, values such as reflection and coarseness need to be applied to each material (Fig. 3.12). To do this, you'll need to use the individual IRP's Material menu (Fig. 3.13). Although the IRPs use different approaches to applying values, the general technique is the same for all of them. Part 6 provides IRP-specific values for a range of textures.

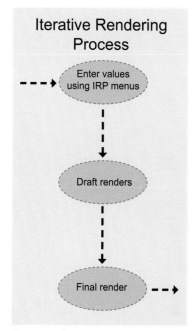

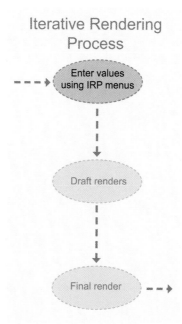

Fig. 3.11: The Iterative Rendering Process flowchart

Fig. 3.12: Highlight of IRP value process

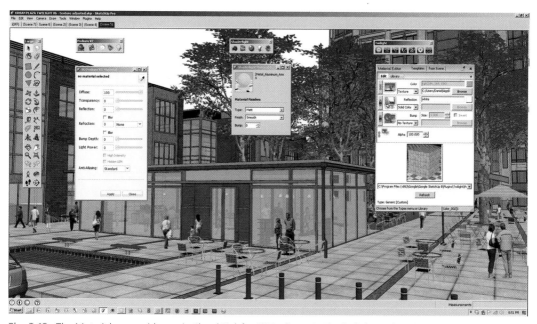

Fig. 3.13: The Material menus (shown in SketchUp) for SU Podium v2, Shaderlight, and Twilight Render v1

Lighting

As previously noted, each individual IRP references the SketchUp Shadow menu to determine lighting. The IRPs adjust the exposure and further refine the lighting quality. The settings allow for a dynamic range of illumination (Fig. 3.14). IRPs handle simulated lighting from bulbs, fixtures, and lights in various ways, but the approach is similar across the applications.

Fig. 3.14: Lighting menus (shown in SketchUp) for SU Podium, Shaderlight, and Twilight Render

Quality and Output Resolution

The size and quality of an image is determined by the IRP (Fig. 3.15). These settings are used to generate draft and final renders, which are key to the iterative process. The rendering quality determines how refined the final rendering will appear. Each IRP allows for a wide range of output resolutions, including standard and custom sizes.

The Iterative Process

Every IRP has a Render button that starts, generates, and allows you to save a rendering. Your rendering is displayed on the screen while it is being processed, which will allow you to monitor the progress.

Rendering images is a repetitive and iterative process. For any given rendering, multiple drafts will need to be produced and lighting and textures will need to be adjusted (Fig. 3.16). The iterative process allows you to quickly assess an image so you can make these changes. Part 5 reviews the process in detail.

Fig. 3.15: Quality and Output menus for SU Podium, Shaderlight, and Twilight Render

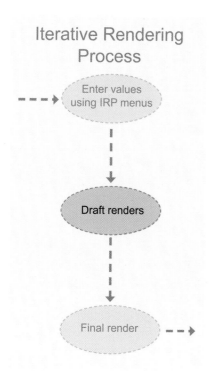

Fig. 3.16: The draft render step

Draft Render

Draft renders are run at a lower quality and resolution than a final render. This cuts down rendering time and allows an image to be turned around quickly for review (Fig. 3.17). As adjustments are made to the model, quality and output resolution are gradually increased, ultimately leading to the final render.

Final Renderings

Final images are the last renderings to be processed at the end of the iterative process (Fig. 3.18). Once all the adjustments are completed, the quality and resolution are set to the desired maximum (Fig. 3.19). Final renderings can take anywhere from several minutes to several hours to process.

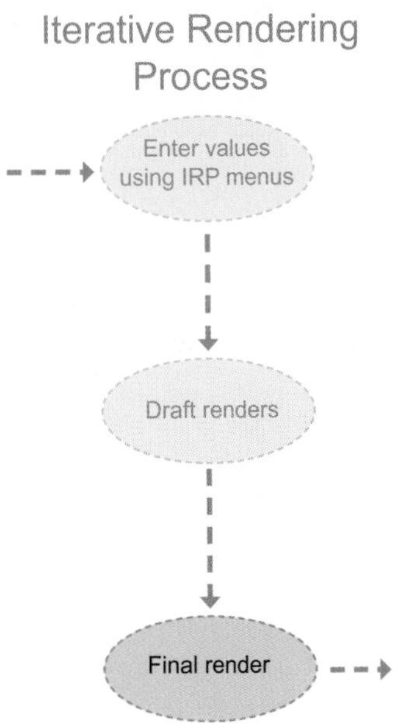

Iterative Rendering
Process

Enter values
using IRP menus

Draft renders

Final render

Fig. 3.18: Highlight of the final render step

Fig. 3.17: Draft renders leading up to the final render

Fig. 3.19: The final rendered image (Twilight Render)

The Post-Rendering Process

Postprocessing is performed on the final rendered image (Fig. 3.20). During this step, Photoshop or similar photo-editing software is utilized to adjust the image. Filtering, color correction, adding entourage elements, and editing contrast are typical adjustments (Fig. 3.21).

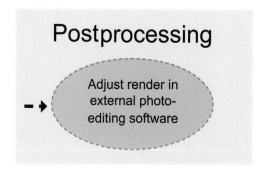

Fig. 3.20: Highlight of the postprocessing step

Fig. 3.21: To produce the completed image in Photoshop, a sky was added, the color and lighting were adjusted, and blemishes were removed.

Many, if not all, rendering professionals consider postprocessing to be a necessary and important step in generating realistic images. In fact, with the right skills, Photoshop can take a poor or dull rendering and transform it into a hyper-realistic image. Part 7 provides some quick tips and instructions for image postprocessing.

How Rendering Works

I n order to understand the rendering process, you need to know how IRPs and computers render images. By understanding the mechanics of computers and their components, you'll be able to save time and ensure that your renders are completed successfully.

The central processing unit (CPU) and random-access memory (RAM) are the two key hardware components that affect rendering. The CPU (the processor) determines the rendering speed. RAM (the computer memory) determines the maximum model size that can be processed. Video cards do not generally affect IRP rendering process but can affect SketchUp's performance.

The computer recommendations at the end of this chapter provide essential basic information so that you can make an informed decision when purchasing a computer for modeling and rendering. (Because computer technology advances quickly, the specific recommendations here will eventually be outdated.)

IRP Render Processing

From the moment you press the Render button to the moment the render itself is complete, the IRP goes through several stages to produce an image. The speed of these stages is determined by the computer's hardware. The following discussion describes the stages. How computer hardware affects those stages is described in the next section.

These stages are not strictly definable. Each IRP renders in a different way and, depending on the setting, stages 2 and 3 can occur simultaneously or consecutively.

Stage 1: Uploading the Model

Before you can begin to work on a rendering, the SketchUp model must first be uploaded to the IRP render engine. *Render engine* refers to the portion of the software that runs the complex calculations used to create and display the rendering.

Once you click the Render button, a new window or menu will appear, indicating the progress of the model upload. Each IRP displays that progress differently, but it is usually displayed as a numeric value or a progress bar. There is no preview image at this stage. The larger and more detailed the model is, the longer the upload time will be. Small models can be processed in seconds, and larger models can take several minutes or longer (Fig 4.1).

Fig. 4.1: The bottom-left corner of the Shaderlight preview screen indicates rendering progress.

Stage 2: Ray Tracing

Ray tracing refers to the action the IRP takes when calculating how light interacts with the model's textured surfaces. At this stage the preview window displays a slowly coalescing image (Fig. 4.2). The IRP will indicate the rendering progress in terms of percentage completed.

Ray tracing speed is affected by the quality and output resolution set for the render and the size and detail of the model.

Stage 3: Anti-Aliasing

Anti-aliasing is the process during which the render engine smoothes the image's jagged edges and lines, helping to soften and refine the image. The anti-aliasing speed varies, depending on the quality and output resolution. Higher quality settings can take a considerable amount of time to complete. Lower settings, common for draft quality, tend to limit or not employ any anti-aliasing, allowing for faster render times (Fig. 4.3).

Fig. 4.2: The Shaderlight preview screen displays the image coalescing during the Ray Tracing stage.

Fig. 4.3: The final rendered image is completed.

Computer Hardware and Rendering

The IRP render engines use complex mathematical algorithms to simulate light (ray tracing) and generate an image, which requires a considerable amount of computer resources to accomplish. The type of computer hardware utilized directly affects the speed of the rendering.

The Computer Processor

The most important computer component that determines rendering speed is the central processing unit (CPU). More commonly referred to as the processor, the CPU affects stages 2 and 3 of the rendering progression.

Processor count is analogous to the number of cylinders in a car engine: the more cylinders, the more powerful the engine and the faster the car can go. The more processors your computer has, the faster renderings will be completed (Fig. 4.4).

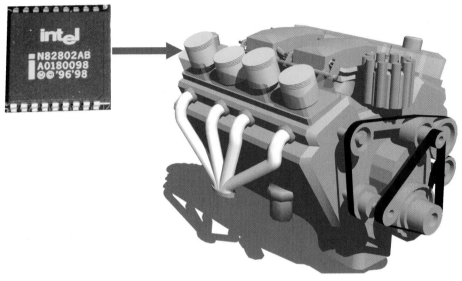

Fig. 4.4: Processors can be compared to car engines.

Generally speaking, each additional processor halves the rendering time. If a render takes one hour with a single processor, it will take 30 minutes with two, 15 minutes with four, and 10 minutes with six. The differences are significant.

Multiprocessing

Multiple-core processing computers have become standard. Currently, computers come with dual-core (2), quad-core (4), or six-core (6) processors. The number of processors used can be expected to continue to increase.

However, more processers do cost more money. The cost for a decent quad-core rendering computer currently ranges from $1,500 to $2,200. In the future, you will see computers with six, eight, twelve, and more cores available for the same price. This revolution in processing is one of the main reasons the average SketchUp user can now create photorealistic images with IRPs. When SketchUp was first released, and for several years after, this was not an option because processing power was either too expensive or not available.

If you're buying a new computer for rendering, make sure you buy the most processors you can afford. Currently, the Intel i5, i7, and Xeon chips are the most cost-effective processors to use for rendering. They are available for both Macs and PCs.

Computer processors are also rated by processing speed, which is measured in gigahertz (GHz). The faster the chip, the better it is for rendering.

Unless you have to have the latest bells and whistles, avoid the top of the line or recently released chips. The cost-to-benefit ratio of these chips is minimal.

RAM and Computer Memory

Random-access memory (RAM) is the amount of memory that is available for the processor to use to read and write data. The more RAM you have, the larger the model the computer can process. Insufficient RAM can cause a render to crash or fail.

RAM is measured in gigabytes (GB). A typical computer possesses 2 to 8 gigabytes of RAM. Large complex models usually require at least 4 GB of RAM. With 8 GB, you should be able to render most models with no problems. If you're rendering light sources such as bulbs and fixtures, or models with large amounts of three-dimensional vegetation, you might need from 8 to 12 GB of RAM.

A typical system comes with 4 to 8 GB of RAM and is relatively affordable.

Performance and SketchUp

No matter how many processors your computer has, SketchUp can use only one processor to process its work. In fact, most CAD applications function in a similar manner.

A gazillion processors will not affect how fast you can model, nor will they allow you to work on larger models with SketchUp. Similarly, RAM does not affect SketchUp in any considerable fashion. Having a high-tech computer loaded with processors and RAM is ideal only for the rendering part of your modeling work.

SketchUp is affected by two factors: the processor speed and the video card. Processor speeds indicate how fast the processor can crunch calculations. The higher the processor number, the faster SketchUp can work. The same is true for video cards. The faster and better the video card, the faster SketchUp will work, pan, orbit, rotate, zoom, and create geometry.

This is particularly true when you're working with large models. NVIDIA gaming cards, like the NVIDIA GeForce series, are strongly recommended when working with SketchUp. Conversely, the video card does not affect rendering process.

Aiden Chopra, the product evangelist for SketchUp, wrote an excellent blog on how to optimize SketchUp to work faster for modeling. It can be found at http://sketchupdate.blogspot .com/2011/10/speed-up-sketchup-use-fast-styles.html.

Desktops and laptops have become comparable in terms of performance and the type of hardware available, but, in general, desktops still have the edge over laptops when used for rendering (Fig. 4.5).

Fig. 4.5: Desktops have the edge for rendering.

First, you get more bang for your buck with a desktop. A laptop with comparable specifications to a desktop is usually 20 percent to 50 percent more expensive. You can purchase a more robust desktop for the same price.

A rendering laptop will be heavier. You can still carry it around, but be prepared for the weight, which is usually around six to eight pounds. Laptop hardware is difficult or almost impossible to upgrade, too.

Because so many calculations are required, modeling and rendering puts particular stress on your computer. The computer will work harder and run hotter. The size of a desktop, relative to a laptop, allows it to more easily be designed to shed heat, making for less wear and tear on the hardware. The consequences of overheating include reduced performance and shortened lifespan of the computer.

Other Rendering Options

There are other ways to render a model that bypass a computer's hardware. As of this writing, no IRP for SketchUp takes advantage of either option discussed here with the exception of Shaderlight. However, this could change and would be an excellent and economical approach to rendering.

Network Rendering

Most studio rendering programs can use multiple computers to produce a single rendering. *Network rendering* utilizes the processors from one or more computers linked together by a typical, internal computer network. These linked computers are called a *render farm* (Fig. 4.6).

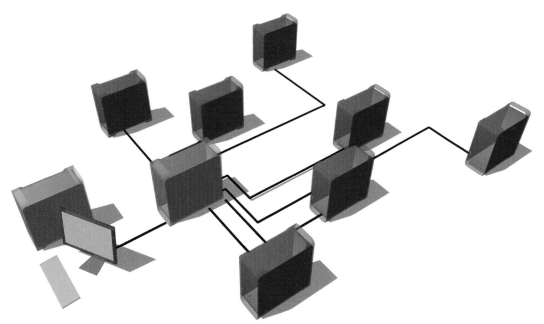

Fig. 4.6: The computer with the rendering file (green) directs the rendering through the server (orange), which is processed by the network of computers (gray).

Even slow computers, when teamed together, can create a formidable array of processing. Major motion picture companies, professional render artists, and large offices utilize render farms using SRPs.

Cloud Rendering

Cloud computing enables your software and data to be run, stored, and processed by computers located someplace other than your home or office. Large companies, like Google and Amazon, offer cloud computing services. You can store, back up, and even run applications remotely, taking advantage of a company's large backbone of powerful and plentiful computers (Fig. 4.7). The sheer amount of processing power made available by the cloud is enormous.

Some companies are starting to offer cloud rendering services. Users can upload their models through a web interface, and the company will generate the renderings using their own render farm. The end user pays for using their systems.

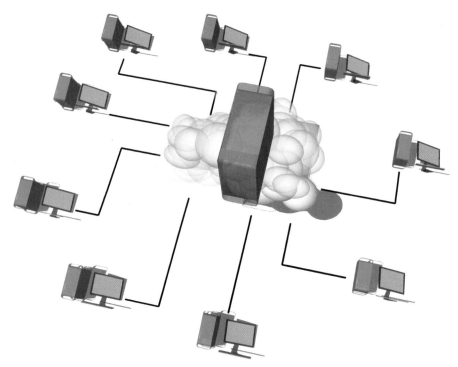

Fig. 4.7: Cloud rendering

Shaderlight, teaming up with Limitless Computing in Boulder, Colorado, has released a cloud rendering service. Check www.artvps.com, the home page for Shaderlight, for more information on this service.

Computer Specifications

Given the current pace of computer advancement, use all the information provided to help you determine your computer needs. These lists are by no means comprehensive. Always consult with specific computer manufacturers when you're configuring a rendering system.

Dell and Mac fit the bill for most of these systems. However, for faster speeds and large model renders, consider specialized manufacturers such as Xi Computers (Fig. 4.8), iBuy-Power, Falcon Computers, CyberPower PC, and others boutique companies. These companies produce gaming- and rendering-specific computers and will ensure a system is configured to your needs.

Fig. 4.8: The Xi Computers web page (www.xicomputer.com)

Minimum Requirements

Systems that meet the minimum requirements will provide slow and limited results, and usually they are not adequate. However, the IRP developers list them as minimum and sometimes even recommended specs.

- ▶ 1 or 2 (core duo) processors
- ▶ 2 GB of RAM
- ▶ ATI or NVIDIA graphics card

Base Requirements

Base-spec computers can render small- to medium-size models with decent speed. Large landscape models and models that contain many simulated lights might struggle or not finish. A second- or third-generation NVIDIA GeForce card ensures that SketchUp will work well.

- Quad Core i5 or i7 processor or similar
- 4 to 8 GB of RAM
- NVIDIA GeForce graphic cards

Recommended Requirements

Ideal for most users, computers that meet the recommended requirements will render most models. However, some large landscape models (see Chapter 14) or models with many simulated lights may not complete rendering. High-end Dell Precision and XPS systems and Macs can be configured for these specs. Other computer manufacturers, previously listed, are ideal for these systems.

- i7 or Xeon Quad or Six Core computer
- 8 GB of RAM
- High-end NVIDIA GeForce graphics card

High-End Rendering Requirements

High-end systems will be overkill for most users, but your renderings will fly! If you want to run small animations, work with large landscape models, or render scenes with tons of simulated lights, these specs are for you. High-end computers can be pricey (but should come down in price in the foreseeable future). They employ duel chipsets—meaning that two CPUs that have quad- or six-core chips. Therefore,

$$2 \text{ quad} = 8 \text{ processors}$$
$$2 \text{ six-core} = 12 \text{ processors}$$

- Dual quad or dual six-core computers—i7 or Xeon
- 12 to 64 GB of RAM
- High-end NVIDIA GeForce graphics card

Learning to Look

O bserving the real world will reveal cues to creating good renderings. By watching how
light interacts with surfaces, revealing reflections while illuminating objects and making
them dull or shiny, you can translate your observations into rendering values. The light and
texture settings in IRPs attempt to re-create the qualities of reality.

Rendering as an Art Form

One of the most sought-after goals of computer rendering is to create hyperrealistic images.
When you first look at a hyperrealistic image, you can't tell if the image is real or not (Fig. 5.1).

Fig. 5.1: Three-dimensional grass created using Advanced Painter Exterior (Akiko Okabe, RNL project)

A cadre of professionals, loosely called *rendering artists*, are devoted to computer rendering. They are dedicated to the rendering craft; they can work weeks, if not months, on a single render to produce images and animations that are hyperrealistic. In short, they are artists in their fields who create incredible images, animations, and movies.

Rendering Artists

This chapter focuses on renderings created by some of these professionals. These images (Fig. 5.1 to Fig. 5.13) incorporate the principles outlined here as interpreted by these artists to further their works and create emotive, realistic images. The following artists are featured.

- ▶ **Aikiko Okabe**: akikookabe.com
- ▶ **Ryan W. Knope**: www.ryanknope.com
- ▶ **Sid Porobic**: chartered architect; director of S. Porobic Associates, Chartered Architects and Designers; lecturer at The School of Arts, University of Northampton; director of Renderclinic, Ltd.
- ▶ **Mateo Soletic**: Mateo Soletic – Designer; director of Soletic Interijeri & SketchupArtists, http://www.sketchupartists.org/
- ▶ **Duane Kemp**: Director of Kemp Productions
- ▶ **Anna Cawrse and team** (Alex Atherton, Chad Murphy, Mike Albert, Victor Perez Amado)
- ▶ **Victor Perez Amado and team** (Anna Cawrse, Alex Atherton, Chad Murphy, Mike Albert)
- ▶ **Kara Letts**: designer from the Washington, D.C., area specializing in commercial interior design, with special interests in technology, sustainability, and universal design.
- ▶ **Jim Leggitt**: FAIA , www.drawingshortcuts.com
- ▶ **Rashad Al-Ahmadi**: Landscape designer

Real-World Inspiration

Many digital artists believe that the key to creating renderings is observing the real world. As you work through this book, learn to look and pay attention to light and how it interacts with materials, surfaces, and objects. Study these interactions as you walk around, drive, sit in your home, and go about your day. Consider how your perceptions of reality can be applied to your renderings.

Start by observing how light is reflected off surfaces. Note the amount and type of light returned. Study how materials interact with each other; try to understand the contrasting and complementary nature of these relationships. These interplays could be defined by how bright or dull, reflective or muted surfaces appear.

Fig. 5.2: Irish pub (Ryan W. Knope)

Most daily observational musings fall into three broad categories. These categories are referenced in the discussion of integrated rendering program values for models in Part 5, "The Iterative Rendering Process." The categories are:

▶ **Quality of Light**: Observe the direction, strength, and color of light and the way light interacts with objects to cause reflections and accent surface character. These can be recreated in renderings using IRP and SketchUp Shadow settings.

▶ **Surface Character:** Study how materials and surfaces look: whether they are smooth or grainy, etched with lines, or contain a variety of character across the surface. You will want to find these qualities in the materials you use for your model.

▶ **Dull to Bright and Flat to Reflective**: Surfaces reflect light in various ways; observe the ways they do. Surfaces range from dull and glossy to bright and shiny. Similarly, they reflect their surroundings, like mirrors that create clear reflections. They can range from clear to muted to indistinct to blurry in appearance.

Part 5 will help you learn to translate your observations into useful but general settings for IRPs. Part 6 and the online supplemental chapters will show you how to further translate these settings into direct values for each IRP.

Fig. 5.3: Initial SketchUp model (top) and Shaderlight rendering overlay (bottom) used for hand-drawn illustration (Jim Leggitt)

Fig. 5.4: Final illustration (Jim Leggitt)

Fig. 5.5: Home on stilts (Sid Porobic)

Fig. 5.6: Interior (Duane Kemp)

Fig. 5.7: Exterior (Duane Kemp)

Fig. 5.8: Light-rail station (Ryan Knope)

Fig. 5.9: Interior rendering for Autodesk 20th Competition (Akiko Okabe and RNL Design Team)

Fig. 5.10: Exterior street scene (Mateo Šoletić)

Fig. 5.11: A cantina and court (Anna Cawrse, Victor Perex Amado, and team)

Fig. 5.12: Exterior site and building (Rashad Al-Ahmadi using Lumion with SketchUp)

Becoming a Student of Light and Color

Go to this book's resource page and follow the link to *Becoming a Student of Light and Color* for more on the very broad topic of observing the world:

http://www.twistedtreephoto.com/quality%20of%20light%201.html

Fig. 5.13: Getting Malled (Ryan W. Knope)

PART 2

Textures

Textures Overview

Textured surfaces represent the most important aspect of the SketchUp model. They define how the model will appear when rendered (Fig. 6.1). A successful model also requires careful preparation and organization, which you will learn about in Part 3. Mastering the use of textures in your models allows you to render quality photorealistic images. With the right textures, even a simple model can come to life (Fig. 6.2).

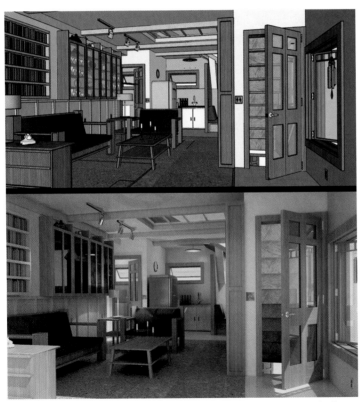

Fig. 6.1: The top image shows the model in SketchUp with textures. The bottom image is the rendered version (SU Podium).

In this book, the texturing chapters appear before the modeling chapters to emphasize the importance of placing textures. However, textures need to be applied to surfaces. Throughout Part 2, assume that a base model of some form is being created (Fig. 6.3). Read the chapters in Part 2 carefully, learn the various tools, follow the provided links, and begin to build a Texture Library.

Fig. 6.2: The top image shows a simple SketchUp model. The model has limited detail. However, once rendered the applied textures help create a photo quality (bottom image).

Fig. 6.3: A textured model (top) and the rendered result (bottom)

Textures in SketchUp

Textures utilize linked images to take on the appearance of real-world materials (Fig. 6.4). The textures are then applied to SketchUp surfaces. Linking textures in SketchUp is a seamless process handled by the Paint Bucket tool. For rendering, the linked images should look like a photograph, representing a specific type of substance or matter found in the real world.

Fig. 6.4: Textures are composed of images that represent the desired material and surface.

The images composing a texture repeat on the applied surfaces. SketchUp takes the linked image and tiles the image on an applied surface in an endless repetition of that image. (Fig. 6.5). This is how a surface can appear to be covered by the image. The size of the linked image can be scaled up or down.

Fig. 6.5: A texture image applied and repeated across SketchUp faces

Not all rendering surfaces require a textured material. Solid colors are useful in some instances. Polished, smooth, or metallic surfaces might achieve the best result using a solid color without an associated linked image (Fig. 6.6). However, most surfaces benefit from a texture linked to an image.

Fig. 6.6: The top image shows the solid surfaces applied to the containers. The IRP texture values applied to these surfaces will render them shiny, as shown in the bottom image (Twilight Render).

The Importance of Textures

Applied textures should accurately represent the desired material in terms of look, proportion, and clarity (Fig. 6.7). The IRP will accentuate the appearances of textures in the model during the rendering process (Fig. 6.8).

Point in fact, a well-textured model possesses an almost photorealistic appearance prior to rendering (Fig. 6.9). As such, using the right textures results in good renderings.

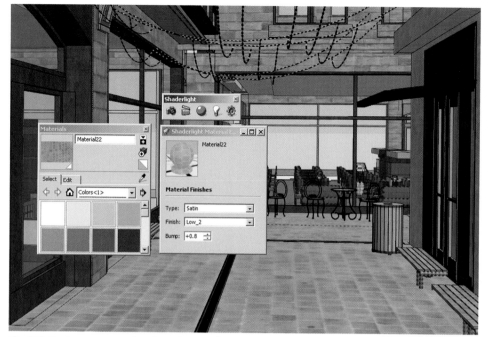

Fig. 6.7: Textures representing the various surfaces (paving, brick for walls, metal window framing, glass, and wood) are applied to the model.

Fig. 6.8: The resulting rendering enhances the textures (Shaderlight).

Fig. 6.9: The model takes on an almost photo-quality appearance in SketchUp with Shadows on and Edges off.

How Textures Work with IRPs

Values are assigned to textures using the IRP Material menu. When the rendering is started, the IRP render engine will adjust the appearance of the texture based on these values (Fig. 6.10). Although each IRP has a different material editing system, the values provide the same results.

The values assigned by the IRP control how reflective, diffuse, blurred, shiny, or coarse the materials appear (Fig. 6.11). The entered values depend on the material—for example, a concrete texture requires diffuse and course settings. Chrome surfaces should be set to Smooth with a high reflection. Transparent reflective settings are typical for glass and windows. Texture values and settings are reviewed in Chapter 21.

Fig. 6.10: The Shaderlight Material Editor

Fig. 6.11: The IRP Material Editors allow for a range of reflections and other effects.

The Texturing Process

The texturing process can be broken down into the following basic steps:

1. Build a Texture Library.
2. Use the SketchUp Texture tools to apply the textures.
3. Edit the textures.

The texturing process is described in greater detail in the next set of chapters.

Build a Texture Library

Download and organize texture files into a coherent Texture Library. Textures should be organized by type and category so that you can quickly sort them and easily access them. You will end up reusing many of your textures. Given the sheer variety of materials that can be arrayed in a model, an organized library will ensure easy access for your future work. Chapter 7 provides detailed information and links to websites offering material images.

Use the SketchUp Texture Tools

Using the SketchUp Paint Bucket tool, you can apply, edit, scale, and replace textures (Fig. 6.12). A right-click context menu allows you to reposition and rotate those textures. External

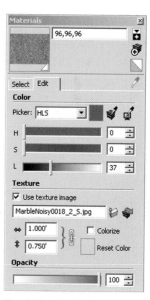

Fig. 6.12: The SketchUp Paint Bucket tool plays a central role in applying and editing texture images.

photo-editing software can be linked to the Paint Bucket tool to provide additional editing options. Chapter 8 provides a detailed review of the various ways to apply and edit textures in SketchUp.

Edit the Textures

Using the available tools, you will need to edit your textures to enhance your renderings and ensure that the textures appear accurate (Fig. 6.13). Chapter 9 demonstrates how to achieve a desired look (Fig. 6.14).

Fig. 6.13: Editing and swapping textures is part of the process when you're generating a rendering. The image on the left shows the original textures applied to the model surface. On the right, all the textures are edited or replaced with different versions.

Fig. 6.14: The adjusted textures create a different version of the rendering as compared to the rendering in Fig. 6.8 (Shaderlight).

General Considerations

When you're working with materials, keep the following considerations in mind. They are discussed further in the next several chapters and are the foremost factors affecting materials.

Textures and the Iterative Process

A big part of the draft iterative process is assessing how materials will appear once rendered. You will end up adjusting assigned IRP texture values or swapping out materials when you're running drafts. It's important to keep the editing process dynamic and ensure that you do not keep textures that do not achieve good results.

Consider Scale

When first applied to surfaces, most textures will require scaling, usually adjusted to appear larger (Fig. 6.15). SketchUp's initial settings for a texture's size in the Paint Bucket menu are set to a low value. This causes them look small and inaccurate.

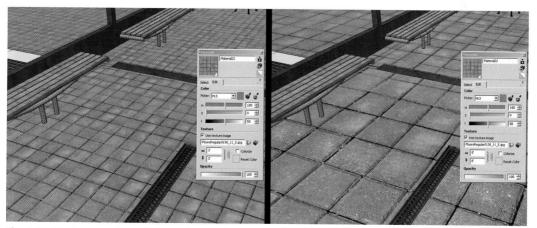

Fig. 6.15: The image on the left shows the initial textures applied to surfaces. They appear small or out of scale. On the right, the textures are scaled upward, providing a more appropriate appearance.

Obtain Multiple Textures

When you're researching and downloading textures, obtain multiple versions of the same texture when possible. This will allow you to swap out a texture when it looks off, without limiting your results (Fig. 6.16).

Fig. 6.16: Multiple versions of the same texture

You will need to swap an applied texture with another version or different material frequently. The substitution process is essential to learn and easy to accomplish.

Quality trumps accuracy. Some textures won't render quite right, no matter what the adjustments. In such cases, it might be better to use a material that is a close, if not a fully accurate, approximation (Fig. 6.17).

Consider File Size

Textures affect the modeling and rendering process. Understanding these factors will help you determine the types of textures you want to download (Fig. 6.18). Of particular concern are the physical size (length and width) and file size of downloadable textures (Fig. 6.19). Keep in mind the following points:

- ▶ Applied textures can increase the file size of the model, causing it to take longer to open or save.

- ▶ Applied textures affect the upload processing time (Stage 1) from SketchUp to the IRP. The more textures and/or the larger the textures, the longer the upload time will be.

- ▶ Materials require RAM to process. Models with many large textures use more RAM to process when rendering. Computers with limited RAM might crash. However, most users and models will rarely encounter this issue.

- ▶ Textures slow down SketchUp's performance. You can mitigate this by turning the Texture View off in SketchUp (see Chapter 8).
- ▶ Smaller texture sizes minimize all these effects.

Fig. 6.17: The top image shows textures less than ideal for rendering. Although not the same, the bottom texture is more realistic.

Fig. 6.18: The SketchUp model with textures (left); the model without textures (right)

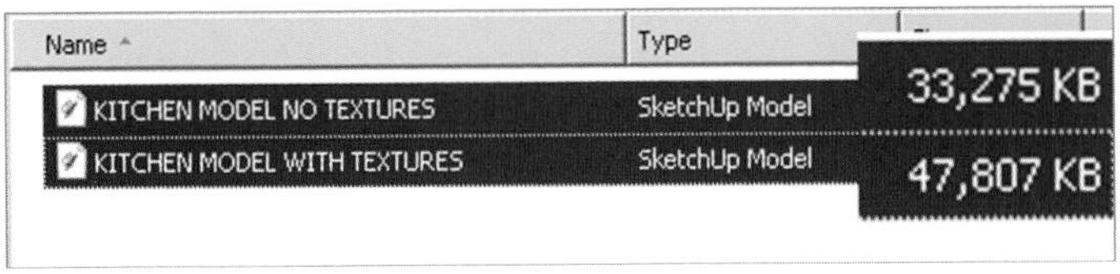

Name ^	Type	
KITCHEN MODEL NO TEXTURES	SketchUp Model	33,275 KB
KITCHEN MODEL WITH TEXTURES	SketchUp Model	47,807 KB

Fig. 6.19: The file size of the model without textures is considerably smaller.

Texture Image Formats

SketchUp supports several file formats for texture images. They include JPEG, PNG, TIFF, PSD, TRG, and BMP. JPEG and PNG files are the typical file formats used for textures. JPEGs are a common file type. They are compressed or optimized and do not take up excessive file space. PNGs are useful because they can be transparent, allowing for various effects when rendering.

The Texture Library

To attain the best rendering results, you'll need to obtain material textures to apply to the SketchUp model. After you download your textures, you'll need to organize them into a coherent library (Fig. 7.1) so that they are easily accessible and can be reused. SketchUp can be linked to the Texture Library, which will enable you to directly insert custom materials into your models.

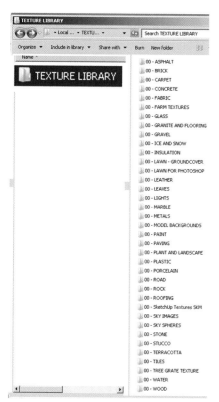

Fig. 7.1: A Texture Library folder on the computer's hard drive

SketchUp Native Textures

SketchUp comes with preinstalled or native textures. To review these materials, open the Paint Bucket tool from the toolbar (or press B, which is the keyboard shortcut). The Paint Bucket pull-down menu lists various texture categories, including Brick and Cladding, Colors, Fencing, Groundcovers, etc. (Fig. 7.2).

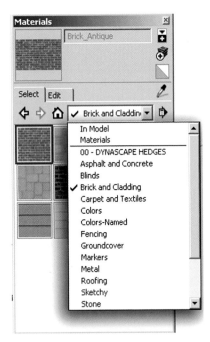

Fig. 7.2: Native textures in SketchUp

Although SketchUp's native textures can be used for rendering, these materials are low in resolution and small in size (256 × 256 pixels). You'll learn about texture size shortly. In general, the native textures are not ideal, nor will they produce the best graphic results. The exception is when you're using these textures with the Shaderlight IRP. Shaderlight supports these textures in a unique fashion, which will be discussed in Chapter 27.

Native SketchUp textures are stored in a unique file format called .skm. The .skm textures are image file types created specifically for SketchUp. The SketchUp Material Library can display only .skm file types.

This limitation means that custom texture libraries can't be listed in it. As stated, custom textures will be stored as JPEGs and other image file formats not recognized by the Paint Bucket tool. This does not mean that the Paint Bucket tool cannot insert, replace, and include custom textures. It just means that you can't store them in the SketchUp Material Library. Because you'll want to keep your custom textures organized, you'll learn how to link the Material menu with a Texture Library at the end of this chapter.

Web Sources

Various websites offer materials specific to rendering, and you can use them to download custom textures. These websites tend to cater to and meet the requirements that are outlined in Part 2. This chapter focuses on the website CG Textures.com due to its large variety of materials. CG Textures.com boasts over 50,000 downloadable textures (Fig. 7.3), and it is a good place to start as you build your initial Texture Library.

CG Textures.com

CG Textures has a large and easy-to-search database. In many cases, it provides sets of downloadable images that come in multiple, but similar varieties and sizes. Textures are available to registered members. Membership is free, and it allows you to search and download materials.

Fig. 7.3: The CG Textures.com website

Your free membership account allows you to download a total of 10 MB of textures per day. It provides access to small texture sizes only, meeting the general requirements for resolutions mentioned previously (between 500 to 1,600 pixels). When you're working with graphics, a 10 MB limit can be quickly surpassed.

Purchasing a normal membership allows you to download 100 MB of textures a day. It provides access to medium and large texture sizes. A normal membership is available for a modest annual fee. It's a low sum worth its weight in gold and is more than sufficient for most users' needs. Although free memberships are available, by obtaining a paid membership to CG Textures you will be helping to support the website so it can grow and expand.

Additional Texture Sites

John Pacyga, RLA, a landscape architect who writes a blog called SketchUp for Landscapes, compiled a vast list of free and commercial texture websites. It includes Facebook, Flickr, and more (Fig. 7.4). You can find his blog here:

http://sketchupland.posterous.com/great-texture-websites-for-sketchup-and-photo

SKETCHUP FOR LANDSCAPES

« Back to blog

GREAT TEXTURE WEBSITES FOR SKETCHUP AND PHOTOSHOP

This is a list of all the texture websites I recommend. Most of these sites offer free seamless textures that can be used in SketchUp (Import -> image) and into Photoshop (Edit->Define Pattern). There are too many textures to even count, so be selective! You are going to need a bigger hard drive... enjoy!

One of my all-time favorite places for seamless textures is Patrick Hoesly's Blog and Flickr site. Visit the blog, zooboingreview.blogspot.com/, to download more free Creative Commons textures.

Fig. 7.4: John Pacyga's blog provides links to many websites offering textures.

Choosing and Downloading Textures

To get the most out of your materials, assess them in relation to the characteristics mentioned here when you're reviewing them for download.

Size Matters

Texture sizes are measured in pixels indicating the texture's length and width. The larger the pixel height and width values, the larger the texture. SketchUp, by default, supports textures no larger than 1024×1024 pixels. Any texture greater in size will be sampled down. In a process *called subsampling,* SketchUp will process the texture at the maximum limit of 1024×1024. However, this limit does not affect the IRPs. If a texture larger than 1,024 pixels is present, the IRP will process the texture up to its maximum size, ignoring SketchUp subsampling.

Smaller Textures as the General Rule

Use smaller texture sizes for most model surfaces with the exception of those discussed here. Small texture sizes can vary from 500 to 1,600 pixels in width.

CG Textures.com provides various sizes for each texture. The sizes range from small, medium, large, and higher. Medium, larger, and greater textures require a paid membership (Fig. 7.5) for use.

Benefits of Large Textures

There are at least three instances when large-sized textures are useful in a model:

- ► For close-up shots of a surface or object
- ► When the texture needs to be scaled upward to expose the finer aspects of a material's detail
- ► For covering large surfaces such as lawn, ground cover, and similar areas

These conditions are reviewed in greater detail in Chapter 9. Under these conditions or when you believe a large texture would provide the best result, download materials larger than 1,600 pixels in width. As stated earlier, CG Textures.com offers multiple-size downloads for material images as reviewed under CG Textures.com.

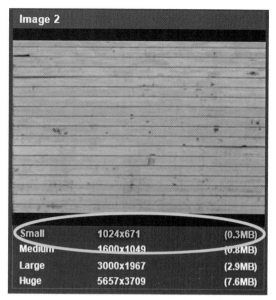

Small	1024x671	(0.3MB)
Medium	1600x1049	(0.8MB)
Large	3000x1967	(2.9MB)
Huge	5657x3709	(7.6MB)

Fig. 7.5: Notice the sizes of wood texture offered by CG Texture.com. When you're working in SketchUp and rendering, small sizes are ideal for most textures.

Texture Types

There are two different types of textures for rendering: seamless and irregular. The four sides of a seamless texture flow into the adjoining sides of the next texture image, creating a continuous pattern (Fig. 7.6). Irregular textures do not match up when placed side by side; this causes a seam to appear where the texture images meet (Fig. 7.7). For this reason, seamless textures are considered superior to irregular ones.

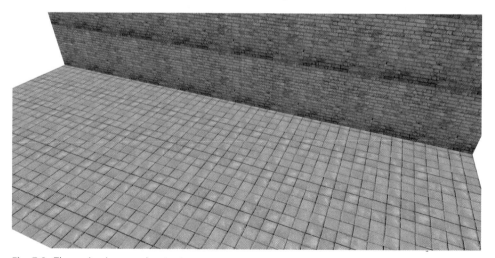

Fig. 7.6: The paving is a seamless texture.

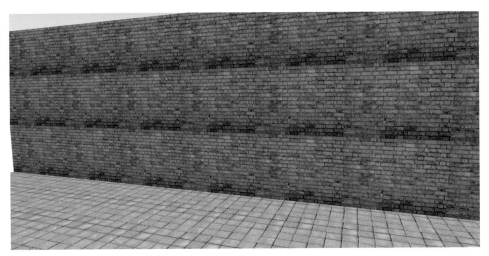

Fig. 7.7: Irregular texture (brick)

However, both types are suited for texturing. There are ways to hide or minimize the seams caused by irregular texture images. In addition, the regular and steady pattern of a seamless texture can be distracting: it might be seamless, but it can appear overly repetitive, creating what's called a moiré pattern (Fig. 7.8). Typically, irregular textures allow for variation across the image surface (Fig. 7.9). Both types of textures have their uses and applications, as explored in Chapter 9.

Fig. 7.8: When a seamless texture is used to define the road, the repeating pattern is distracting and unrealistic.

CG Textures.com indicates which textures are seamless by labeling them with a star and the word "Tiled" next to their names (Fig. 7.10). CG Textures.com includes tools you can use to view tiled textures in perspective; just select 3D Tiling Preview.

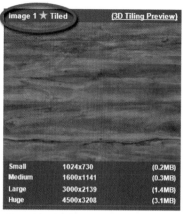

Fig. 7.9: The seamless texture is replaced with an irregular asphalt texture, providing an appropriate look.

Fig. 7.10: CG Textures.com indicates if a texture is seamless.

Multiple Versions

When you're looking for a specific texture, download multiple and different versions. Once you've started the draft iterative process, you'll be swapping out textures as a common practice. A texture might not render well, be the wrong type, or be too small. By having multiple versions of materials, you'll be prepared with several variations and be able to quickly swap for better results.

CG Textures.com is a great resource because most of their textures have two, three, or more versions. In addition, these variations come in different sizes (Fig. 7.11).

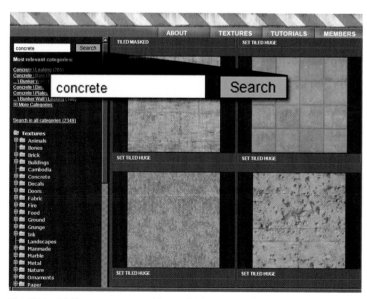

Fig. 7.11: CG Textures.com provides multiple versions for many of its textures.

Saving a Texture Library

You will want to create an organized and easy-to-access library for your texture images (Fig. 7.12). Save your materials and textures in a single folder location. Create any additional folder subcategories organized by material type—for example, folders for concrete, fabrics, carpets, wood, ceramic, etc. (Fig. 7.13). Of the many steps in the rendering process, this might be one of the most important. Having an organized and plentiful Texture Library makes the rendering process considerably easier.

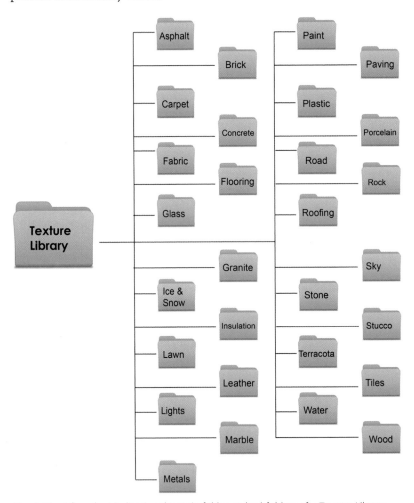

Fig. 7.12: A flowchart indicating the main folder and subfolders of a Texture Library

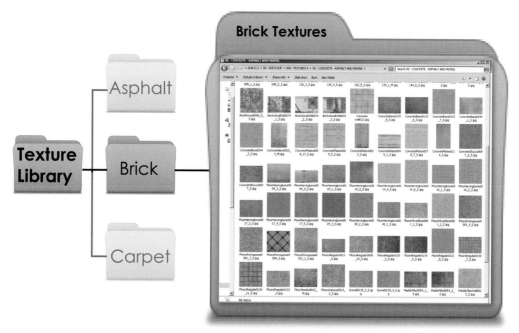

Fig. 7.13: An expanded flowchart showing brick texture images located in the Brick subfolder located in the Texture Library

Save the Material Library in an easily accessible location. You will be linking the Material Library to SketchUp's Paint Bucket tool; see below.

One of the most effective ways to build a Texture Library is on a project-by-project basis. Different models and projects will require different materials. The average model uses between 10 and 20 textures. After three or four renderings, your library could exceed 100 images. Before long, you will be reusing textures from the library, knowing which ones work best for a given model.

The bottom line is, download often and keep it organized!

Searching CG Textures

Searching for a texture is relatively simple. You can enter a search term in the search bar or search the database list below it (Fig. 7.14). Using the Search menu can be quicker and more accurate. A list of possible matches will be displaced as images. In many cases, there will be multiple options from which to choose.

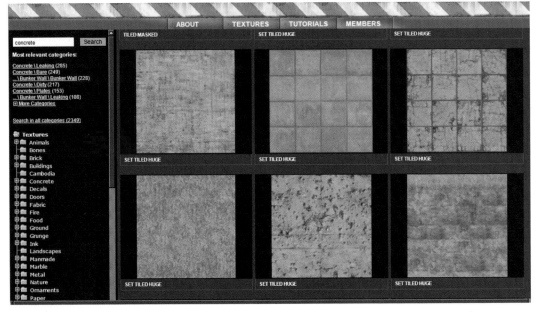

Fig. 7.14: Searching CG Textures.com for "concrete"

For example, doing a search for "concrete" yields more than 36 pages of results comprised of different concrete image sets. Each set contains at least one but usually multiple images. Clicking on a set will launch a new browser window displaying the images part of that collection.

For most, but not all, images in a set, there will be three size options: small, medium, and large. Some images will have limited sizes, typically small and medium. Once you have the results displayed and are ready to download a texture, follow these steps:

1. Download small image sizes. As indicated, for most textures you only need the small size versions.

2. Download multiple versions. If the texture has multiple versions, download the variations to give yourself more flexibility.

3. Save the file to your Texture Library in the correct category.

CG Textures.com and similar websites frown upon downloading whole sets in a single sitting, and they ask that you not do it. Site administrators will suspect that such downloads are being used for resale or being posted on other sites. It is never okay to share or repost downloaded textures.

You won't always find the texture you need at CG Textures.com. Before giving up, though, try searching with different search terms. Something will likely appear. If you can't find what you need, explore other texture sites; see John Pacyga's blog and search the various links mentioned previously.

Linking the Texture Library

To insert and swap textures with ease, you will want to link your Texture Library to SketchUp's Paint Bucket file browser and texture options. Doing this allows for a simple and easy workflow when applying and editing textures. Swapping textures to a linked Texture Library is reviewed in Chapter 8 and Chapter 9. Please note, this process differs for Mac's. See the next chapter about Mac Texture tools.

To link the library:

1. In SketchUp, select Window → Preferences.

2. In Preferences, select File Option.

3. On the right of File Option, select Texture Images and click the Browse button (Fig. 7.15).

4. Navigate to the root folder of your Texture Library (Fig. 7.16).

5. Click OK. The Paint Bucket browser (under the Edit tab described in Chapter 8) is now linked to the Texture Library.

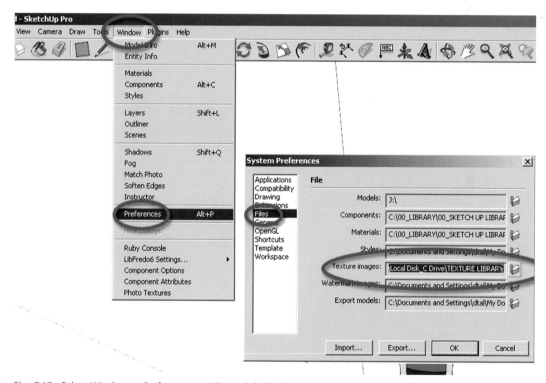

Fig. 7.15: Select Window → Preferences → Files to link SketchUp to the Texture Library.

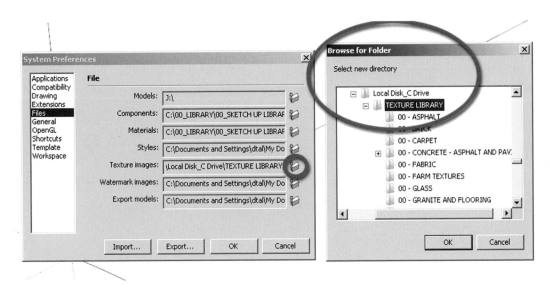

Fig. 7.16: Linking SketchUp to the Texture Library folder

The SketchUp Texture Tools

Textures need to be applied, edited, scaled, moved, rotated, color corrected, and swapped. The SketchUp Texture tools used for these tasks are straightforward and easy to use.

This chapter reviews what the Texture tools do. You can use it as a reference manual when you're working with Chapter 9 and learning to apply and edit textures on surfaces. You should read through this chapter at least once to familiarize yourself with all the options.

Macintosh Texture Tools

The PC and Mac versions of the SketchUp Paint Bucket tool are different: their submenu locations and options are accessed differently. This chapter reviews the tools from the perspective of the PC. While it is still relevant and useful for Mac users, if you are using a Mac, you should download and use the online chapter "Mac Texture Tools" (Fig. 8.1). You can find it with the other accompanying chapters at www.ambit-3d.com (Fig. 8.2).

Fig. 8.1: The online "Mac Texture Tools" chapter

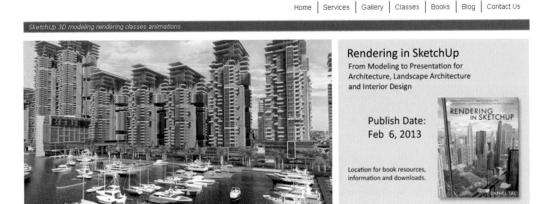

SketchUp 3D modeling rendering classes animations

Rendering in SketchUp

From Modeling to Presentation for Architecture, Landscape Architecture and Interior Design

Publish Date:
Feb 6, 2013

Location for book resources, information and downloads.

Future location for Rendering In SketchUp Book resources including:

- Free Accompanying Chapters
- Texture and Component website links
- SketchUp Files related to the book
- Ruby Scripts Plugins
- Links to Rendering Software for SketchUp

**Trimble**. SketchUp.

Welcome to our SketchUp related resources and services site.

Check out our latest BLOG covering SketchUp tools, tips and news.

Fig. 8.2: The online website (www.ambit-3d.com) where you can download the Mac chapter

PC Texture Tools

Before delving into tool descriptions, you should understand the general tasks that are typically performed on textures. These tasks are referenced in Chapter 9 where you'll learn to assess and adjust textures.

▶ **Applying**: Applying refers to the placement of textures onto surfaces. The Paint Bucket tool applicator is used to place textures onto model faces.

▶ **Scaling**: Scaling increases or decreases the size of the texture image. By adjusting the size, you can make the pattern/photo of the material image larger or smaller on the applied surfaces. The Paint Bucket tool's Edit function and SketchUp's right-click Texture menu are used to scale textures.

▶ **Swapping**: Solid colors and texture images can be easily replaced or swapped with a click of the button. An existing, applied material can be replaced with a new material using the functions under Edit in the Paint Bucket. Swapping is done in the Paint Bucket tool under the Edit menu.

- ▶ **Adjusting Color**: Amending texture colors can help ensure that a material has the correct appearance. Color can be adjusted with the Paint Bucket tool or with external photo-editing software, such as Photoshop.

- ▶ **Moving/Rotating**: You can modify the position and orientation of textures on surfaces using the right-click Texture options.

- ▶ **Computer Performance and Texture Views**: When they are applied to model surface, textures can effect computer and SketchUp performance. You can mitigate these effects using the SketchUp Tools Style menu, which controls how surfaces are displayed. Several different tools are used to edit texture. The remainder of this chapter focuses on how these tools work. Important functions and ones performed often are noted (look for the asterisk*) so you'll know that mastering them is important. Here is a quick list and overview:

- ▶ **The Paint Bucket Tool**: The main Texture tool used for applying, editing, scaling, adjusting color, inserting custom textures, and swapping textures.

- ▶ **Styles Menu**: This menu controls the visibility of textures and the appearance of faces.

- ▶ **Right-click Texture Options**: This context-sensitive tool is a finicky tool that rotates, repositions, and scales textures using the mouse.

- ▶ **External Photo Editing**: The Paint Bucket menu can be linked to external photo-editing software such as Photoshop. The physical appearance of a texture can be reconfigured in programs like Photoshop and then updated in SketchUp.

The Paint Bucket Tool

The Paint Bucket tool allows you to select a color or texture and apply it to a model face. The Paint Bucket tool is used for three primary tasks when modeling and rendering:

- ▶ Replacing a solid color or texture with a downloaded texture image from your Texture Library

- ▶ Scaling the texture image and resolution

- ▶ Swapping out textures when you're editing the model during the draft iterative process

A comprehensive description of all the Paint Bucket menu operations follows.

The Applicator

The Paint Bucket applicator is used to apply selected materials onto surfaces (Fig. 8.3). It automatically becomes active when the Paint Bucket tool is open. It can also be reactivated by pressing the B key on the keyboard.

Fig. 8.3: The Paint Bucket applicator

The Select and Edit Tabs

The Paint Bucket menu is organized under two categories: Select and Edit. The various Paint Bucket tools are described here (Fig. 8.4).

The Select Tab

When the Paint Bucket Tool is opened, Select is the default category. Under the Select tab, you can choose and apply native SketchUp materials using the Paint Bucket applicator. Native textures can be selected from the material pull-down menu (Fig. 8.5).

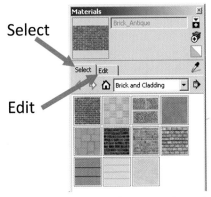

Fig. 8.4: The Paint Bucket tool and the Select and Edit tabs

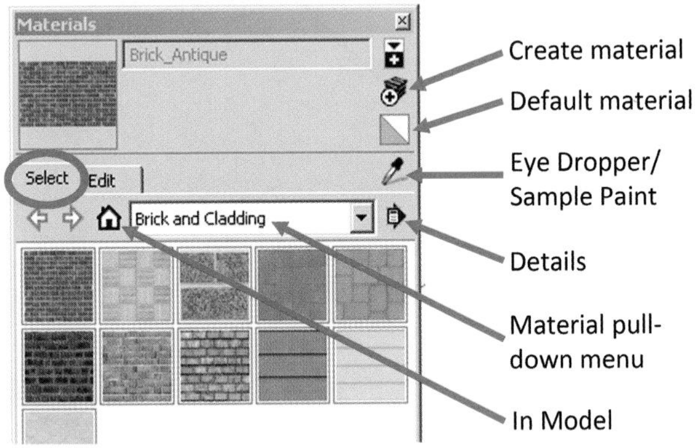

Fig. 8.5: The Select tab options

Create Material*

Selecting the Create Material button will launch a new Materials menu with the Edit tab and associated options. The menu will contain a swatch of the current selected material including the default (no color). Create Material allows you to generate a new version or copy of the selected material or create a new texture (Fig. 8.6).

Default Material

As you'll see in Chapter 9, initial model surfaces in SketchUp have no color, meaning they are set at the default. Selecting the Default button removes any color or material that was on an applied face; it is a model's starting point, but it does not serve any useful purpose when rendering. You should not remove colors, textures, or surfaces using this option because all the surfaces should have a texture or color.

Eye Dropper/Sample Paint*

The Eye Dropper allows you to select a material or color that has already been applied to a face. The tool can be accessed when both the Select and Edit tabs are active. As long as the Paint Bucket tool is open, you can use the Alt key as a quick shortcut to activate the Eye Dropper. The Eye Dropper is a key tool used often when texturing a model (Fig. 8.7).

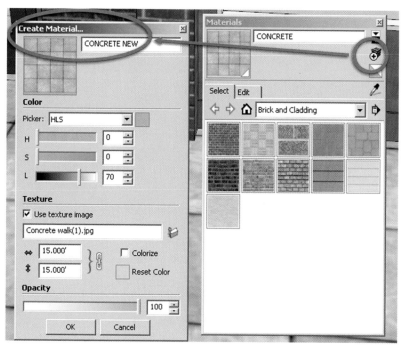

Fig. 8.6: Clicking on the Create New Material button (top-right circle) will open the Create Material window (left menu).

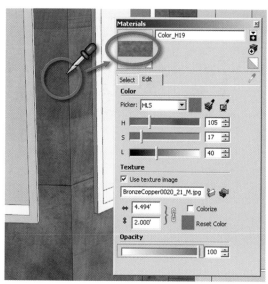

Fig. 8.7: The Eye Dropper allows you to select any material in the model, making it active in the Paint Bucket window.

Details

The Details button controls how the material swatches will appear. They can be displayed in a list and even as extra-large thumbnails (large thumbnails are the default), which will allow you to open new material SketchUp libraries. This option is not useful for working with materials from your custom Texture Library.

Material Pull-Down Menu

The Material pull-down menu provides access to SketchUp's native Material Library categories. Textures are displayed when a category is selected. Selecting a material makes it active so it can be applied to surfaces.

In Model

Selecting the In Model button will display a selectable view of all the materials applied and present in the model.

The Edit Tab

The Edit tab allows you to swap, insert, adjust, and scale native and custom textures. You should become familiar with this tab and its related functions. The Edit tab is organized by its own subcategories of Color, Texture, and Opacity. You can access the Edit tab only after a material is applied to a surface and/or selected using the Eye Dropper (Fig. 8.8).

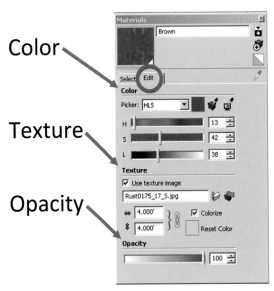

Fig. 8.8: The Edit tab

Color

Below the Color heading on the Materials menu are options that affect the hue, saturation, contrast, and values of a selected color or texture map (Fig. 8.9).

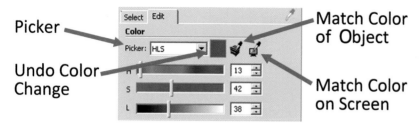

Fig. 8.9: The Color Category options under the Edit tab

Picker* This option allows you to choose how you view and select solid colors for materials. There are four selections: Color Wheel, HLS, HSB, and RGB. The default is the Color Wheel (Fig. 8.10). HLS stands for Hue, Lightness, and Saturation. HSB stands for Hue, Saturation, and Brightness. RGB, which stands for Red, Green, Blue, is the typical color assortment found in most programs. However, selecting HLS from the pull-down menu is usually a better option.

Depending on which setting you pick from the drop-down menu, the area below will have a menu customized to the selected color value option.

Surface Shading A common complaint about SketchUp is that colors appear overly bright or do not accurately represent RGB values as displayed in Photoshop or similar software. This is because SketchUp applies shading to all surfaces to allow for depth and 3D. This shading can create many variations in a single color, depending on its location and position in a model. Because of this shading, using the Color Wheel or RGB does not allow for a precise adjustment of a colors, tone, and value.

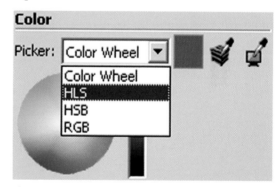

Fig. 8.10: Color Picker is the default setting for SketchUp color editing.

The HLS option is used most often for editing and adjusting colors in SketchUp (Fig. 8.11). It allows for the greatest control of color and texture display in your model (Fig. 8.12). Using HLS, you can tone down bright colors, create more

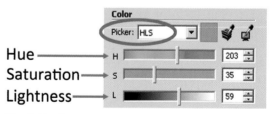

Fig. 8.11: The HLS option is the preferred color-editing option.

sedate and muted tones, and lighten or darken a color. It is strongly recommended that you set HLS as the default for your colors and adjust the settings to see the results. Play around with the three sliders to better understand the results.

Undo Color Change If you do adjust a color or texture value, you can reset the material or color to its original values by clicking the Undo button.

Fig. 8.12: The HLS option is used to edit oversaturated colors (top image), resulting in more muted, realistic texture colors suitable for rendering (bottom image).

Match Color of Object and Match Color on Screen* These two buttons are very useful. They allow you to globally match or swap one color for another. Select a color with the Eye Dropper, and then select one of the Match Color buttons.

Match Color of Object in Model Selecting this option allows you to replace the selected color with a color applied in your model. Simply click on a face with the color you want and swap out the color displayed in the Materials window with the one you pick.

Match Color on Screen This option allows you to pick a color from any place on your screen or other applications; it will apply the color to the material selected in the Paint Bucket (Fig. 8.13, Fig. 8.14).

Fig. 8.13: The yellow brick texture in the SketchUp can be matched to the brick color shown in the photo viewer on the left.

Fig. 8.14: The yellow brick texture is active in the SketchUp Paint Bucket. The Match Color on-screen alters the yellow brick to match the red brick color in the building photo.

Texture*

Below the Texture heading are several options for creating and editing texture images (Fig. 8.15). These tools are the most important ones in the Paint Bucket menu for establishing materials for rendering. Practice using these options until you are comfortable with them.

Assuming you have linked your Texture Library as described in Chapter 7, the Use Texture Image, Browse, and File Path tools will reference or use your custom Texture Library.

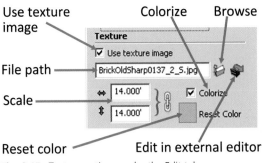

Fig. 8.15: Texture options under the Edit tab

Use Texture Image*/Swapping This option is the primary way to insert and swap custom texture images from your Texture Library. The check box will always have a check mark if the selected material is a texture image—that is, a linked image associated with the texture (Fig. 8.16). Unchecking the box will remove the image from the texture, causing the material to revert to a solid color (Fig. 8.17).

Checking or rechecking the box will launch a file browser requesting that an image be added (Fig. 8.18). This is useful when replacing or swapping texture images to adjust the materials on a surface throughout a model (Fig. 8.19).

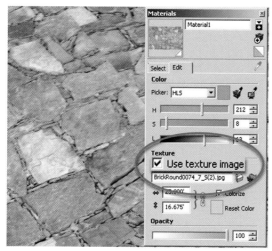

Fig. 8.16: Under the Edit tab, the Use Texture image box is checked, indicating that a texture image is present (in this case, the bluish paving image).

Fig. 8.17: Unchecking the box removes the image. The texture becomes a solid color.

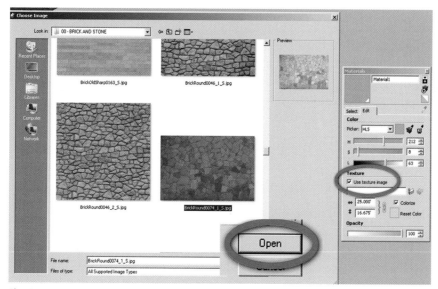

Fig. 8.18: Rechecking the box launches a file browser that should be linked to the Texture Library. You can select a new texture image from the browser window.

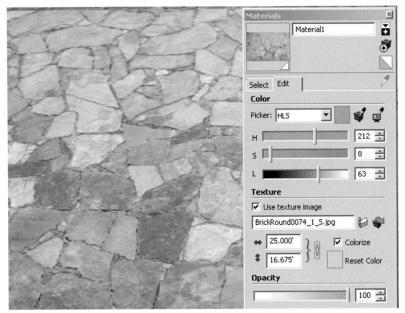

Fig. 8.19: The new texture image replaces the solid color. All versions of the texture are updated with the new material image.

File Path* Any time a material texture or any material that has a JPEG (or other image file type) associated with it is selected, the area below the Texture heading will show a file path to the location of the JPEG image that comprises the texture.

Browse* Selecting the Browse button will launch the file browser. You can replace or add a new image to create a texture map. Clicking the Browse button achieves the same result as unchecking the radio button next to the Use Texture Image option.

Edit Texture Image in External Editor Clicking on this button launches the photo editor (i.e., Photoshop). The selected texture will appear in the external program. You can then adjust the texture image in the editing application. Saving it will automatically update the image in SketchUp. See Chapter 10.

Scaling* SketchUp allows you to scale the size of a texture image. Scaling affects the way the texture image displays on applied faces. The larger the scale, the bigger the image becomes. Conversely, the smaller the scale, the smaller the image appears (Fig. 8.20). Image scale is measured in the same units in which the model is set (imperial or metric). Texture images are scaled proportionally; adjusting the horizontal scale will automatically adjust the vertical scale and vice versa. This proportional scaling can be turned off by clicking on the Link button next to the scale values.

Most if not all textures used in your models will need to be scaled using this option (Fig. 8.21).

Fig. 8.20: The Scale Value boxes are enlarged showing the selected texture size (1f).

Fig. 8.21: The textures are scaled to appear larger.

Colorize   Some textures are composed of multiple color grains and, once they are edited, can take on a disharmonious composition of pixilated colors. For example, an adjusted grass texture might have flecks of magenta and blue. These flecks can become distracting and ruin the material's appearance. Colorize causes the dominant color, in this case the lawn's green tones, to replace the other color flecks. The best way to use this tool is through experimentation and observing the results.

Reset Color   This button restores the original texture color, removing any color adjustments. It will not reset scale.

Opacity

Opacity allows you to control how transparent a material appears. The opacity is set using a slider. A zero (0) value indicates the material is fully transparent; a value of 100 makes it 100 percent Solid. (Fig. 8.22, Fig. 8.23).

Fig. 8.22: The window texture is set to 100 percent opacity, making it completely opaque.

Fig. 8.23: The opacity for the window texture is lowered to 53 percent, making the material transparent and revealing the model detail behind it.

The Styles Menu

The SketchUp Styles menu controls how surface colors and texture are displayed. The options range from x-ray views peering through model surfaces to wire frame, displaying the edges and lines composing surfaces (Fig. 8.24).

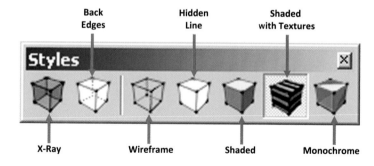

Fig. 8.24: The Styles menu with options

Shaded and Shaded with Texture are the two most important options because they affect performance. They are the two primary settings used for modeling.

To access the Styles menu, select View → Toolbars → Styles. Don't confuse it with the Window → Styles menu, which has very different functions. The Styles menu options are described from left to right as they appear in the menu bar.

X-ray The X-ray button can be toggled on and off. Once turned on, it will work with the other options listed here. X-ray turns all faces in the model transparent, allowing you to see objects normally hidden by other geometry. Furthermore, X-ray allows you to select lines and faces through the transparency. The X-ray button needs to be toggled off (clicked) to turn the x-ray off.

Back Edges Back Edges displays dashed lines through geometry illustrating the back lines that compose a volume or 3D object. Like the X-ray style, it can be toggled on or off and will work with the other style options listed.

Wire Frame This style turns off all model faces. Only the edges and lines that compose the model are visible.

Hidden Line The Hidden Line style turns all colors and textures in the model to white.

Shaded* Shaded turns off all texture images (texture maps) in the model. Any applied textures will appear as solid colors (Fig. 8.25). The color displayed is the boldest or strongest tone of the texture.

Fig. 8.25: The texture images are toggled off in this SketchUp model with Styles set to Textures.

This is an important setting to use when modeling with textured models because SketchUp does not need to process the texture maps on surfaces. Using this style will dramatically increase performance while still providing a clear view of what the model looks like. Use this as the default Styles option and turn on Shaded with Textures only when applying and assessing model textures.

Shaded with Texture* As the name implies, the texture maps of the applied textures in the model are displayed (Fig. 8.26). For slower (and even faster computers), this can cause SketchUp to run slowly as SketchUp needs to regenerate the display every time you orbit, pan, zoom, or otherwise work in the model. Turn on this style when you want to review how textures appear in the model.

Fig. 8.26: Shaded with Textures displays the texture images in the model.

Monochrome The Monochrome style reverts all faces to SketchUp's default face style. This allows you to assess which faces are Front or Back in your model, which is important for some rendering programs.

The Right-Click Texture Menu

The context-sensitive Texture menu allows you to adjust texture images on a selected surface. While the options of moving, scaling, projecting, and rotating a texture are handy, the functionality of these options can be temperamental and nuanced. You'll need to approach these tools with patience and diligence, but they are worth it.

To access the right-click Texture menu, select an active face with an applied material and right-click over the texture. A series of options will appear, including one called Texture. Select Texture to access a second menu with the four options: Position, Reset Position, Projected, and Edit Texture (Fig. 8.27).

You must select one active face. You cannot have multiple faces or edges selected.

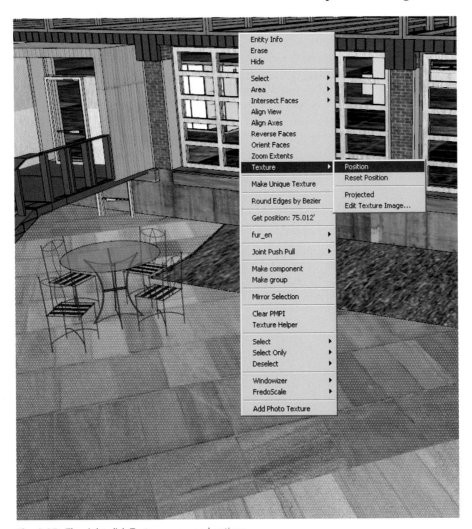

Fig. 8.27: The right-click Texture menu and options

Applying Changes

The adjustments you make to a texture using these options will affect only the texture of the selected face. No other surface containing the same texture will be affected. In order for the changes to be applied to similar surfaces, you will need to select the adjusted texture face with the Eye Dropper and reapply the texture to the other faces.

This means that changes using these options are not universal. However, most changes done to material images with these textures are intended to be localized. See Chapter 9 for more details.

Position*

Position includes a unique set of options that allows textures to be scaled, distorted, rotated, and repositioned on a surface. As noted by the asterisks, the most useful options are scaling and positioning.

Once you select Position, three things will occur:

Four Pins Four different color pins will appear on the texture representing the four tools (Fig. 8.28).

Fig. 8.28: The four colored pins (blue, yellow, red, and green) become visible once Position is selected from the right-click menu.

Texture Map The selected texture will appear beyond the surface on which it's placed. SketchUp is showing the tiling used to lay texture images onto model surfaces (Fig. 8.29).

Fig. 8.29: The texture image tiling extends outward once the right-click Texture menu's Position option is activated.

Move Texture Tool A cursor will change to the Pan icon (a hand). Holding down the left mouse allows you to drag and move the texture (Fig. 8.30). Whenever a pin is inactive, the Pan/Move Texture function is enabled. The Move Texture option combined with texture rotation is useful for placing textures correctly onto a surface for maximum effect. This is outlined in Chapter 9.

Any of the four pins can be selected, and each one provides a different set of options. The Green Pin, Red Pin, and Initial Pan options provide the most utility. The yellow and blue pins are seldom used.

You might need to pan out to view the pins. To select and activate one of the pins, click and hold the mouse button directly over the Pin icons. Moving the mouse while holding down the left mouse button will cause the tool to perform its function.

If you click and release a pin, you will be able to move the pin to a new location (Fig. 8.31). This is useful for setting the center of rotation, as discussed in the "Green Pin" section. If you need to zoom out to view and select the pins, move the red and green pins closer together. Position them so that they are easier to view and use.

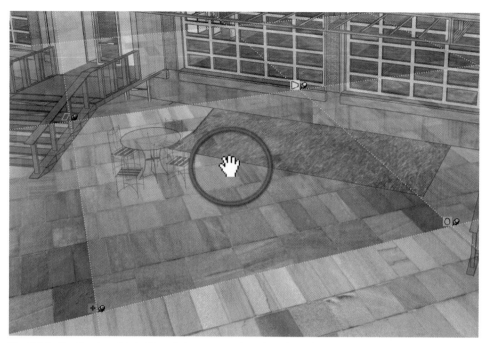

Fig. 8.30: The Pan icon (circled in red) becomes active when the right-click Texture Position tool is activated.

Fig. 8.31: Moving the pins to different spots can make it easier to use the various pin functions.

If you want to set changes you've made using the pins, press the Enter key. This will also deactivate the Texture Context tool. If you do not want to apply any changes, simply press the Esc key at any time.

Red Pin–Move* The red pin sets the "center point" of the texture for editing. When using the green pin Rotate function, the red pin will act as the center axis of rotation of the texture. To use it effectively, center the red pin on your screen, place the green pin in close proximity, and zoom in. This will give you more control over the texture rotation.

Green Pin–Rotate and Scale* Holding down the green pin causes a protractor to appear at the center of the red pin. Moving the mouse will cause the texture to rotate, scale, or both (Fig. 8.32). Using the tool requires some finesse and patience. You can rotate the texture without scaling, and you can rotate a texture using the increments on the protractor (Fig. 8.33). It takes slow, steady mouse motions. Generally, moving the mouse left or right will cause the texture to scale (Fig. 8.34); moving the mouse in wide arcs will cause it to rotate. Placing the red and green pins in close proximity, as previously mentioned, helps provide greater control.

Fig. 8.32: Selecting the green pin causes a protractor to appear, allowing you to scale and rotate the texture image.

Fig. 8.33: Slowly moving the mouse in an arc will cause the texture image to rotate.

Fig. 8.34: Slowly moving the mouse left or right will cause the texture image to scale up or down in size.

Unfortunately, you can't enter values in the Measurements bar to provide exact scale and rotation values.

Yellow Pin–Distort   The yellow pin will distort a texture, adjusting toward a perspective-type vanishing point. This can be useful when trying to put an image or texture in perspective.

Blue Pin–Shear/Scale   This option can create some interesting distortions and ripples in a texture, but like the yellow pin, it is not as useful as the red and green pins.

Applying Textures to Terrains and Organic Surfaces

The Projected option is used to apply textures to irregular surfaces, such as terrain and the curved surfaces of objects or buildings.

Applying textures to irregular, rounded, or organic surfaces can be tricky in SketchUp. Rounded surfaces are composed of many flat faces that create the illusion of curvature. When textures are initially applied to these surfaces, the material will appear distorted and fractured (Fig. 8.35): every face takes on the texture image but does not work in tandem with neighboring surfaces to display a singular pattern or motif. The result can make the applied texture look like shattered glass (Fig. 8.36).

The Projected option allows textures to be applied to irregular, organic, rounded, and terrain-like surfaces (Fig. 8.37, Fig. 8.38). The process is simple, but there are some special considerations.

Fig. 8.35: An aerial image is applied as a texture to the terrain surface.

Fig. 8.36: Each facet/face of the terrain displays the aerial image differently, causing the image to appear distorted.

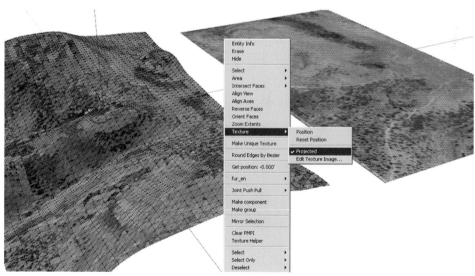

Fig. 8.37: Selecting the Projected option from the right-click Texture menu can fix the aerial appurtenance on the applied surface.

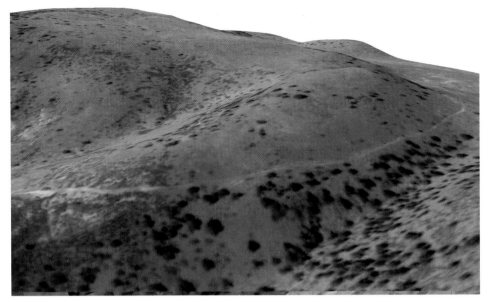

Fig. 8.38: The aerial image is fixed, correctly displaying on the surface.

Texture and Surface Orientation

The texture to be placed onto the irregular surface must first be applied to a flat surface. This flat surface must then be parallel to the irregular surface. For example, if you want to place a texture or an aerial image (which is a giant texture) onto a terrain model, the aerial must first be applied to a flat horizontal surface.

Another example would be vertical curtains. The texture must be applied to a surface that is both vertical and in-line with the curtain, making it parallel (Fig. 8.39).

Fig. 8.39: The curtain model on the far left will have the texture to its right applied to its surface. The applied texture must be parallel (both vertically and horizontally) to the applied image. The right side of the image shows the texture correctly applied to the curtain model.

Here is the process broken down into easy-to-follow steps:

1. Apply the desired texture to a flat surface.
2. Orient the surface parallel to the irregular surface.
3. Select the flat face with the applied texture, right-click, select Texture, and then Projected.
4. Select all the edges and faces of the irregular surface. If it's a group or component, enter the group/component instance. Triple-click to select all the edges and faces. Make sure that faces you do not want to be painted are not selected.
5. Use the Paint Bucket Eye Dropper and select the flat surface with the projected texture.
6. The Paint Bucket applicator will become active. Apply the material to the selected irregular surface. The material will be applied correctly to the irregular surface.

Things to Consider

Several important factors affect the way textures are displayed using the Projected option for organic surfaces.

Surface Orientation

The orientation of the flat surface with the texture that will be projected needs to be parallel to the irregular surface onto which it will be projected.

If the irregular surface is (mostly) oriented along the horizontal plane of SketchUp (terrain, for example), then the surface with the projected texture must be oriented along the horizontal plane. If the irregular surface is mostly vertical, then the projected surface must be vertical. The direction of vertical surfaces must be consistent as well.

Select All Edges and Faces

When applying the projected texture onto the irregular surface, all the edges and faces must be selected (Fig. 8.40). This includes all hidden edges, which will be present 100 percent of the time with any irregular surfaces (unless they are all visible). The best way to select all the faces and edges on these surfaces is to do a triple-click selection. However, because triple-click will also select all noncomponent or grouped geometry objects connected to the irregular surface, you should ensure that the irregular surface is its own group or component.

Nothing Is Perfect

This method is not foolproof or perfect. The more an irregular surface curves away from the orientation of the projected flat texture surface, some distortion will appear on the edges of the irregular geometry. This is most common when trying to project a texture onto a sphere. Depending on the orientation of the projected texture, the sides of the sphere not aligned with the projected surface will still be distorted.

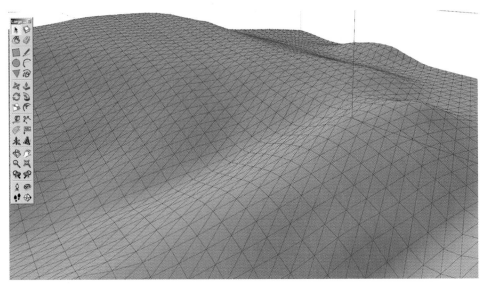

Fig. 8.40: The entire surface is selected, including the edges that compose the surface.

Right-Click Texture Bugs

The right-click Texture option does have some bugs worth noting.

Texture Option Missing When a surface with a texture is being selected, the Texture option will not always appear in the right-click menu. Reapplying the same texture to the surface usually fixes this problem (but not always). This bug is common with surfaces nested inside a group or component. Make sure that the surface is selectable and that you are not selecting the group or component.

Green Pin-Rotate and Scale The Green Pin option can be hard to control. When you're trying to rotate a texture's position on a surface, the Scaling option activates. It takes a slow and steady mouse to simply rotate the texture without scaling it and vice versa. Compounding that, you cannot use the Value Control box or Measurements area in SketchUp (bottom right of the screen) to enter values for either rotation or scale. Hopefully, the SketchUp developers will fix these options in the future because these tools are necessary for applying textures onto surfaces in SketchUp for rendering.

You should explore the Green Pin option as much as you can.

Ruby Script UV Tool for Organic Texturing

Dale Martens, a structural engineer and Ruby Script tools writer, created the UV Tools for SketchUp. These tools allow you to map textures onto complex organic surfaces. Go to Resources to find this tool and other Ruby Scripts useful for rendering.

Apply, Assess, and Adjust

In what follows, "the three As" (Apply, Assess, and Adjust) refers to the steps taken to achieve rich, realistic textures laid out onto model surfaces. The three As are part checklist and part actions to be performed. This chapter will teach you the specifics for each step. Use this chapter as a reference manual and refer back to it as you progress through the rendering process.

You should follow all of the Apply steps. The Assess and Adjust steps are optional if you are new to rendering. Assess and Adjust are good practices to adopt as you gain more experience and practice. *However, if you are new to rendering, be patient with yourself and gradually implement these additional steps*. Your time is better spent mastering the basic techniques before trying to fully implement these additional Assess and Adjust steps. Eventually, with time and practice, the three As should become an integral and habitual part of your rendering process.

The Three As

The tools used for the three As are reviewed in Chapter 8. Make sure you have read the chapter to ensure that you are familiar with the general function of the tools outlined in this chapter. The three As are

- ▶ **Apply**: Place textures onto surfaces.
- ▶ **Assess**: Evaluate textures for clarity and quality.
- ▶ **Adjust**: Based on your assessments, scale, position, rotate, edit, and swap the textures to achieve your desired look.

The Goal of the Three As

The three As encompass the process of texturing with the goal of laying down material images to bring a rendering to life and convey a sense of realism (Fig. 9.1, Fig. 9.2). *Realism* refers to how a rendered material would look in a factual and tangible sense when evaluated against its real-world counterpart.

Fig. 9.1: These five images show the progression of textures added to the model. Solid colors are swapped with texture images.

Fig. 9.2: Once the texture images are all in place, the model is rendered (SU Podium).

The Nonlinear Process

Indeed, the three As process is nonlinear. As you work, you should always be assessing how a material appears on surfaces after it's initially applied. You will tweak the textures during the iterative rendering process (see Chapter 20). Make sure to scrutinize your material images before inserting them into a model. "Assess" refers to the aspect of learning to look and see, meaning you should look with a critical eye at your model's detail.

Apply

Three steps are taken to apply textures. They are key to quickly setting up the model for rendering. Skipping the initial step will create extra work, even leading to rendering inaccuracies of missing textures and colors on faces. The steps are:

1. Apply color to the model faces.
2. Replace colors with textures.
3. Scale the inserted textures.

Apply Color to Model Faces

Many users make the mistake of modeling and extruding surfaces without applying a color or texture. This omission results in extra time spent placing colors or materials on every extruded nook and cranny of a model. For fully articulated models, this can be a time-consuming process. Also, some surfaces will require only a color, not a texture, and it makes sense to apply that color during this step. For best results, do the following:

1. Always apply solid colors.
2. Apply colors before extruding.
3. Apply many colors.
4. Apply colors to the outside of components and groups.

Always Apply Solid Colors

Always apply a solid color to surfaces when actively modeling. You can easily replace all instances of a particular solid color in one step with a custom texture material from your Texture Library. The default SketchUp material has no color; none of its associated default material instances can be replaced with a texture material in one step. The default SketchUp material is not considered a solid color for purposes of this step.

Although you should not use SketchUp's default material, you can use SketchUp's native textures for this process if you want to include some level of texture accuracy in the initial model. These textures can be edited with a new custom material.

You will not always know what materials you will be using for your model. Instead of agonizing over the materials required up front, simply paint some colors now and allow yourself to worry about needed materials later. This will free you to focus on the model shape and form, and it will make it easier to prepare the model for rendering when you're ready.

Apply Colors Before Extruding

Flat surfaces will extrude all sides with the color applied to the initial flat surfaces (Fig. 9.3). This step will save you valuable time and headaches. While it's not always possible, you should apply solid colors to flat surfaces before you extrude them (Fig. 9.4, Fig. 9.5).

Apply Many Colors

Consider what you are modeling and use color to differentiate between model surfaces. If you know a surface will be a wall or counter, apply one color to surfaces that are walls and another to countertops (Fig. 9.6). If the next surface will be a ceiling or cabinet, add a different color for each.

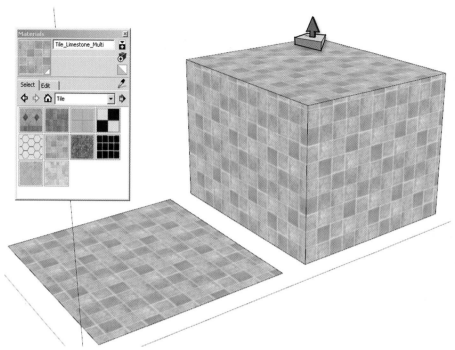

Fig. 9.3: The texture is applied to the flat surface (left). Once the surface is extruded, all of the sides possess the texture.

Fig. 9.4: Make sure solid colors are applied to all model surfaces.

Fig. 9.5: Do not use the default SketchUp option. Always apply colors to the model surfaces.

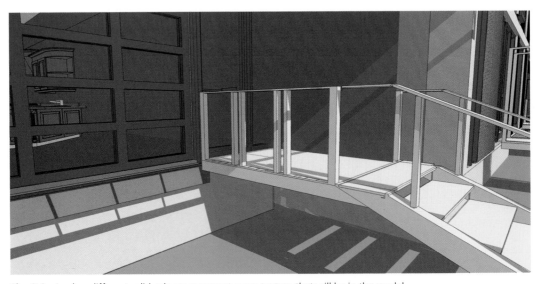

Fig. 9.6: Apply a different solid color to represent every texture that will be in the model.

Part 2: Textures

You will want to swap out the solid color with a specific texture appropriate to that surface (Fig. 9.7, Fig. 9.8). So while you do not need to apply the correct material, you should put some consideration into coloring your model to prepare it for textures appropriate to the surfaces.

Fig. 9.7: The solid colors are replaced with texture images from the Texture Library.

Fig. 9.8: The rendered version of the applied textures (Twilight Render)

It's important to note that some surfaces will not require a texture image. A solid color will work fine as long as IRP values are applied to the color. This is a subjective decision. Some metals render better with an image, others do not. Examples of such surfaces are metals, plastics, porcelains, windows, and similar smooth surfaces that are reflective, polished, or transparent. In these instances, choose a solid color that best represents the color of the material.

Apply Colors to the Outside of Components and Groups

Objects and geometry that are bundled as components and groups have the unique ability to have a color applied to the outside of the component or group instance. The surfaces inside a component/group without a color (the default) will all take on the applied color, and you won't have to color apply all of them (Fig. 9.9, Fig. 9.10). Any surface already containing a color will ignore the color application.

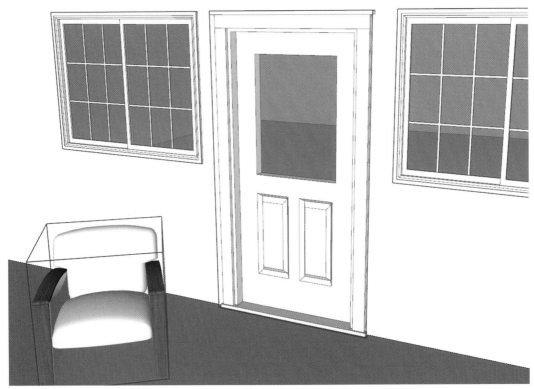

Fig. 9.9: Most of the window, door, and chair component surfaces do not possess any color. Except for the window glass, door glass, and chair arms, they are all painted with the SketchUp default material.

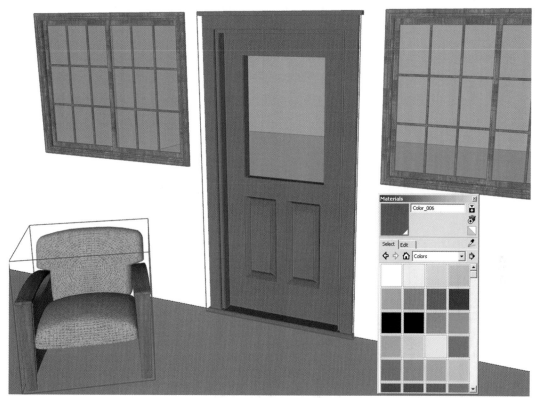

Fig. 9.10: Applying a color to the outside of the component will cause all the default surfaces to take on that color/texture.

Replace Colors with Textures

Inserting a custom texture to replace a solid color or native SketchUp texture is simple. Once you are ready to apply specific textures to the model surfaces, follow these quick steps.

1. Using the Paint Bucket Eye Dropper, select the model surface with a solid color (Fig. 9.11). Next, go to the Edit tab and under Texture, select the Browse button. SketchUp *should* be pointed toward your Texture Library. If not, do so now, as outlined at the end of Chapter 7 under Linking the Texture Library. (Fig. 9.12).

2. Quickly navigate to the appropriate texture folder. Select the desired image and press OK. Every surface with the same color will now contain that texture image (Fig. 9.13).

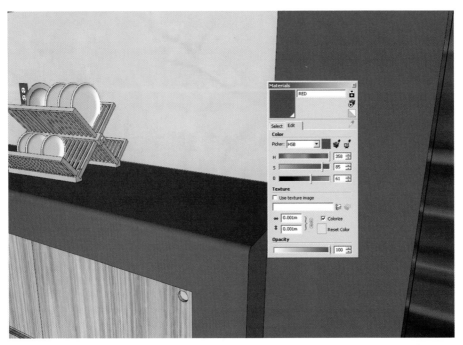

Fig. 9.11: The SketchUp Paint Bucket Eye Dropper tool is used to select the solid red color of the counter.

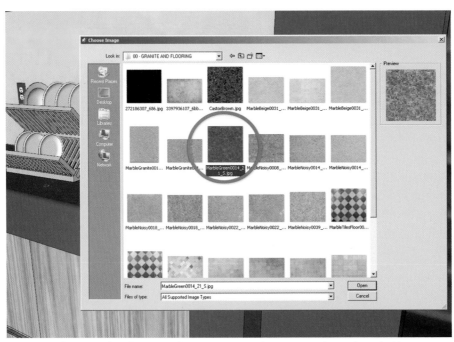

Fig. 9.12: After you select the Browse button, you can select a texture image from the Texture Library to replace the red color of the counter.

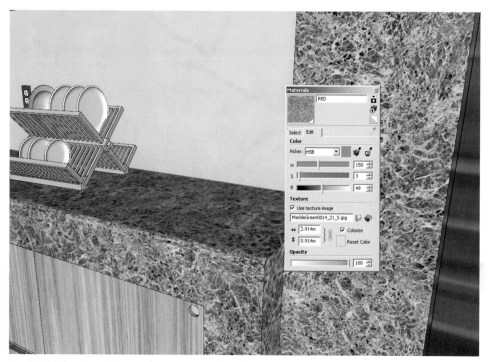

Fig. 9.13: The selected texture image now replaces the red color.

Scale Inserted Textures

Nine times out of ten, the inserted texture image will be indistinct and too small. SketchUp displays inserted textures at a default of 1′ (Fig. 9.14). For most CG Texture images (and textures from other websites), this scale is not large enough (Fig. 9.15).

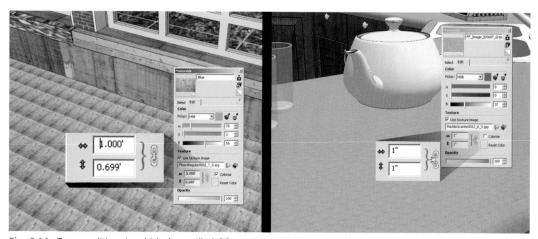

Fig. 9.14: Two conditions in which the applied CG textures are incorrectly scaled and appear too small on the surfaces

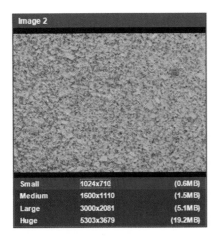

Small	1024x710	(0.6MB)
Medium	1600x1110	(1.5MB)
Large	3000x2081	(5.1MB)
Huge	5303x3679	(19.2MB)

Fig. 9.15: The small CG Texture.com textures are ideal for SketchUp surfaces and are easily scaled for appearance.

If the texture appears indistinct, too small, or overly patterned, adjust the scale. Go to the Edit tab and under Texture, change either length or width to a higher scale. For *most* small texture downloads from CG Textures.com, the appropriate scale number ranges from 8′ to 24′ or higher. Start with 8′ and incrementally increase the texture size until it looks correct for its context. Unfortunately, this is not always the case, as can be seen in Fig. 9.16 countertop Texture is correctly scaled at 2′. You will further assess the image scale during the adjust and assess process.

Fig. 9.16: The textures from Fig. 9.14 are scaled upward, providing a clear appearance on the model surface.

Swap Textures

If a texture does not look correct even after scaled or after being rendered, swap it out with a different version (Fig. 9.17). Simply select the texture with the Eye Dropper tool; in the Paint Bucket Edit menu, under Texture, click on Browse. Select a new texture to swap the current version with the new texture (Fig. 9.18).

Fig. 9.17: The rendering of the wall with brick texture looks off and doesn't provide the correct material character (Shaderlight).

Fig. 9.18: The wall texture is replaced with a new brick material and rerendered (Shaderlight).

Assess and Adjust

Assessing and adjusting textures is both an objective and a subjective process. Objectively, textures should possess particular characteristics. Subjective qualities can be assessed only by the modeler; only you know if the texture meets your exact needs. Here are some characteristics and qualities to assess and some recommended adjustments.

General Clarity, Quality, and Character

Assess the texture and decide if it meets the needs and goals of the model and model context. Some textures might appear correct and accurate in the SketchUp model, but appear different and discontinuous when rendered. Frequently, it will be appropriate to swap out a texture for a different version based on these assessments. Swap out any textures that render poorly.

Color/Contrast/Hue Saturation

The color, tones, contrast, and hues of a texture can be altered to provide a specific look. A texture might have the correct appearance but the wrong color. For example, gray-blue pavers can be altered to have a warm yellow-gray look (Fig. 9.19). Red corrugated metal can be adjusted to a green patina (Fig. 9.20). Polished, light-tan granite can be edited to dark granite (Fig. 9.21, Fig. 9.22).

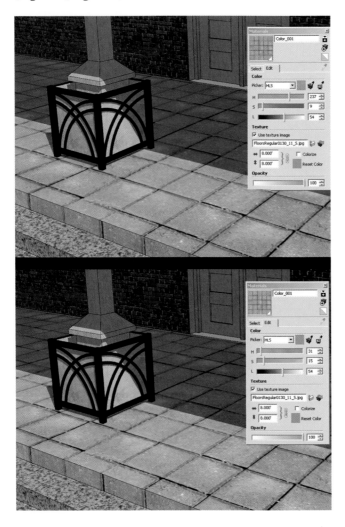

Fig. 9.19: The blue paving color is adjusted to a warm gray.

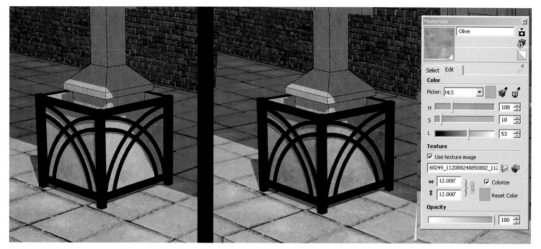

Fig. 9.20: The corrugated metal is adjusted to appear green patina.

Fig. 9.21: The countertop granite-yellow color can be adjusted to a different hue.

Fig. 9.22: The HLS options in the SketchUp Paint Bucket menu can be used to alter the countertop to a darker color.

In some instances, the material might be better with sharp contrasting edges or require a more muted variation across the surface. For example, mortar between bricks can be adjusted to possess greater contrast allowing for stronger delineation between the bricks and joints. A groundcover, carpet, fabric, paint, or metal might require muted textures. A texture might have a strong hue that can be toned down (Fig. 9.23). The variations are endless. The point is that the original texture colors and tones can be adjusted to suit the needs of the render.

The Paint Bucket Edit menu can be used to adjust the hue, saturations, and colors of textures. Use the HLS (HSB on a Mac) or RGB color Picker functions to make these adjustments. Remember that using the SketchUp Paint Bucket produces limited results and that an external photo-editing program linked to SketchUp is the ideal approach for adjusting color, contrast, and hue on textures (see Chapter 10).

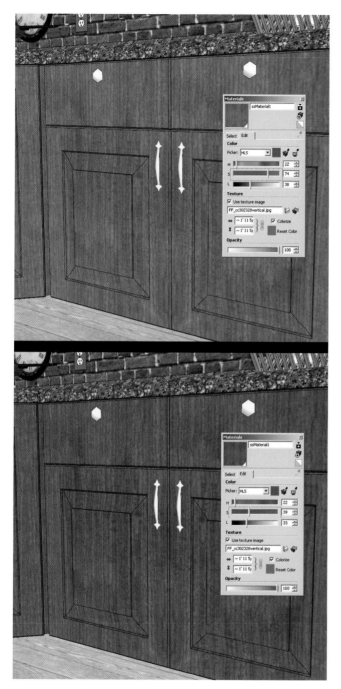

Fig. 9.23: By using the HLS editing options, you can adjust the hue/saturation of the wood material to appear darker and grayer.

Surface and Model Context

Textures represent real-world materials and surfaces constructed into a context befitting their purpose. A sometimes overlooked aspect of texture placement is addressing the specific circumstances of the material. Consider the following to determine whether textures fit with the model context and reposition textures as appropriate.

Orientation

Is the applied material oriented in the correct manner relative to the environment in which it is placed? For example, if an applied flooring texture is skewed, creating an awkward and unrealistic appearance, rotate the texture, using the Position texture tool, so it's aligned to the room's orientation and reflects a real-world condition (Fig. 9.24, Fig. 9.25).

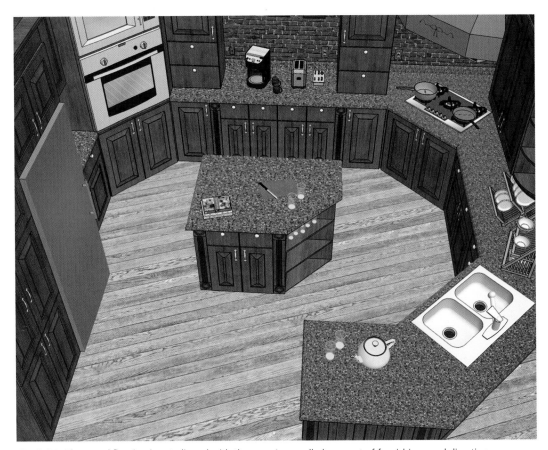

Fig. 9.24: The wood flooring is not aligned with the room's overall placement of furnishings and direction.

Fig. 9.25: The right-click Texture tool can be used to rotate the wood flooring texture to match the room's orientation.

Alignment

Align textures to meet at edges or at the confluence of surfaces. Here are two examples:

▶ Scaling and aligning concrete scoring so that it's aligned both vertically and horizontally provides a more realistic situation (Fig. 9.26, Fig. 9.27)

▶ Repositioning textures to create a congruent appearance where two walls meet with a ceramic tiles texture, but the alignment of the tiles does not meet (Fig. 9.28)

Fig. 9.26: The concrete curb and horizontal paving do not align.

Fig. 9.27: The right-click Texture tool is used to reposition the concrete surface applied to the vertical face of the curb. The texture joints are aligned with the adjacent concrete paving.

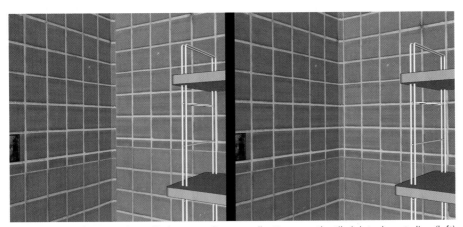

Fig. 9.28: The tile texture is applied to two adjacent walls. However, the tile joints do not align (left). One of the applied texture faces is adjusted using the right-click Texture Move option to align to the joints to the adjacent wall (right).

Variety

The placement of a texture on multiple surfaces visible in a view can cause the appearance of unnatural repetition. In essence, the moiré pattern becomes visible even though the texture is not a single texture. Two examples are:

▶ The beams making up a trellis all have the same wood texture. However, each beam looks identical, which causes a distracting pattern (Fig. 9.29). Using the Position Texture tools, move the wood texture on each beam to create variety (Fig. 9.30, Fig 9.31). If the beams are components, adjusting one will adjust the others. You might need to make each beam a unique component to edit the textures. (Select the component, right-click, and select Make Unique.)

▶ The backs of the steps visible through the door have the same pattern. Using the Position Texture tool (right-click and select Texture), adjust the texture for each back of step to create more variety and remove the visible pattern (Fig. 9.32).

Fig. 9.29: The trellis wood beams appear to be identical in terms of textures.

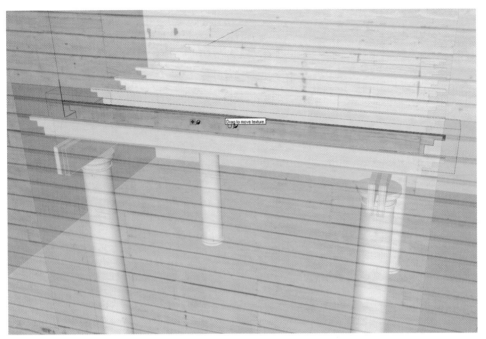

Fig. 9.30: Using the right-click Texture tool's Move option, you can adjust the wood pattern on the beams.

Fig. 9.31: The result is that each beam looks unique, making the object more realistic.

Fig. 9.32: The backs of the steps have the same appearance due to the wood texture placement (left). The textures for each step are adjusted to give it a more realistic appearance (right).

Multiple Versions

Using multiple versions of the same texture can create more variety. Referring back to the trellis example, several versions of the wood texture can create the desired variety and remove the repetitive patterns (Fig. 9.33). CG Textures.com usually has multiple versions of a texture available for download.

Fig. 9.33: The two walls have the same texture material type. However, two different versions of the texture were applied to each wall surface giving them a more diverse look.

Blemishes

Textures can have small areas of imperfection, fault, or stain. These blemishes become readily apparent when the textures are placed and scaled on surfaces. They are usually easy to notice before you render, but they are especially noticeable after rendering.

There are two options for removing blemishes. The first is to swap out the material for a different image. The second is to remove the blemish from the image in an external photo-editing program. This is reviewed in Chapter 10.

Distorted Hues

Some textures images are composed of contrasting colors. The contrasts can become visible after a texture is adjusted in a photo-editing program or using the HLS / HSB sliders: spots of rainbow pixels infect the texture, detracting from its appearance (Fig. 9.34). You can repair the effect using the Colorize option in the Paint Bucket Edit menu. Checking the Colorize box will allow the dominant color of the texture to fill in and replace the multihued speckles (Fig. 9.35).

Fig. 9.34: The texture color adjustment resulted in a distorted, splotchy hue.

Fig. 9.35: Using the Colorize option under the Edit tab of the Paint bucket, you can remove the distortion.

Moiré Patterns and Seamless Textures

A moiré pattern is a seemingly endless repeating pattern of the texture image on a surface (Fig. 9.36). Moiré patterns occur when you are using tiled or seamless textures. The larger the surface area, the more likely it is that a moiré pattern will become apparent because of the repeating tiles of the texture. Ground covers, lawns, asphalt, and concrete paving are common culprits (Fig. 9.37).

Fig. 9.36: The texture for the lawn has a clearly visible repeating moiré pattern.

Moiré patterns caused by a seamless texture that is scaled too small are common when you're first learning to apply textures (which is why scaling is the first thing you should do after applying a texture to a face). There are two approaches to dealing with moiré patterns. Each can cause other problems, warranting further adjustments, which are discussed later in this chapter.

Scaling   Increase the overall scale of the texture until the pattern is less recognizable (Fig. 9.38, Fig. 9.39, Fig. 9.40). If this causes the texture to look too large or unrealistic, consider using an irregular texture as described next or try swapping out the texture.

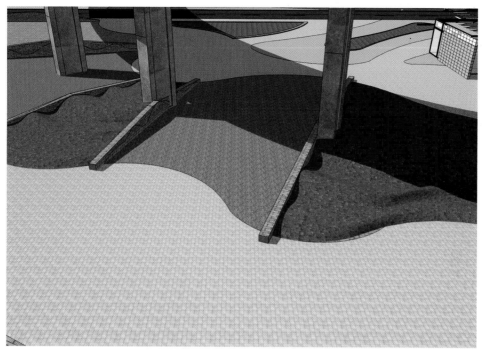

Fig. 9.37: The ground plane textures for the park all have clearly repeating patterns.

Fig. 9.38: The ground planes are scaled upward for a more appropriate appearance.

Fig. 9.39: The scaled ground plane textures in context with the other model amenities

Large irregular texture   Download a large size texture that is not tiled or seamless. This is one instance where using a large texture image is desirable; the larger the size, the better. A large texture is greater than 1,024 pixels in width and height.

The goal is to scale and position the large irregular texture to allow the variety of character to dominate the appearance of the surface (Fig. 9.41). In other words, use a texture that does not contain a repeating, notable pattern. One issue with this method is that any seams can be visible where the irregular texture repeats on the surface. This can be mitigated by following suggested adjustments as discussed next.

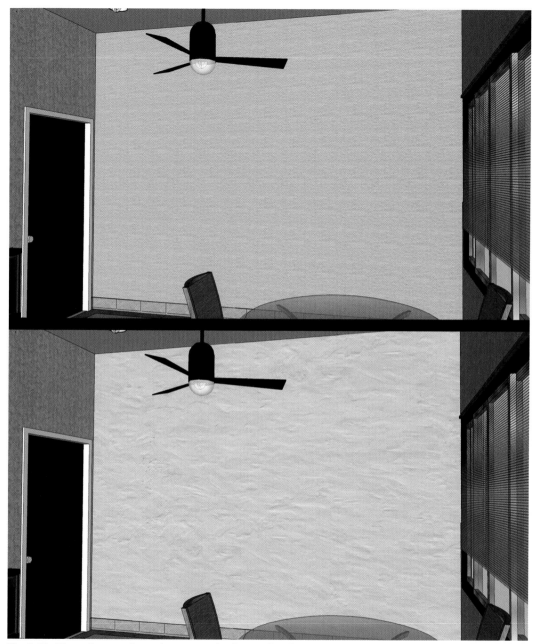

Fig. 9.40: The wall texture has a clear pattern (top). Rescaling the image allows the wall paint texture to look better (bottom).

Fig. 9.41: A large, irregular lawn texture swaps out the previous lawn texture (Fig. 9.36), giving the surface a clearer appearance.

Seams and Irregular Textures

Seams occur when the edges of an applied, irregular texture image meet and cause a noticeable or faint discrepancy to appear (Fig. 9.42). The most obvious way to fix this problem is to use seamless textures: the four edges of the image will match perfectly. When placed next to each other, there will be no seam. However, seamless textures can lead to moiré patterns (as noted previously).

When you make any adjustments to a seam, make sure to consider the camera view to be used for rendering (see Chapter 15). Using any of the following methods, you can hide the seam so it is not visible in a particular camera view.

Scaling One option is to scale the texture so the seam does not appear in the camera view.

Position Using the right-click Texture tools, reposition (move or rotate) the texture so the seam is not visible in camera view (Fig. 9.43).

Hide Using model detail (see Part 3), place components or objects to obscure the seam in the camera view (Fig. 9.44).

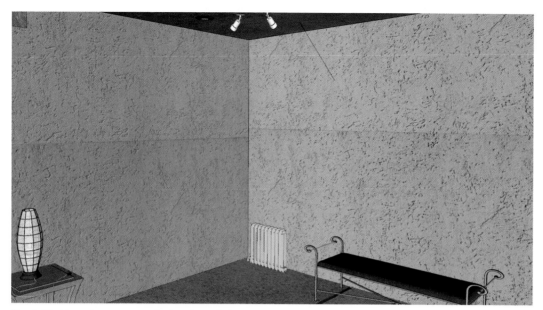

Fig. 9.42: The paint texture applied to the walls has a subtle but visible seam.

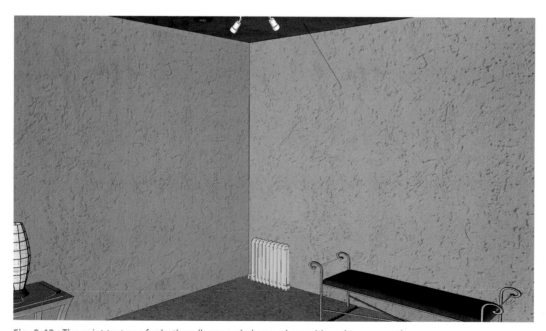

Fig. 9.43: The paint textures for both walls are scaled up and repositioned to remove the seam.

Fig. 9.44: Painting components are placed on the walls to help hide or minimize the view of the seams.

Transitions Subdivide the surface at the location of the seam (Fig. 9.45, Fig. 9.46). Then do one or both of the following: reposition (move or rotate) one of the surfaces to minimize the visibility of the seam and/or apply a different version of the same texture onto one of the surfaces. The goal is to create an intentional seam, allowing the two surfaces to transition into each other.

Fig. 9.45: The floor texture has multiple visible seams.

Fig. 9.46: A transition band is modeled into the floor at the seams' locations.

Texture Tips

Here are several useful tips to help you work with textures, save time, and have additional options.

Multiple Versions of a Texture

In some instances, having multiple versions of the same texture with varying colors (or other adjustments) can be useful. An effective way to create multiple versions is to copy, adjust, and save alternative versions.

Select the texture or color you want to duplicate and adjust it. From the Paint Bucket menu, select Create Material. A Create Material window will appear using the same texture image (Fig. 9.47). You can give this version a new name and make any other adjustments as needed (Fig. 9.48). Next, apply the texture to surfaces (Fig. 9.49). Any adjustments made to this version of the copy will not affect the original source texture.

Fig. 9.47: The texture to be duplicated and altered is selected. The Create Material button is clicked, opening the texture in the Create Material menu.

Fig. 9.48: The newly created texture (which is a duplicate of the original) has its color adjusted (using the HLS option).

Fig. 9.49: The new material is applied to the floor surface. The material is the same image as its original, but it has a totally different color.

Swapping Between Models

Once you have several rendered models under your belt, consider moving materials between models. This is an effective way to save time and effort. If you are going to use the same render program for your next model render, copying and pasting the texture from one model to the next has several advantages:

▶ The texture will have the appropriate scale and appearance.

▶ The render values (specific to the IRP) will move between models, saving you time because you won't have to reapply these values.

Here are the steps you can take to copy between models:

1. Open up the SketchUp model with already-applied textures.

2. Use the Rectangle tool and create as many surfaces as textures you want to copy.

3. Using the Material Eye Dropper, select one of the desired textures and apply it to one of the rectangle surfaces created in the previous step.

4. Repeat the process for all the textures.

5. Select all the rectangle swatches and go to Edit → Copy (Fig. 9.50).

6. Either open up a new version of SketchUp or go to File → Open, and open the model to which you want to transfer the material textures.

7. Once the model is open, go to Edit → Paste.

8. The rectangle swatches will be placed in the new model. The render values (if they were applied), scaling, and other texture edits or effects will transfer (Fig. 9.51).

9. You can use the Material Eye Dropper to sample the textures and apply them to surfaces.

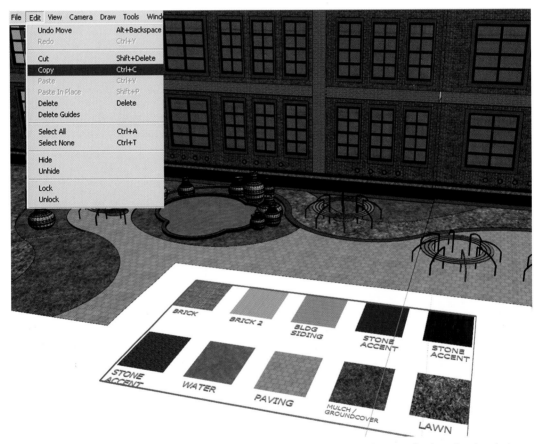

Fig. 9.50: The textures in the model are placed onto rectangular surfaces. Then they are all selected and copied.

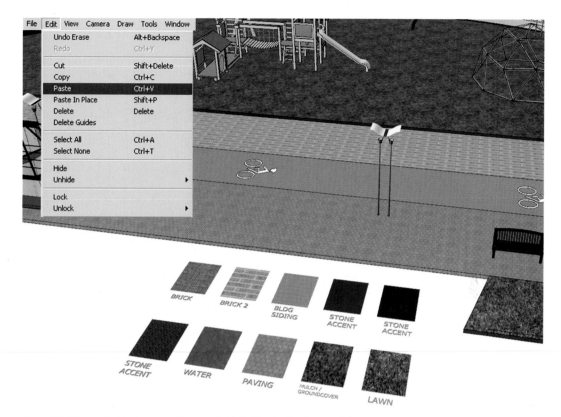

Fig. 9.51: The copied textures are then pasted into the destination model.

Saving a SketchUp Swatch Library

The method of swapping between models can be taken a step further. Consider creating a dedicated SketchUp file that contains only swatches with ready-to-render textures. Because texture images cannot be saved out of SketchUp and retain scale or render values, this becomes an effective way to have a ready-made and ready-to-go set of textures for future rendering models.

Saving a Texture

You can save edited textures back into your Texture Library. To do that, you'll need to use the external photo-editing option. You'll learn how to do that in the next chapter.

Editing Textures in an External Photo Editor

CHAPTER

10

Sketchup can be linked to an external photo-editing software package, such as Adobe Photoshop, to create greater variety in an image. Photoshop tools can improve textures and generate new materials to be saved into the Texture Library. Although a photo editor is not essential when preparing a model for rendering, the options one provides can make for better renderings, through high-quality edits—such as adjusting color, adding grain, and fixing blemishes—that simply are not possible within SketchUp alone.

The chapter references Adobe Photoshop to demonstrate alteration methods. Other editing software, such as Gimp or something similar, can be used instead.

Linking an Editor to SketchUp

Go to Window → Preferences (PC) or SketchUp → Preferences (Mac), and select the Applications tab on the left (Fig. 10.1). A single option will appear on the right. Select Open and use the file browser to navigate to the directory location of the desired photo editor. Select the application's executable file and press OK (Fig. 10.2). Close the Preferences window. SketchUp will be forever linked to the software.

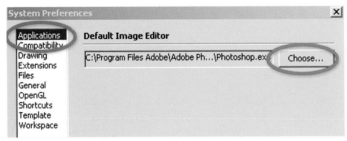

Fig. 10.1: SketchUp can be linked with external photo-editing software, in this case Adobe Photoshop.

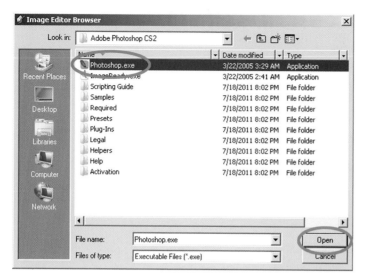

Fig. 10.2: Once you've selected the Browse button under Application, navigate to the photo-editing software application folder and select the program. Then click OK.

Launching, Editing, and Saving

To launch the editor, select a texture in the model using the Eye Dropper (Fig. 10.3). Do not select a solid color; it has no image to edit. In the Edit tab of the Paint Bucket menu under Textures, select the Edit Texture in External Editor button. The photo editor will launch with the selected texture open (Fig, 10.4).

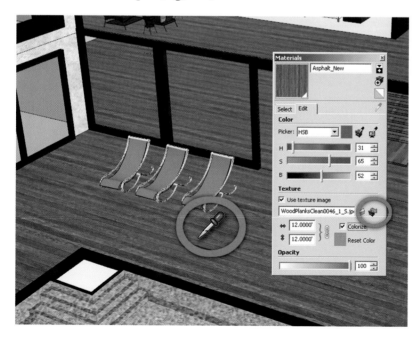

Fig. 10.3: Using the SketchUp Paint Bucket, select the material. Click the Edit Texture button in the external editor.

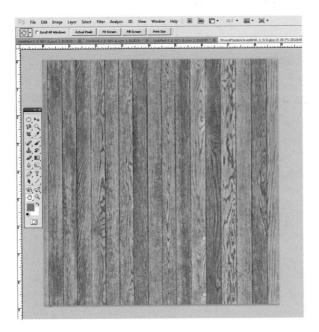

Fig. 10.4: The photo-editing program will automatically launch, displaying the selected texture, which is not yet ready to be edited.

Saving and Updating the Texture

In the editor, make any needed alterations (Fig. 10.5). Then save the file (File → Save) or close the Texture window and save upon closing. Overwrite the file if asked (Fig. 10.6). Return to SketchUp. The material will be updated automatically with the alterations (Fig. 10.7).

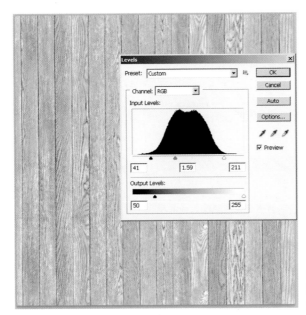

Fig. 10.5: The wood texture is adjusted in Photoshop. By adjusting the Levels, you can make the texture appear light.

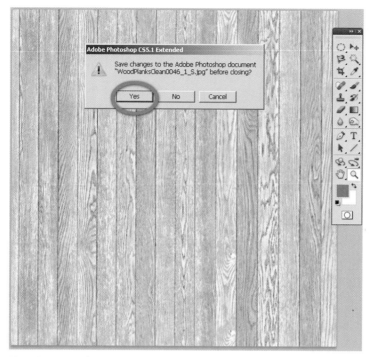

Fig. 10.6: Once the edits are completed, save the file.

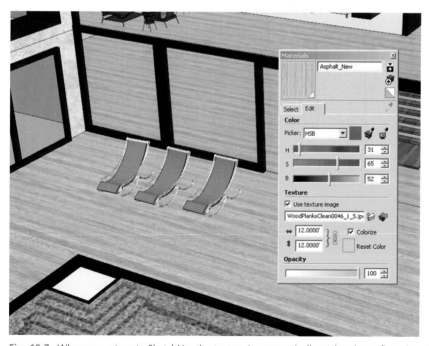

Fig. 10.7: When you return to SketchUp, the texture is automatically updated to reflect the edits.

The changes you make to the material will affect only the applied texture in the model. Editing the texture does not alter or update the core material saved in your Texture Library.

Saving to the Texture Library

Adjusted textures can be saved to the Material Library. Simply perform a Save As into the appropriate Texture Library folder.

Undoing Texture Edits

If you do not like the appearance of an adjusted texture once you are back in SketchUp, you can undo the changes (Alt+Backspace or Edit → Undo).

Removing/Flattening Layers

If you are a skilled Photoshop user, you might add or duplicate layers when editing. Before saving them, make sure all of the layers are flattened. If you do not flatten any layers before saving, Photoshop will require that the material be saved as a new file. This will delink the image from SketchUp and prevent any updates from being applied to the texture in the model. By flattening the layers, you will allow normal saving and updating.

Typical Alterations

Below are some typical changes that you can make to material images. Many of these alterations are subjective; others are objective, as described in Chapter 9. Complete as many alterations as needed to improve the texture.

Adjusting Levels/Brightness/Contrast

In Photoshop, select Image → Adjustments → Levels or Adjustments → Brightness/Contrast.

Adjusting the brightness and contrast of a texture allows you to sharpen or mute a texture's surface details (Fig. 10.8). Contrasting allows texture character to stand out. For example, contrasting brick, concrete, tiled floor, wood grain, or home siding materials will cause the joints, seams, and grains to have greater depth. When rendered, the contrast will give more relief to the material (Fig. 10.9).

Increasing contrast can also increase color saturation. Decreasing the hue and saturation of material after you've adjusted the levels is recommended (Fig. 10.10).

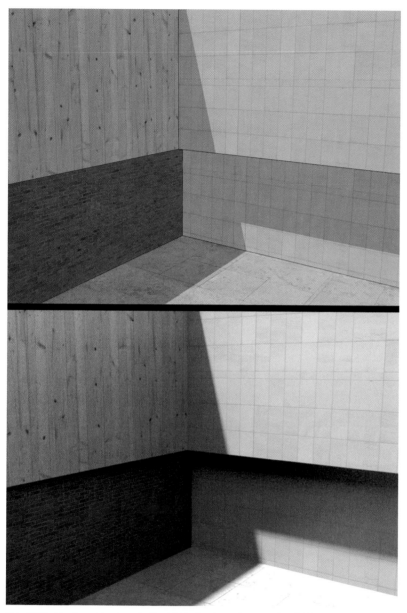

Fig. 10.8: Unaltered textures in SketchUp (top) are then rendered (Shaderlight).

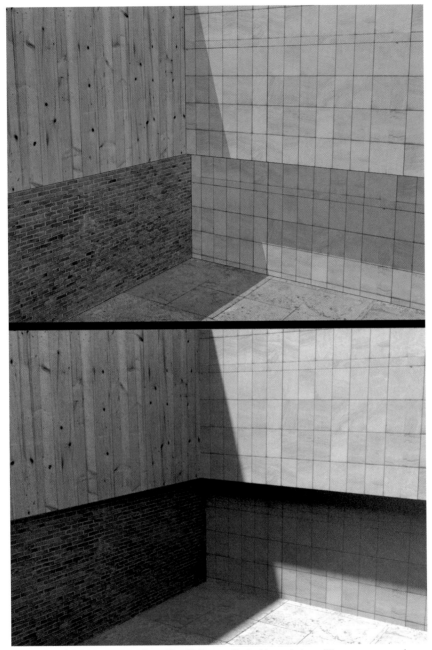

Fig. 10.9: The same textures from Fig. 10.8 are adjusted in a photo-editing program and given greater contrast. The top image shows the edited textures in SketchUp. The bottom image shows the textures rendered in Shaderlight with greater depth due to the adjustments.

Fig. 10.10: The original texture (left) has its levels adjusted (middle) and then slightly desaturated (right).

Decreasing the contrast can help soften a texture, giving it a more uniform look without drawing attention to any single aspect of the material (Fig. 10.11, Fig. 10.12). This might be useful on textures like paint, brushed metals, kitchen counters, asphalt, and other materials with more uniform and faded surface character.

Fig. 10.11: The Asphalt texture has too much contrast (top). It is adjusted in a photo-editing program and given less contrast (bottom).

Fig. 10.12: The resulting render with the adjusted asphalt texture

Adjusting Hue/Saturation

In Photoshop, select Image → Adjustments → Hue/Saturation.

Using Hue/Saturation is an excellent way to create a variety of textures from the same material, each displayed in a different color and tone (Fig. 10.13, Fig. 10.14).

Changing Color

Adjusting the hue/saturation allows you to completely change the base color of a texture. Black granite can be changed to light yellow countertop; red paving can be adjusted to a light gray-blue. The variations are endless.

Desaturating

A common initial result when draft rendering is the oversaturated appearance of some materials. Colors can appear overly bright or rich. These values can detract from a rendering. Hue/Saturation allows you to tone down a color's vibrancy. Slightly desaturating colors helps moderate the vivid nature of colors in renderings.

Fig. 10.13: The green metal texture as it is applied to the building facade (top); a close-up of the texture (bottom)

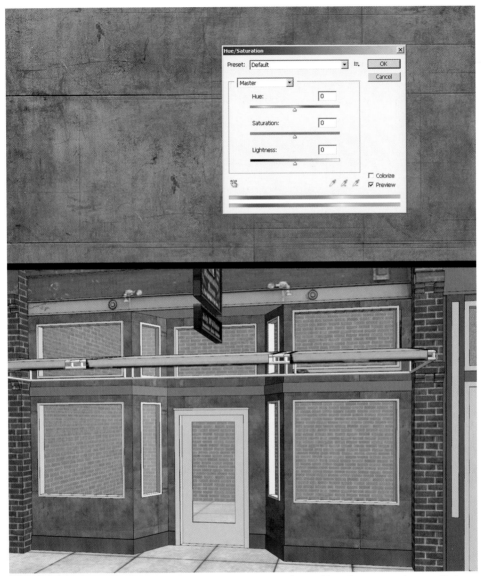

Fig. 10.14: The texture is adjusted in Photoshop, altering the color and how it appears when applied to the building (top). A close-up of the texture shows the results (bottom).

Lightness/Darkness

Lightness/Darkness affects the overall tone of a texture image. It can be useful in toning down vivid textures or lightening materials that appear dark.

Inverting

In Photoshop, select Image → Adjustments → Invert.

Inverting a texture can create a whole new material appearance. Inverted materials take on a contrasting look, where dark becomes light and light becomes dark. Colors take on their opposite appearances. A good example is gray tiles: once inverted, the score joints are lighter while the overall surface is darker. The material looks more like tiles than concrete—i.e., a whole new material (Fig. 10.15, Fig. 10.16).

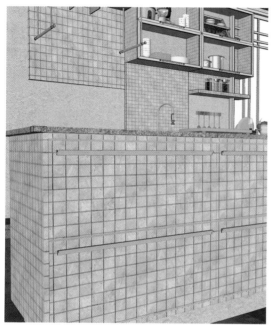

Fig. 10.15: The gray tile applied to the cabinets will be adjusted in Photoshop.

Fig. 10.16: With the Invert function in Photoshop, the tile texture coloration is flipped causing the light gray tiles to appear as dark gray and the dark joints to appear white, thereby creating a new texture.

Correcting Blemishes and Patterns

The Clone Stamp can be found in the Photoshop toolbar; it looks like a rubber stamping device. The Clone Stamp can address two typical texture issues: removing blemishes and hiding seams.

Removing Blemishes

As described in Chapter 9, blemishes can be distracting but with the Clone Stamp they are easy to remove. Simply clone one location of the image and stamp it onto the blemish. Clone an area over the blemish that makes the blemished area fit with the overall material look (Fig. 10.17, Fig. 10.18, Fig. 10.19).

Fig. 10.17: The texture blemishes as applied to the SketchUp surfaces.

Fig. 10.18: The blemishes will be removed using the Clone Stamp tool in Photoshop.

Fig. 10.19: The adjusted, blemish-free textures in SketchUp once they are adjusted and saved.

Hiding Seams

The Clone Stamp is ideal for equalizing the edges of a texture where seams appear. In many instances, seams become visible due to the variation of dark and light in a texture pattern. The Clone Stamp can be used to sample lighter or darker areas and stamp the variation out from the edges or sides of the texture image.

Cropping

The edges of some textures, particularly from CG Textures.com, contain distracting artifacts, elements, or adjacent materials. The easiest way to remove these blemishes is to use the Photoshop Crop tool. Create a crop box to remove the edges with blemishes (Fig. 10.20, Fig.10.21, Fig.10.22).

Fig. 10.20: The wood flooring texture has an odd blemish.

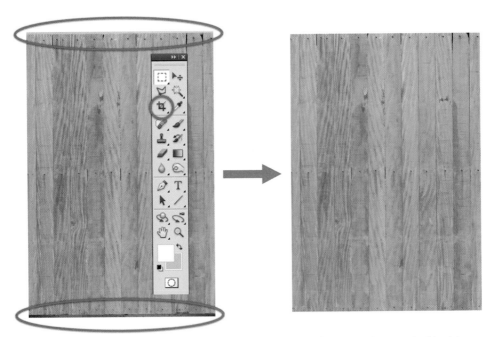

Fig. 10.21: The texture is opened in Photoshop. The Crop tool is used to cut out/remove the blemish from the texture.

Fig. 10.22: The adjusted texture as displayed in Photoshop.

Rotating Textures

Some textures might be oriented toward the wrong direction on surfaces. For example, after applying a wood texture to a bench or chair, the wood grain might be oriented in an awkward way on all the bench slats. Or, siding added to a home could be oriented vertically instead of appearing horizontal.

You can change texture orientation in SketchUp by using the right-click Texture Position tools to rotate the image on a selected surface. However, these rotations will affect only the selected surface. By using Photoshop, you can quickly reorient all applied versions of the textures.

Select the texture and launch the external editor. Using the Photoshop Transform (Edit Transform) or Rotate Canvas (Image → Rotate Canvas) commands, rotate the texture and then save it. In SketchUp, the texture will rotate in all applied instances (Fig. 10.23, Fig. 10.24, Fig. 10.25, Fig. 10.26, Fig. 10.27, Fig. 10.28).

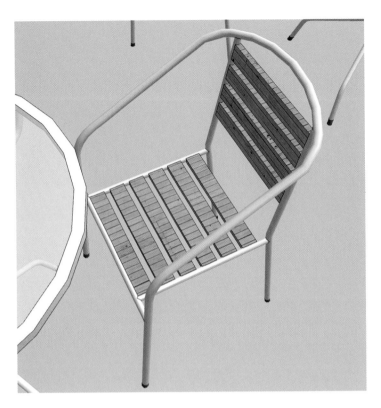

Fig. 10.23: The applied wood texture is oriented incorrectly on the chair surfaces.

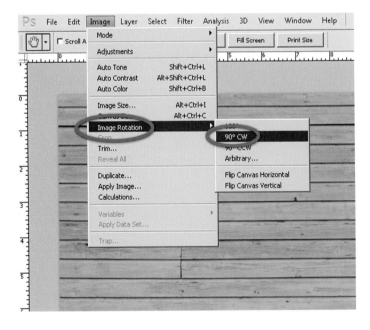

Fig. 10.24: The texture is opened in Photoshop. The Rotate Canvas tool is used to rotate the texture 90 degrees.

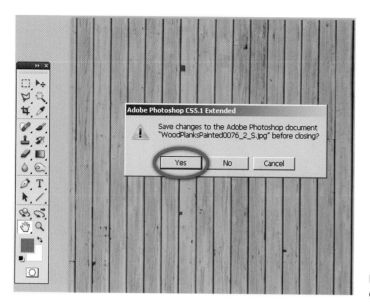

Fig. 10.25: The texture is saved and closed in Photoshop.

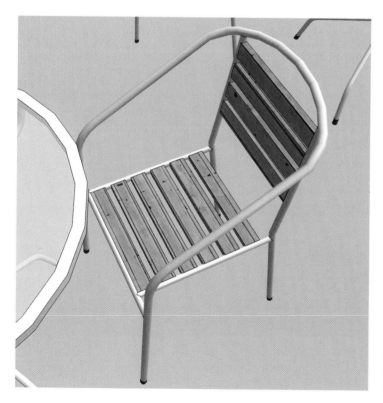

Fig. 10.26: The wood texture is now more accurately aligned to the chair's seat and back.

Fig. 10.27: The top image shows the house siding running up and down, which is incorrect. The bottom image is the rotated siding texture. It was rotated in Photoshop.

Fig. 10.28: The resulting rendering of the house with the correct siding orientation

Modeling Detail

An Overview of Modeling Detail

The physical world is filled with details, colors, objects, and materials of all different sizes. As it constructs our sense of reality, the human mind assimilates these details both consciously and unconsciously. Three-dimensional models can, with time and work, have an almost equal level of intricate detail (Fig. 11.1, Fig. 11.2, Fig. 11.3, Fig. 11.4). By adding detail to a model, you can greatly accentuate your renderings and promote realism.

Fig. 11.1 through Fig. 11.4 are modeled by interior designer Kala Letts (additional detail and rendering by Daniel Tal). The model was the winning entry in the Easter Seals SketchUp-a-Space competition in 2012. Kala's intent was to show how to create an accessible design office and space useful for people with disabilities. The striking aspect of these models is the thoughtful level of detail.

Fig. 11.1: The SketchUp model view of interior model without component detailing (model by Kala Letts, rendering by Daniel Tal)

For example, the rendering shown in Fig. 11.2 has the bare minimum of amenities and furnishings. The chairs, table, shelves, and drawers provide a level of scale and suggest use but do not convey an inviting atmospehre. In contrast, in Fig. 11.4, the inclusion of easels, office supplies, books, pictures, and other amenities typical of active habitation bring the scene to life. The details help create an inviting graphic that clearly conveys design intent.

The chapter provides an overview of the methods used to achieve such detail for both interior and exterior spaces.

Fig. 11.2: Rendered version of SketchUp model (Twilight Render) from Fig. 11.1 (model by Kala Letts, rendering by Daniel Tal)

Fig. 11.3: The same interior model (SketchUp) with added component details (model by Kala Letts, rendering by Daniel Tal)

Fig. 11.4: The detailed interior model from Fig. 11.3 is rendered in Twilight Render. The model appears to be more complete and have a greater sense of realism due to the added component details (model by Kala Letts, rendering by Daniel Tal).

What Is Detail Modeling?

Detail refers to the many elements that compose a typical scene. A model should include components and objects that provide viewers with context and scale typical of real-world settings. For example:

► For interior design models, this could mean including objects and elements, such as books, carpets, lighting fixtures, décor, or whatever details are found in the particular setting. It could mean including exterior or site details that can be seen through a window.

► For site models, this could mean using the right vegetation components, adding realistically detailed people to activate a scene, and having the right background context and typical street elements (Fig. 11.5, Fig. 11.6).

► For architectural models, this could mean including detailed building components and providing the structure with a sense of place, adding detailed fenestrations, including partial interiors visible through windows, using site elements for context and scale, and setting the building in a backdrop (Fig. 11.7, Fig. 11.8).

The processes in the following chapters are outlined in methodical order with specific goals:

► Create a full and rich model with as much detail as possible.

► Model quickly and efficiently.

► Maintain computer and model performance.

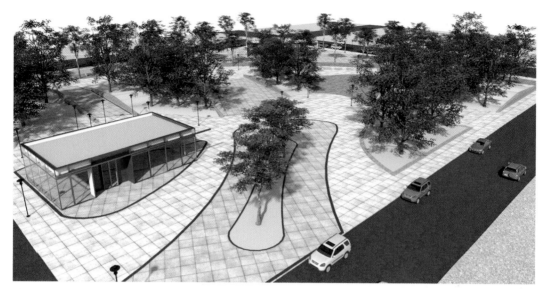

Fig. 11.5: Rendered park model (Shaderlight) without detail

Fig. 11.6: Rendered park model (Shaderlight) with detail, making it appear more complete while increasing the sense of realism

Fig. 11.7: Architectural model (SU Podium) without interior and site component detail

Fig. 11.8: The architectural model (SU Podium) with interior and site detail, giving it context, scale, and realism

Methods

The chapters in Part 3 are intended to be used collectively as they individually address the following methods:

- ▶ The Detailing Tools
- ▶ The Component Details
- ▶ Organizing the Model

Detailing Tools

Chapter 12 introduces the various tools, such as layers and scenes, that you can use to add a lot of detail to your models, while maintaining computer and model performance (Fig. 11.9).

Fig. 11.9: The SketchUp component browser is an important tool that you can use to quickly add details to your models (model by Kala Letts, rendering by Daniel Tal).

Component Details

Components are the details. Chapter 13 discusses premade components. Premade components are widely available, extremely effective, easy to find, and easy to insert into a model. By using filler components from 3D Warehouse, you will be able to quickly insert appropriate detail. Creating and leveraging a Component Library with components from FormFonts and/or DynaSCAPE Sketch3D will ensure that you are using well-made, detailed objects that provide maximum effect for SketchUp renderings.

Organizing the Model

Organization is everything. Adding detailed components, particularly vegetation, can slow down SketchUp and your computer's performance. By correctly organizing your model, you can help maintain optimum performance so you can construct detailed rich models with fewer headaches. Using layers and scenes is the key to organizing a model—and while not difficult, the technique is often overlooked (Fig. 11.10). Chapter 14 discusses model organization using layers and scenes to maximize computer performance.

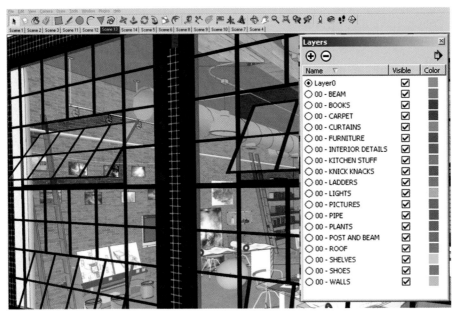

Fig. 11.10: Using layers in SketchUp is the single most important thing you can do while modeling.

Composition and Backdrop

Chapter 15 discusses composing your scenes and using backdrops, which are important when you're creating the simulated reality of a rendering. *Composition* refers to the particular placement or arrangement of visual elements in a scene. *Backdrops* are 2D images that help fill in the gaps in your model and give it context (Fig. 11.11, Fig. 11.12).

Advanced Detailing

Chapter 16 reviews concepts for adding another layer of detail to promote realism in rendering. It includes a review of various Ruby Scripts and modeling processes. This chapter is intended for users who are comfortable with SketchUp or want to understand how a model can be further refined.

Fig. 11.11: The vegetation in the background of this rendered house model (Twilight Render) was created with 2D backdrops .

Fig. 11.12: The model of the house is shown in SketchUp. The 2D backdrops are visible around the model edges.

CHAPTER 12

The Detailing Tools

Several tools and concepts are especially important to help you achieve the model detail you want. Use the following information as a reference when you're working through the rest of Part 3, which explores when and how you should use these tools.

The Component Library

Build a library! A Component Library is an essential tool for working correctly and quickly with SketchUp (Fig. 12.1). Chapter 13 reviews websites and lists specific components you can download. The goal is to download components into a central organized folder on your computer. A Component Library is separate from, but just as important as, a Texture Library.

Place the Component Library on your computer hard drive. Organize the folder into model types and categories. Call the root folder "Component Library," and as you collect and download components, save them into an appropriate subfolder category such as Sofas, Desks, Carpets, Kitchens, Lamps, Trees, Shrubs, Windows, etc. (Fig. 12.2, Fig. 12.3).

Fig. 12.1: Component Library folders on the PC

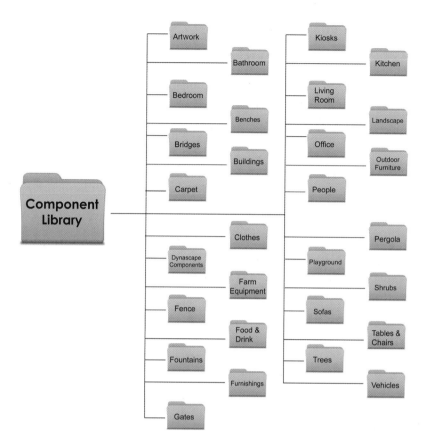

Fig. 12.2: A Component Library org chart

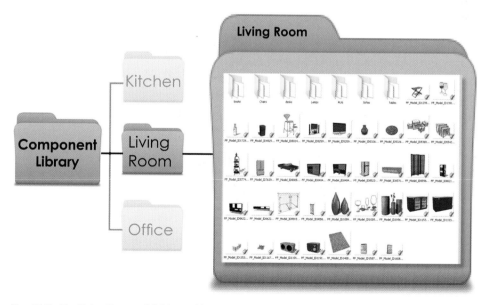

Fig. 12.3: The Living Room subfolder and its components

The Component Browser

The component browser allows you to easily access and insert components into your model, which will quickly add detail to it. The component browser can be linked to the Component Library. To access the component browser, go to Window → Components (Fig. 12.3).

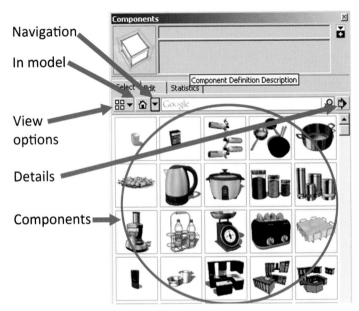

Fig. 12.4: The SketchUp component browser

Linking to the Component Library Folder

To create a link to your Component Library, select the Details button (Fig. 12.5). Select Open or Create a Local Collection. A file browser will open. Navigate to and select the folder containing your components. The components in the folder will appear in the component browser. You can insert these components into your model.

Using Favorites

Return to the Details button and select Add to Favorites. This will create a Favorites link under the Navigation button. Click on Navigation (the small down arrow). The favorites will appear between Transportation at the top and Recent at the bottom (Fig. 12.6). You can add as many favorites as you want.

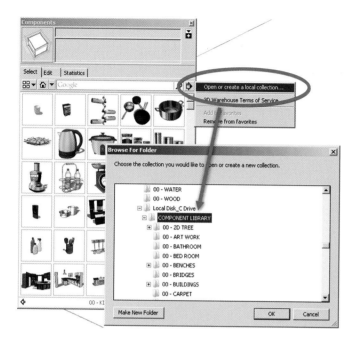

Fig. 12.5: The Details button allows you to navigate to the Component Library where you can locate components to insert into a SketchUp model.

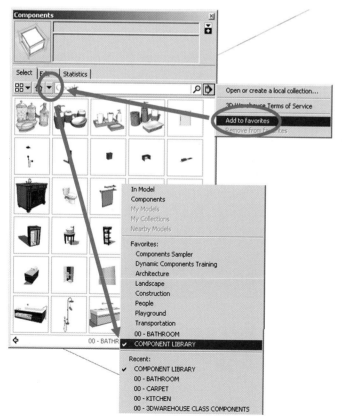

Fig. 12.6: To add the Component Library folder and its subfolders to your Favorites, select Details → Add to Favorites. This will enable you to quickly access the component models.

Placing Components

Once the components appear in the component browser, simply click on a component and move the cursor into your model. The component will move into the model. Once the component is in your model, the Move tool is automatically active, allowing you to place and/or copy the component.

Viewing Options

The View options control how components are displayed in the component browser. Use Large Thumbnails as the default view so that you can easily identify and select your components (Fig. 12.7).

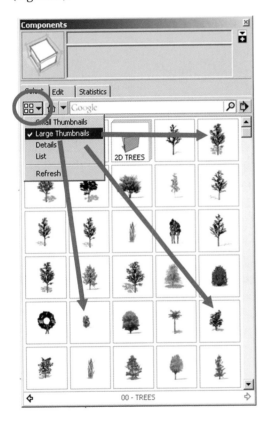

Fig. 12.7: Adjust the View option in the component browser.

Using Layers

The layers in SketchUp do two important things:

▸ They keep models organized.

▸ They help maintain computer performance.

All of the components and groups in your model should be placed on layers (Fig. 12.8). This will enable you to quickly sort your components and turn them on or off as needed. You can add as many layers as needed. You'll learn more about this in Chapter 14.

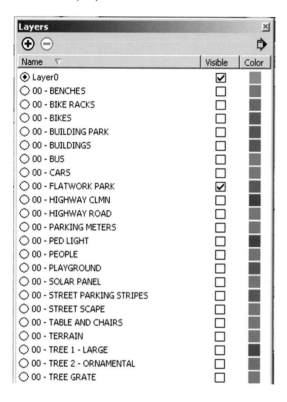

Fig. 12.8: A list of layers in SketchUp

Toggle off the Layers option in order to hide the components on those layers. Components on "off" layers are not processed by SketchUp, which enhances computer performance (Fig. 12.9, Fig. 12.10). This resource-saving option makes layers an essential ingredient when you're working with large models with many components, particularly 3D vegetation components.

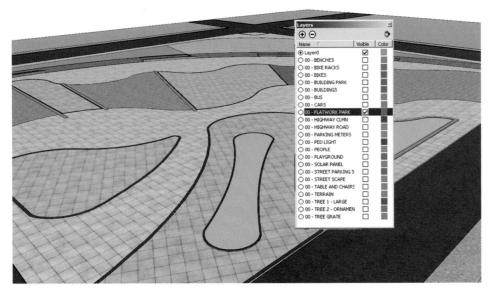

Fig. 12.9: The layers for this model are all turned off, hiding the component detail.

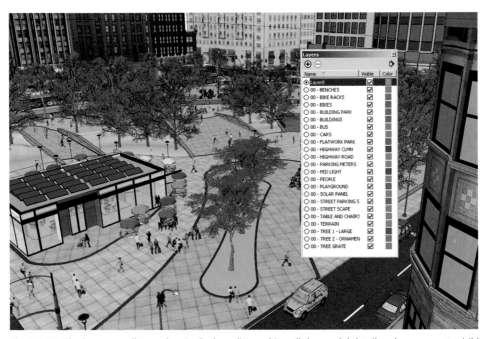

Fig. 12.10: The layers are all turned on in the layer list, making all the model detail and components visible.

Creating and Naming Layers

The Layer menu is accessed under Window → Layers. To create a new layer, click on the **(+)** button at the top. A new layer line will appear so that you can name it. Double-clicking on a layer name allows you to rename it (Fig. 12.11).

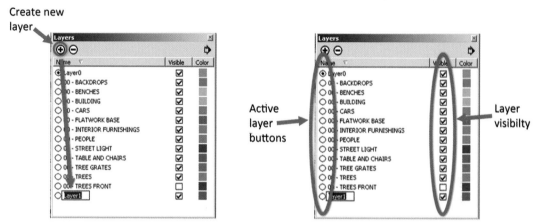

Create new layer

Active layer buttons

Layer visibilty

Fig. 12.11: The image on the left shows how to create a new layer. The image on the right shows the active layer and Visibility buttons in the layer list.

Active Layer

Clicking on the radio button to the left of a layer will make it active. Layer 0 is the default drafting layer and should always be active unless components are being inserted into the model. When premade components are added to the model, they are placed on active layers as outlined in Chapter 14 (Fig. 12.11).

Toggling Off

Unchecking the box to the right of a layer name will toggle the layer off. All objects on the layer will be invisible. It is not possible to turn off a layer while it's active.

Deleting Layers

Selecting a layer and clicking on the (-) button will delete it. If the layer has no geometry or components on it, the layer will be removed automatically. If it contains any geometry, a new dialogue will appear with three options:

- ▶ **Move Contents to Default Layer:** Use this option when you're deleting a layer. Any geometry or components on the deleted layer are placed on Layer 0. It will ensure that no necessary geometry is removed from the model (Fig. 12.12).

- ▶ **Move Contents to Active Layer:** The contents of a deleted layer will be moved to the active layer. Use this option when you want to merge layers into a single layer.

▶ **Delete Contents:** The layer and its contents will be removed from the model. Use this option with extreme caution. Use it only when you want to delete objects from a model and are certain that all the associated geometry is located on the layer to be deleted. Remember that geometry composing objects might be located on multiple layers; using this option when some geometry is located on a different layer can ruin a model.

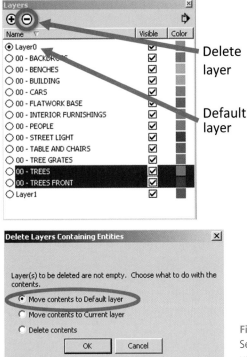

Delete layer

Default layer

Fig. 12.12: Layers can be selected and deleted. Select Move Contents to Default Layer to remove any unwanted layers.

Entity Info and Layers

Entity Info is used in tandem with layers to keep a model organized. It displays properties of selected components, groups, and geometry and allows components to be moved to different layers. Entity Info can be opened from Window → Entity Info or by right-clicking on a selected object and choosing it from the top of the context menu.

When you select an object and open Entity Info, the Layer menu in the Entity Info box will display the layer on which the object is nested (Fig. 12.13). If multiple objects that share the same layer are selected, the layer name will be displayed. If multiple objects are selected that are on different layers, the layer box will appear blank because it can display only one layer at a time.

Clicking on the arrow next to Layer in Entity Info displays a drop-down menu listing all of the layers in the model. When objects are selected and a layer is selected from the pull-down menu, all of the selected objects will be moved onto the selected layer (Fig. 12.14). This works even if the objects are on different layers.

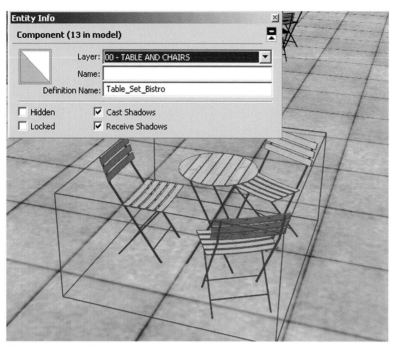

Fig. 12.13: The Table and Chairs component is selected and appears in the Entity Info box, indicating that the layer the component resides on 00 - TABLE AND CHAIRS.

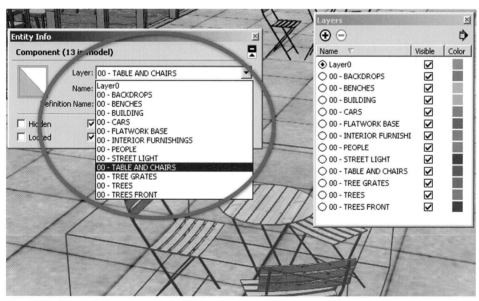

Fig. 12.14: The pull-down menu under Entity Info shows all the layers in the model. Selecting a component and then a layer from this list will place the component on that layer.

SketchUp Scenes

The Scene menu allows you to toggle on or toggle off specific model properties with a single click. At its simplest, it's used to save camera views (Fig. 12.15). To access the Scenes menu, select Window → Scenes. Simply clicking the **(+)** button creates a tab on the top left of the screen under the main menu called **Scene 1**. Clicking the scene **(+)** button again will continue to create more scenes, each sequentially numbered(Fig. 12.16). Clicking on the tab at any time will rotate the view back to the saved camera position.

You can control and save additional scene settings using Scene Properties in the Scene menu (Fig. 12.17). If you don't see Scene Properties, click on the arrow at the top right of the Scene menu to make them visible (expand menu option as shown in Fig 12.15). This menu has many options, including updating, naming, and deleting scenes. The remainder of this section focuses on settings that are useful and frequently used for this book's methods. To learn more about scene properties in general, refer to the *Google SketchUp for Dummies* series (Wiley) by Aidan Chopra.

Create scene

Delete scene

Expand menu

Rename scene

Scene properties

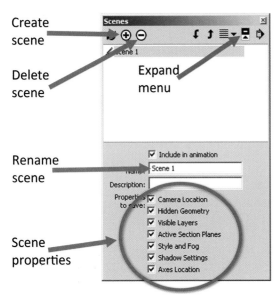

Fig. 12.15: The Scene Menu options

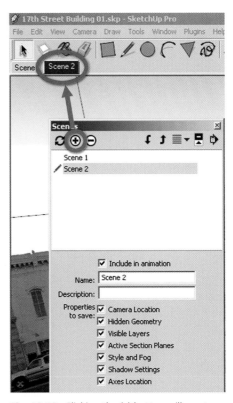

Fig. 12.16: Clicking the (+) button will create a new scene. The Scene tab appears at the top left of the SketchUp screen below the main menu.

Fig. 12.17: Properties options in the Scene menu

Each property has a check box. A checked box means the setting property is retained when a scene is created. Unchecking the box will prevent that particular value from being retained when a scene is created.

The three properties outlined here are referenced in the remainder of Part 3 and Part 4. The remaining properties can be kept at default (checked) when you're working through Part 3 and Part 4.

Camera Location

When your scene is created and Camera Location is checked, the camera position and view will be retained. This option will also save focal length, camera perspective, and section views. Unchecking this option means the camera position will not be recorded in the scene.

Visible Layers

Visible Layers causes the scene to remember which layers were on or off in the Layers menu when the scene was created (Fig. 12.18). This option allows you to control layer and component visibility by clicking on the scene. Chapter 14 reviews how to create On/Off scenes useful in maintaining performance and working with vegetation.

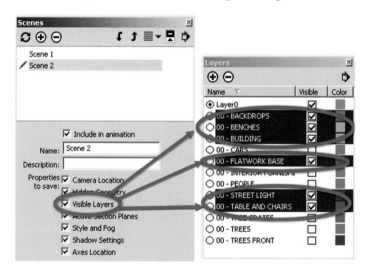

Fig. 12.18: The Visible Layers option under Scene properties will remember which layers are toggled on and off in the Layers menu when the scene is created.

Shadow Settings

This scene property remembers the specific Shadow Settings (Windows → Shadows) used at the time the scene was created (Fig. 12.19). If the Shadows were On, clicking on the scene will turn on the Shadows. All other Shadow settings are retained as well.

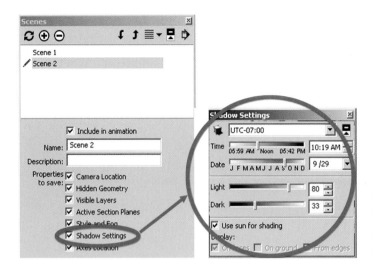

Fig. 12.19: The Shadow Settings option under Scene Properties remembers what Shadow settings were set when the scene was created.

The Camera Tools

The following three tools are useful for creating camera effects and adjusting views. They should be used when setting up scenes for rendering and establishing composition.

Position Camera

Once the Position Camera tool is activated, clicking on a surface or object will cause the camera view to be positioned to 5.5′ above a selected surface (Fig. 12.20, Fig. 12.21). The height of the position can be adjusted in the Measurements menu. Once you position the camera, simply enter a new height (start typing) and press Return. This tool is ideal for setting eye-level camera views.

Look Around

The Look Around tool allows you to pivot in place, looking in any direction. It activates after Position Camera is used, and it can be used with or independently from Position Camera to look around from a specific vantage point (Fig. 12.22, Fig. 12.23).

Fig. 12.20: When the Position Camera tool is activated, you can select a surface on which to position the camera.

Fig. 12.21: The Position Camera tool displays an eye-level view of the building.

Fig. 12.22: The Look Around tool allows you to adjust the view as if you were turning your head. Look Around is automatically activated after Position Camera is used.

Fig. 12.23: The camera view is adjusted with Look Around.

Focal Length

Focal length, can be adjusted at any time in SketchUp. Click on the Zoom icon. You can then enter a value into the Measurements menu (simply start typing). Values are entered in ##mm + enter. Typical focal lengths range from 35 mm to 60 mm (Fig. 12.24, Fig. 12.25, Fig. 12.26).

Fig. 12.24: The view is adjusted to a focal length of 55 mm, creating a narrow view of the scene.

Fig. 12.25: The view is adjusted to a focal length of 45 mm, expanding the scene view.

Fig. 12.26: The view is adjusted to a focal length of 35 mm, widening the scene view.

Component Details

Premade components are widely available and can add context, scale, and action to a model. They are easy to obtain and insert, and they can effectively be used to convey a sense of realism and context. Although you can and sometimes should make your own components, creating original components is beyond the scope of this book. See *SketchUp for Site Design* (Wiley, 2009) to learn more about creating original components.

This chapter reviews the type of component detail from which architecture, site, and interior models can benefit. It includes reviews of websites with premade components and search parameters that will help you quickly build a library of recommended components for detailing. Chapter 14 will teach you the best practices for placing and organizing these premade objects.

What Is Component Detail?

Component detail refers to the many premade models that represent specific elements associated with buildings, interiors, and outdoor settings (Fig. 13.1, Fig. 13.2). They range from windows to street lights and benches to kitchen appliances, fixtures, books, and crockery. These representative models can be downloaded from the web and inserted into models.

Fig. 13.1: Rendered image of interior detail components (Twilight Render)

Fig. 13.2: Rendered image of exterior detail components (Shaderlight)

Base-Model Articulation and Detailing

There is a difference between using components for base-model articulation and for detailing. Components used for base-model articulation help the building, interior, or site-plan model reflect the form and space of the design intent. Components used for detailing are intended to accentuate the model's design. Listed here are some general base-model typologies. Their use is intended as a general approach; the appropriateness and results will depend on the space and its use.

Interior Base Models

Interior models are defined by floors, ceilings, walls, partitions, doors, windows, and a minimal amount of furnishings and objects paralleling the space's intent (Fig. 13.3, Fig. 13.4). Some examples of minimal furnishings are the following:

- ▶ **Living Room**: Sofas, tables, chairs, televisions, lamps, and lights
- ▶ **Kitchen**: Refrigerators, stoves, sinks, cabinets, and lighting
- ▶ **Restaurant**: Tables, chairs, and lighting
- ▶ **Office**: Desks, office chairs, computers, and monitors
- ▶ **Bathroom**: Sinks, medicine cabinets, cabinets, toilets, and showers

Fig. 13.3: SketchUp model of interior with base furniture and shape, but no component detail

Fig. 13.4: SketchUp model of same interior with detail components

Base Site Exteriors

A base site model defines contextual buildings, walks, roads, trails, walls, grades, minimal vegetation, and site elements (Fig. 13.5, Fig. 13.6).

Fig. 13.5: Rendering of site model base forms and objects (Shaderlight)

Fig. 13.6: Rendering of site model with component details (Shaderlight)

Base Architecture

Base architectural models contain the building form adorned by simple roof, windows, portals, and doors.

People Components

Various types of people components, ranging from 2D photographs to 3D components, are reviewed at the end of this chapter. People components are important for adding scale and activity to a render.

Premade Components and Textures

The texturing process outlined in Part 2 applies to premade components inserted into the model. This means that any premade components should possess textures appropriate for your model and rendering. Most premade components (in particular, the ones reviewed in this chapter) have two characteristics that make them easy to work with in regard to textures:

- ▶ Most premade components already have textures applied to them. This means, like the textures applied to the base mode, these textures should receive IRP rendering values as outlined in Chapter 22.

- ▶ At the very least, premade components have solid color or image texture that can be easily swapped (see Chapter 8) for a more appropriate texture (Fig. 13.7, Fig. 13.8).

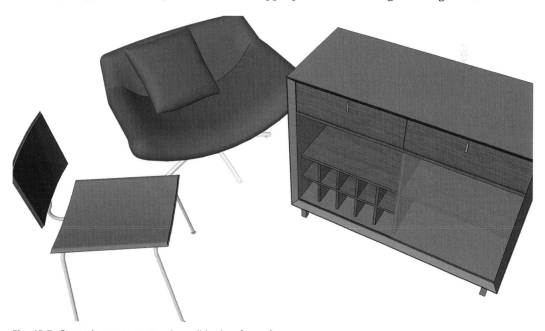

Fig. 13.7: Premade components using solid colors for surfaces

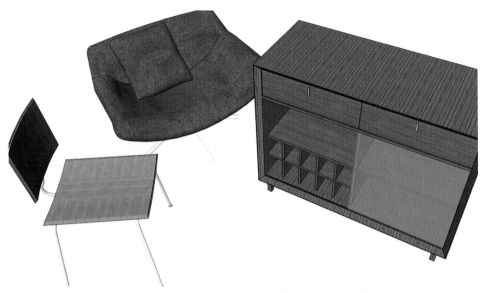

Fig. 13.8: By using the Texture Swapping method, you can add texture to solid colors.

Component Detail Types

Tables 13.1, 13.2, and 13.3 list some common details used for interior, site, and architectural settings. There are endless objects in the real world. However, collectively, the items listed here will help you complete a rendered scene. The component equivalents for all these elements are available on the websites discussed later in this chapter.

Table 13.1: Interior Details and Potential Components

air conditioning	appliances	area carpets	artwork and pictures	base boards	bedding	bedroom sets
beds	blinds and window coverings	books shelves	books	chairs	coffee tables	computers
crockery	doorjambs	doorknobs	doorstops	electric cords	electric outlets	fixtures
flat screens	food	furniture	glass walls	glasses	lamps	laptops
living room sets	office furniture	partitions	pillows	plants	silverware	sofas
table	thermostats	trash cans	vases	vents	wall lights	window backdrops and exterior scenes
steps	mechanical furnace	mechanical water heater	piping	washers and dryers	decor	

Table 13.2: Site Details and Potential Components

arbors	backdrops	banners	bike racks	boulders	buildings - general	canopy structures
cars	chimneys	fences	fire pits	fountains	kiosks	lighting: in-ground
lighting: pedestrian	lighting: street	lighting: wall lights	manholes	newsstands	outdoor kitchens	parking meters
people	pergolas	playgrounds	railing	sculptures and art	street signs	swimming pools
traffic lights	transportation stops	trash and recycling containers	tree grates	utility meters and boxes	vegetation/ flowers	vegetation/ shrubs
vegetation/ trees	vegetation/ vines	fire hydrants				

Table 13.3: Architectural Details and Potential Components

chimneys	doors	exterior light fixtures	gutters	HVAC	sky lights	solar panels
windows	plaques	ornamentations	light fixtures	awnings	rails	steps
fire escapes						

Building Volumes and Fenestrations

Buildings benefit from additional details unrelated to components. By including *fenestrations* (openings) in the form of 3D volumes, you can greatly enhance a building's graphic appeal. Typical elements that can be modeled are parapets, overhangs, and reveals. Good components can provide similar detail, such as extruded windows found at DynaSCAPE Sketch3D's website (http://www.dynascape.com/sketch3D.html).

For more information on adding detailed volume and extrusion to buildings, refer to *Google SketchUp for Site Design* (Fig. 13.9, Fig. 13.10, Fig. 13.11).

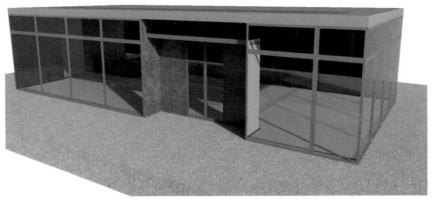

Fig. 13.9: The rendered building has only base details (Shaderlight).

Fig. 13.10: The building fenestration and extrusions are added to the base model improving the building look (Shaderlight).

Fig. 13.11: Additional exterior details, such as wall lightings and downspouts, are added. Contextual interior furniture is added, rounding the building detail.

Premade Component Websites

The following three websites (Trimble 3D Warehouse, FormFonts, and DynaSCAPE Sketch3D) are well suited to provide the types of component details you can use. Collectively, they offer a broad assortment of free and commercial components. The resource website for this book (see Chapter 2) provides direct links to these resources.

These three websites require that you download components one at a time. Although this can be inconvenient, it is to prevent piracy and illegal sharing of models that might occur if components were packaged in groups.

Using the reference material in this chapter, make sure you download any components into an organized Component Library (Fig. 13.12). Regularly spend time downloading them, and collect them when you're modeling a project. You will quickly build up your Component Library.

3D Warehouse

3D Warehouse is a search engine for 3D models. It's the single, largest repository of SketchUp models on the Web (Fig. 13.13). SketchUp users, companies, and institutions upload their models to the Warehouse for others to view, download, and freely use.

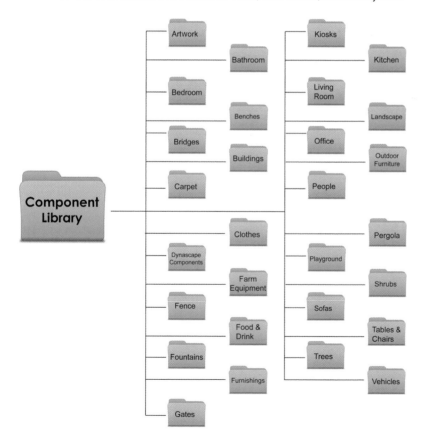

Fig. 13.12: A Component Library

Fig. 13.13: 3D Warehouse is easy to search directly from inside SketchUp.

Accessing 3D Warehouse is simple. In SketchUp, select File → 3D Warehouse → Get Models. A browser will open in SketchUp that will allow you to type in search terms. You can search any model type. You can then download objects directly into your model (Fig. 13.14).

Fig. 13.14: Once a model is located on 3D Warehouse, you can download it directly into SketchUp.

3D Warehouse is not the ideal source for components, with the exception of building models. Use it as a supplemental resource in tandem with commercial component sites.

3D Warehouse Advantages

3D Warehouse does have some distinct advantages.

Quick and Dirty Detailing   Using 3D Warehouse is the quickest way to insert detail into a model. Open the internal SketchUp 3D Warehouse browser, search for a specific model component, pick the best one, and insert it directly into your model. If you need a quick kitchen appliance or site element, you can search the Warehouse and place it within seconds.

Contextual Buildings   3D Warehouse is an excellent site to obtain buildings useful for backdrops and context (Fig. 13.15). There are thousands of great buildings to use. Many of them are used in Google Earth. These buildings have photo-textures for facades, making them ideal for rendering because they possess an implied realism (Fig. 13.16). Check out the book's resources links for specific links to useful backdrop buildings.

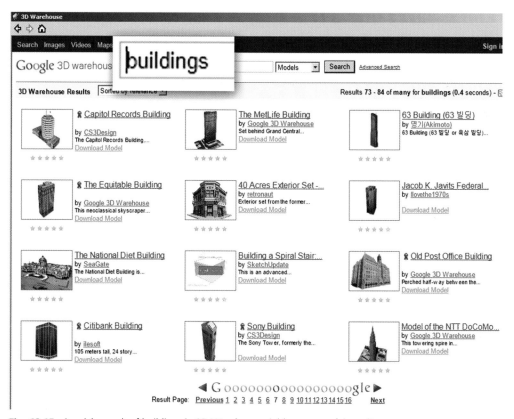

Fig. 13.15: A quick search of buildings in 3D Warehouse yields many useful results.

Fig. 13.16: 3D Warehouse buildings inserted into SketchUp model with FormFonts Geometrees (see FormFonts section) and rendered in Twilight Render

Manufacturers' Components   Many furniture, appliance, construction, and manufacturing companies have developed and uploaded professional grade, product-specific models into the Warehouse (Fig. 13.17). However, they can be hard to find. When looking for a specific item, use the Collections search option. Look for manufacturer names or logos in the results. Or, search by using a specific manufacturer and product name.

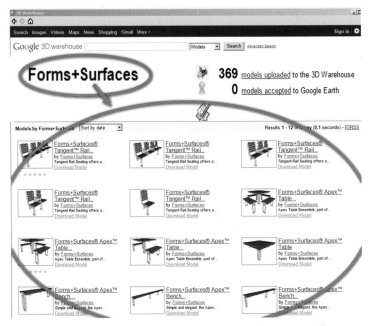

Fig. 13.17: 3D Warehouse search results showing manufacturer-specific components

3D Warehouse Disadvantages

Using the 3D Warehouse (http://sketchup.google.com/3dwarehouse) offers several challenges. First, many models on the Warehouse are poorly constructed or lack aesthetic appeal. Most vegetation falls in this category. Some are useful, most are not. The online book resources provide links to specific plants in 3D Warehouse useful for modeling and rendering.

Second, learning how to search through 3D Warehouse and find the right type of models, given the sheer quantity available, can be time-consuming.

Third, directly inserting models makes it easy to skip the step of saving the models into a Component Library. However, you can avoid this problem by searching the Warehouse using a typical web browser (Chrome, Firefox, Windows Explorer) and downloading the models directly to the Component Library.

FormFonts

FormFonts (www.formfonts.com) offers a wide assortment of professionally made 3D components. Many, if not most, of the components found at FormFonts are useful for rendering (Fig. 13.18).

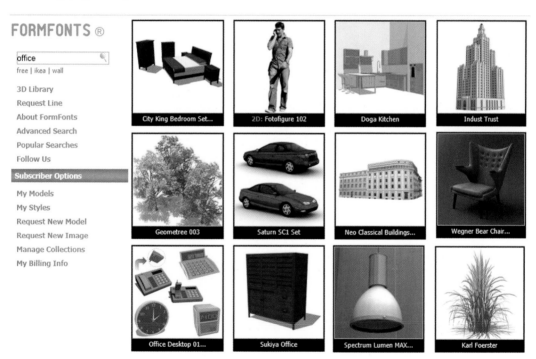

Fig. 13.18: The FormFonts website and some of the component model types offered

FormFonts is a subscription website. A one-year subscription allows you to download 30 models a day for a total of 10,950 downloads for the year. A subscription investment will pay for itself in the sheer number, quality, and variety of components available.

Search Terms

General model categories are listed here with specific search terms that can provide useful results for that category.

Interiors

Professional interior designers and do-it-yourselfers should check out FormFonts. It has a large variety of modern, classical, and contemporary furnishings, appliances, and fixtures. It has the best collection of interior components available for SketchUp (Fig. 13.19).

Some useful search terms are interior, furniture, sofas, table and chairs, fixtures, appliances, kitchen, decorations, and office furniture.

Fig. 13.19: A sampling of the interior components found at FormFonts. There are many more!

Buildings

FormFonts includes a modest assortment of detailed buildings. They are a must to check out because most of them are excellent components that will help you build context or backgrounds for exterior renderings (Fig. 13.20).

Fig. 13.20: FormFonts has premade buildings components for download.

Vehicles and Transportation

FormFonts offers many transportation modes ranging from trains, cars, buses, to airplanes and more.

Some useful search terms include: cars, trains, buses, and planes.

People

Adding people components to your models is reviewed below under "People Components and Rendering." You can search FormFonts for people components using the term Fotofigure. Download all of them (Fig. 13.21).

Fig. 13.21: The Fotofigures on FormFonts are excellent for rendering.

Vegetation

FormFonts offers high-quality 3D vegetation, including trees and shrubs, for SketchUp. The Geometrees are excellent generic trees for rendering. Fully 3D, they take on an almost real character when rendered (Fig. 13.22, Fig. 12.23).

Some general search terms include: vegetation and Geometree.

Use the following search terms to locate the recommended models.

Trees   flowering dogwood, Geometree, areca palms, coconut palm 2, joshua tree 01, young palms, palms, tree in box 01, tree in box 02, palo verde tree, architectural birches, eucalyptus, ghost gum, birch (all), stone pine, acanthus molis, date palm, birch (bare)

Shrubs and Grasses Crape myrtle, magnolia, juniper, frangipani, daphne, generic bush, shrub 01, zebra plant, buddleia, fanpalm02, monstera, forsythia, day lily, HQ plant 0 - 04, bird of paradise, pampas grass, Karl Forester, sand cord grass, blue lymegrass, sunflower, arum or calla lily, clivia miniata, maidenhair fern, zebra rush, monkshood, agave, saguaros, potted areca palms, agave 02, papyrus, generic cordyline, Aglaonema pictum, common fern, bamboo, bullrushes, tulips, agapanthus (For some shrubs and grasses, you will need to delete the pot that comes with the plant.)

Fig. 13.22: FormFonts Geometrees, while generic, are ideal for rendering.

Fig. 13.23: Geometrees used in a park rendering (SU Podium)

Other Models and Requests

Just to emphasize the point, do not hesitate to type in any search term for any object in FormFonts. There is a good chance they have it. If not, use the request form and ask for specific model types.

Sketch3D

DynaSCAPE Sketch3D DynaSCAPE software (http://sketch3d.dynascape.com) is the maker of a 2D Cad drafting program for residential and site design. Sketch3D is a collection of over 1,000 plant components specific for SketchUp (Fig. 13.24).

Although Sketch3D is pricey, there is no daily limit to the number of components you can download. Part of your subscription to Sketch3D includes access to custom SketchUp textures related to site and exterior spaces. Also included is access to a custom CAD clean-up Ruby Script.

All of Sketch 3D's site amenities, structures, and furnishings are great for rendering. In particular, the vines and trellis structures stand out as unique. It is harder to indicate which plants are useful for rendering from the Sketch3D collection. You will need to experiment with the plant types and see what works well for you. One excellent quality is that many of the 2D FaceMe shrubs and some of the 2D FaceMe trees are perfect for photorealistic rendering.

The Sketch3D components are optimized for SketchUp. The 3D plants are well constructed and possess minimum geometry. You can populate your model with many of the 3D plants and without dramatically affecting your computer's performance. (However, optimized components are no substitute for a well-organized model, as described in the Chapter 14.)

Fig. 13.24: DynaSCAPE Sketch3D is the single best collection of vegetation components available for SketchUp.

Vegetation

Sketch3D offers a huge assortment of specific plants ranging from grasses, perennials, annuals, vines, shrubs, and deciduous trees to evergreen trees and more. The plants are listed by both their common and Latin names (Fig. 13.25, Fig. 13.26, Fig. 13.27, Fig. 13.28).

Fig. 13.25: Some shrub components from DynaSCAPE Sketch3D

Gladiolus x hortulanus

Hakonechloa - forest grass

Helictotrichon sempervirens - blue oat grass

Hemerocallis - Daylily (pink)

Hemerocallis - Daylily (red)

Hemerocallis - Daylily (white)

Hemerocallis - Daylily (yellow)

Hemerocallis - Orange Daylily

Hemerocallis - pink daylily

Hemerocallis - Pink Daylily-B

Hemerocallis - red daylily

Hemerocallis - White Daylily

Lantana camara 'Patriot Sunburst'

Lavandula angustifolia

Lavandula angustifolia - lavander

Leucanthemum - shasta daisy-1

Leucanthemum - shasta daisy-2

Leymus condensatus - giant wild rye

Liatris - purple gayfeather

Ligularia stenocephala

Lilium - Asiatic lily (pink)

Lilium - Asiatic lily (red)

Lilium - Asiatic lily (white)

Lilium - Asiatic lily (yellow)

Fig. 13.26: Rendering of building with plant components from Sketch3D (Twilight Render)

Fig. 13.27: A SketchUp model filled with DynaSCAPE Sketch3D vegetation, with FormFonts Geometrees in the background

Fig. 13.28: Rendering of model from Fig. 13.27 (Twilight Render)

Site Accessories

Sketch3D offers well-made site furnishings and structure components including rocks, boulders, pools, trellises, pergolas with well-articulated vines, fire pits, patio furnishings, and more (Fig. 13.29).

Windows and Doors

Sketch3D offers door and window components. Although 3D Warehouse has such models, they are usually poorly constructed. The Sketch3D versions are ideal for architecture models. The collection is growing and is one of the most unique online architectural component collections available for SketchUp (Fig. 13.30).

People Components and Rendering

Adding people components will help bring your rendering to life. People provide scale, activity, and context. People components can be included in a model and rendered with the scene.

Types of People

There are several categories of people components: two-dimensional photoreal, two-dimensional non-photoreal (NPR), and three-dimensional people. 2D photoreal people are ideal for rendering but are not available in large quantities. 2D NPR and 3D people can be useful for rendering as described here (Fig. 13.31, Fig. 13.32, Fig. 13.33).

2D people, like 2D trees and shrubs, are called FaceMe components. Each component is a single vertical surface, typically a photograph or image of the object. When orbiting and panning in SketchUp, the component will always face the camera—i.e., will always "face me."

PR 2D People Components

Using the search term "PR People" or "Fotofigure" in FormFonts will bring up 50 results of 2D Face Me photographic people. Using these components is strongly recommended because their implied realism makes them render well.

The quantity and type of PR 2D people is limited. All available PR people are walking or standing, but not sitting. Use 3D people and Arc Vision RPC people (Google search ArcVision RPC for more information) in tandem with PR 2D people to fill in scenes with sitting people.

Decorative Private Screen (SF-41)brown | Decorative Private Screen (SF-41)white | Garden Shed 11x11 (SC-10) | Garden Shed 8x10 (SC-2)

Garden Shed 8x12 (SC-11) | Garden Shed 8x12 (SC-17) | Garden Shed 8x12 (SC-20) | Garden Shed 8x12 (SC-6)

Garden Shed 8x12 (SC-9) | Gazebo Oct 10X10 (P-22) | Gazebo Square 10x10 (P-23) | Pergola 10x12 (P-2)-brown

Fig. 13.29: DynaSCAPE Sketch3D has many other useful component types like these structures.

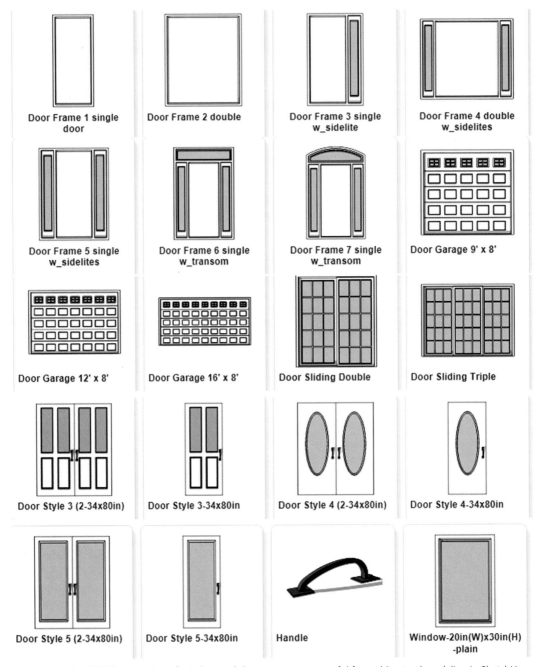

Door Frame 1 single door

Door Frame 2 double

Door Frame 3 single w_sidelite

Door Frame 4 double w_sidelites

Door Frame 5 single w_sidelites

Door Frame 6 single w_transom

Door Frame 7 single w_transom

Door Garage 9' x 8'

Door Garage 12' x 8'

Door Garage 16' x 8'

Door Sliding Double

Door Sliding Triple

Door Style 3 (2-34x80in)

Door Style 3-34x80in

Door Style 4 (2-34x80in)

Door Style 4-34x80in

Door Style 5 (2-34x80in)

Door Style 5-34x80in

Handle

Window-20in(W)x30in(H) -plain

Fig. 13.30: Sketch3D has a variety of window and door components useful for architectural modeling in SketchUp.

Fig. 13.31: Rendering of riverwalk without people (Shaderlight)

Fig. 13.32: 3D FormFonts people components sitting at the tables and chairs are added to the riverwalk scene. These components help provide scale and context (Shaderlight).

Fig. 13.33: FormFonts Fotofigures are added to round out the rendering and provide activity and scale (Shaderlight).

2D Non-Photoreal

You can obtain 2D non-photoreal people from 3D Warehouse. Use the Paint Bucket Edit options to alter the color to either a solid black or white. Adjust the transparency to make them slightly see-through. While they do not aid in creating realism, they do have a good aesthetic quality that can help convey a sense of space and scale.

3D People

You can download 3D people from FormFonts and 3D Warehouse. The options from FormFonts are the best available for SketchUp. 3D people are versatile, especially ones that convey specific positions such as being seated. They are well suited to work in tandem with FormFonts PR people. 3D people work well placed in the background or somewhat distant in the midground. They are distracting when placed in the foreground or closer to the camera view.

3D people don't render well due to a lack of textures and the general difficulty of rendering people. If you have time, add fabric textures to clothing and provide render-texture values prior to rendering.

Organizing the Model

The layering system outlined in this chapter will allow you to create detailed, component-rich models. Using simple layer conventions will help you maintain SketchUp performance. Even if you are new to SketchUp, you should learn to apply this method.

Using layers is essential when you're modeling with vegetation components (Fig. 14.1). Plant components are the source of most performance issues. By placing vegetation on layers, you help maintain function. If you need a refresher on how to use the tools referenced here, refer to Chapter 12.

SketchUp relies heavily on the computer's graphics video card and CPU to display your model. Rotating, zooming, and panning when good amounts of model detail are visible causes the video card and CPU to work much harder, causing SketchUp to slow down. Placing components and objects on layers, and then turning layers on and off, as needed, allows some objects to be hidden, requiring less of the computer's resources and thus maintaining performance.

Similarly, being able to turn layers off and effectively hide details and components makes it easier to compose and stage scenes for rendering.

Fig. 14.1: All of the shrubs in this SketchUp model are placed on layers.

What Is a Large Model?

A large model is any model that experiences performance problems and slowdowns due to the amount of geometry present. SketchUp has thresholds, measured in *faces,* of how much geometry it can easily display and still function. To find the Face value, select Window → Model Info menu under Statistics (Fig. 14.2). The total number of faces in the model is listed to the right of the Face value line. Make sure the Show Nested Components box at the top is checked to ensure the Face tally is accurate.

Threshold

Chapter 4 talks about how SketchUp is affected by processor and video cards. The better the processor and video card, the better SketchUp can handle large. The threshold for SketchUp 8 using a recommended computer is around three to five million faces. Beyond that, the model can become unresponsive, even hard to open. This means, even if you are using layers, you should try not to exceed that number. With some exceptions, models achieving such large sizes are those using substantial quantities of three-dimensional vegetation.

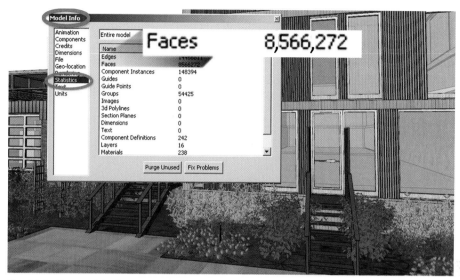

Fig. 14.2: The Model Info → Statistics option displays the sizes of the model. The model contains over 8.5 million faces of geometry, mostly due to the 3D vegetation.

Model Size and Rendering

When first learning to render, try to keep the model sizes no bigger than 500,000 faces. You can render larger models, but they take time and need to be strictly organized. In addition, you might need to use a computer that meets the specifications listed in Chapter 4 (Fig. 14.3).

Fig. 14.3: This interior model contains 340,000 faces, making it an ideal size for rendering (model by Kala Letts and Daniel Tal).

Limitless Layers

Even with the threshold and rendering size limits, it is possible to build models of immense size by using layers. As shown in this example, the model used for the render has 161 million faces (Fig. 14.4, Fig. 14.5). However, you might not want to try this at home. The accompanying online material "Part 9: Twilight Render" explains how to create such large models using layers.

Fig. 14.4: Due to all of the trees, this SketchUp terrain model contains 161 million faces (house model by Avraham Zohar, site model by Daniel Tal).

Fig. 14.5: Twilight Render instances all the trees, making this render possible (Twilight Render v1).

Layering Strategy

Put everything on layers (Fig. 14.6). It's that simple!

This strategy has several goals:

▶ Use layers so that you can toggle the geometry and objects On and Off. Your ability to toggle the geometry will make it easier to model and help maintain SketchUp performance.

▶ Place all inserted and created components on their own layers. Each component detail type should be on its own layer. The layer name must convey the description of the component.

▶ Keep layer names simple and straightforward.

▶ Clean up the layer list. Relocate layers that are imported from any CAD program.

Fig. 14.6: Components and the layer names for those components

Draft with Layer 0

When you're drafting in SketchUp (adding faces, drawing lines, extruding faces), Layer 0 should be the active layer. Keep Layer 0 active and activate other layers only when you're placing or inserting components into the model. Keeping the geometry on Layer 0 keeps the model clean (Fig. 14.7). Only the component itself, as a selected whole, should be placed on a layer.

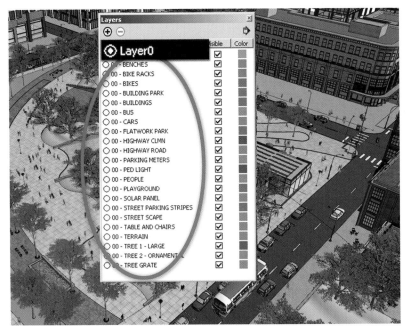

Fig. 14.7: Layers 0 is highlighted at the top of the layer list.

Create Layers

Before you insert any premade components into the model, create layers. Create a layer for every component types you will insert. Use a logical naming convention, such as one based on the model typology (Fig. 14.8). Separate and name the layers by types: place cars on the Car layer, people on the People layer, light fixtures on the Light Fixture layer, etc. The exception to this rule is vegetation, which you will learn about in a moment.

00 - Layer Prefix

Add a **00 –** before layer names (two zeros), especially if you insert linework and objects from CAD programs. Imported CAD files contain their layers when they are inserted into SketchUp. Mixing component layer lists with CAD layer lists can cause layer lists to be long and cluttered.

Including the **00 -** prefix in front of the layer name will help you keep the model component layers sorted. Clicking on the Name tab in the Layer menu will sort layers alphabetically. The **00** designation will usually be listed in front (on top) of any imported CAD layers, allowing the component details layers to be sorted easily.

Some premade components will already have their own layers. These layers were added when the model was made (by whoever created it). If additional layers were used, those layers will insert into the model with the component. This convention will ensure that they appear below layers with 00 convention.

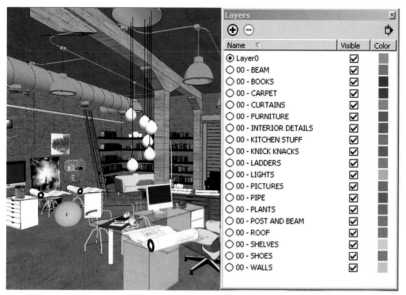

Fig. 14.8: All the components in this interior model are placed on layers with corresponding, straightforward names.

Vegetation Layers

Every vegetation type—be it shrub, tree, perennial, annual, or vine—must have its own layer. For example, if five tree types are in the model, you should create five layers, placing each type on a separate layer. Any copies of the tree type will automatically be placed on the same layer. Site models frequently have 15 or more layers devoted to plants.

Here are some suggestions for vegetation layer names. This naming convention will keep species organized by type and include the vegetation name (Fig. 14.9). If the vegetation is generic, use a number instead.

- ▶ **00 - TREES -** [species name, i.e., *OAKS*] or **00 - TREES - 01, 00 - TREES - 02,** etc.

- ▶ **00 - SHRUBS -** [species name, i.e., BUSH] or **00 - SHRUBS - 01, 00 - SHRUBS – 02,** etc.

- ▶ **00 - PERENNIALS -** [species name, i.e., AGAVE] or **00 - PERENNIALS - 01, 00 - PERENNIALS – 02,** etc.

- ▶ **00 - ANNUALS -** [species name–, i.e., BEGONIA] or **00 - ANNUALS - 01, 00 - ANNUALS – 02,** etc.

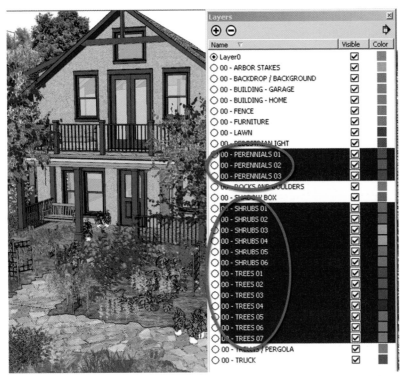

Fig. 14.9: The vegetation in the model is categorized by type. Each shrub, tree, and perennial type has its own layer.

Layer Conventions by Model Typology

Each of the three model typologies (interior, site, and architecture) benefit from different layers approaches. In tandem with the points already discussed, keep your model organized and functional.

Interior Models

For interior models, place the ceiling and walls on their own layers (Fig. 14.10). Turning them off will give you greater access to the model interior to make changes and insert component details (Fig. 14.11). All furnishings and objects should be components on their own layers (Fig. 14.12).

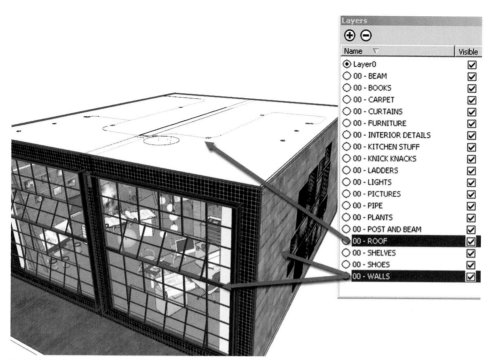

Fig. 14.10: Layers are created for the roofs and walls of the interior model. The roof and walls are made into components and then placed on these layers.

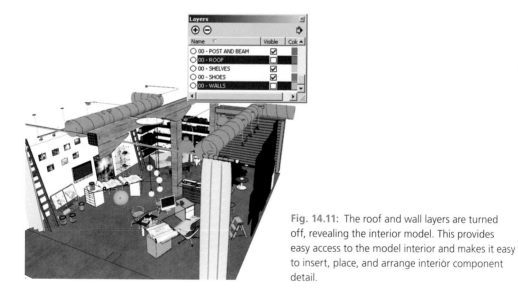

Fig. 14.11: The roof and wall layers are turned off, revealing the interior model. This provides easy access to the model interior and makes it easy to insert, place, and arrange interior component detail.

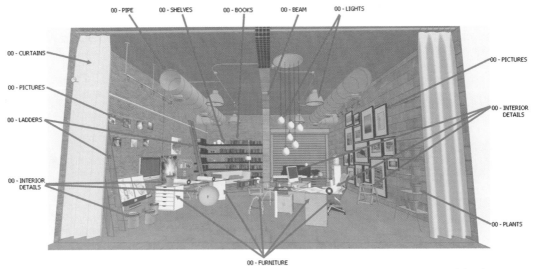

Fig. 14.12: A diagram of (most) interior detail components in the model and the layers names used for those components

Architectural Models

A good strategy for building models is to have all the various elements that compose the building on layers. This will allow you to peel back the building facade all the way to the structure as needed. This strategy provides the greatest amount of control and gives you the ability to view different building elements (Fig. 14.13, Fig. 14.14, Fig. 14.15, Fig. 14.16, Fig. 14.17). Make sure all drafted geometry that defines the base model is on Layer 0.

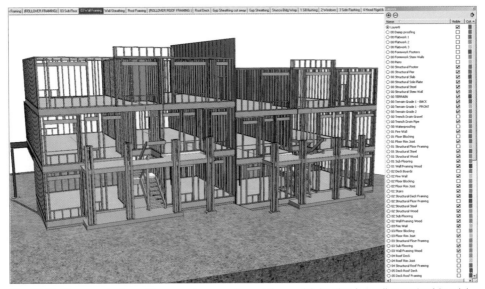

Fig. 14.13: The organization of layers and scenes allowed the model detail to be well organized (model by Mark Carvalho).

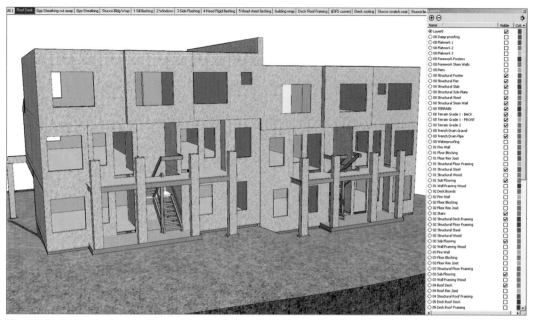

Fig. 14.14: Each scene turned off a specific set of layers revealing more and more of the model (model by Mark Carvalho).

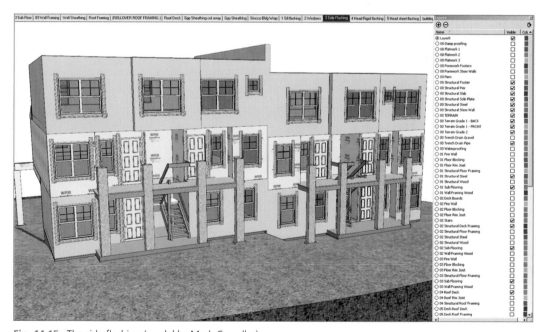

Fig. 14.15: The side flashing (model by Mark Carvalho)

Fig. 14.16: The stucco scratch coat (model by Mark Carvalho)

Fig. 14.17: This type of organization is paramount for working with building models (model by Mark Carvalho).

Site Models

These models benefit from having all objects composing the landscape, in particular the vegetation, on layers to maintain computer performance (Fig. 14.18).

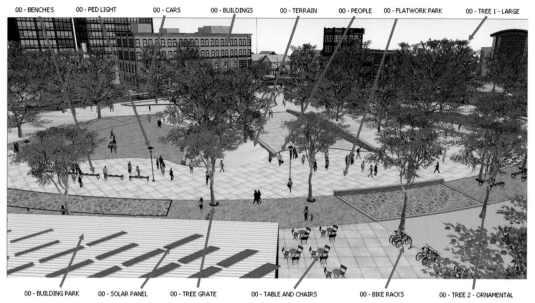

00 - BENCHES 00 - PED LIGHT 00 - CARS 00 - BUILDINGS 00 - TERRAIN 00 - PEOPLE 00 - FLATWORK PARK 00 - TREE 1 - LARGE

00 - BUILDING PARK 00 - SOLAR PANEL 00 - TREE GRATE 00 - TABLE AND CHAIRS 00 - BIKE RACKS 00 - TREE 2 - ORNAMENTAL

Fig. 14.18: Site model diagram showing typical layer names for the components found in the park model

Cleaning Up Layers

Once your layer strategy for the model is in place, it's time to clean up the layer list. You may want to import CAD files into SketchUp. Regardless of which program you use (AutoCAD, Revit, DynaSCAPE, or similar programs), the imported CAD information includes the CAD layers. In many instances, the imported CAD file will cause the layer list to grow rather large and confusing. Similarly, many premade components include their own layers, which will show up in the layer list once the component is placed in the model (Fig. 14.19).

If you use the suggested layering convention, cleaning up the layer list is easy. Select the CAD and any other imported/extra layers, and click the Delete button on the Layer menu. The default action, Move contents to Default layer, should be selected. Next, click OK (Fig. 14.20). The layers will be merged with Layer 0 (Fig. 14.21, Fig. 14.22).

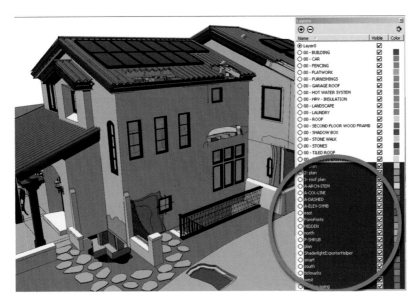

Fig. 14.19: The extra layers at the bottom of the SketchUp layer list were imported with the AutoCAD linework.

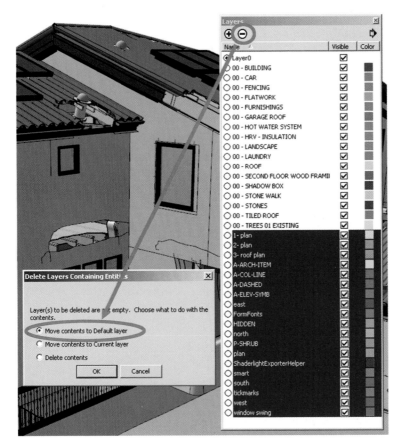

Fig. 14.20: To keep the model layers clean and organized, use the Layer Delete option. They are no longer needed because the model detail and geometry is well organized.

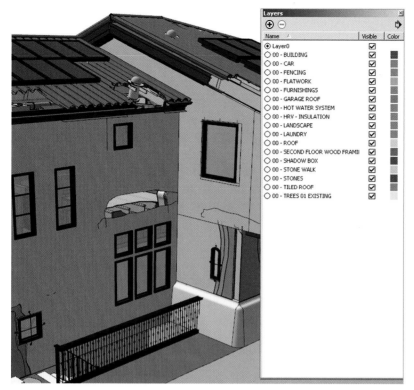

Fig. 14.21: Once the AutoCAD layers are deleted, move them to Layer 0.

Fig. 14.22: Clarum Home rendering (Shaderlight) of the organized model (model by Mark Carvalho and Daniel Tal)

Controlling Layers with Scenes

When you save a scene, SketchUp will remember which layers were visible or hidden when the scene was created or last saved. Clicking on a scene will return the visible or hidden layers to that scene's setting. You won't have to turn layers on or off through the Layer menu; the software with do that task for you in one simple click.

Creating On/Off Scenes

When you're creating On/Off scenes during the modeling phase, uncheck the Camera Location button (Fig. 14.23). This will allow the detail to be toggled off or on from any position in the model, instead of being returned to a set view every time. Recheck the Camera Location box before you create a scene in which you want to retain the camera view. Failure to do so will prevent the camera position from being preserved.

Off Scenes

Off scenes should be used to turn off (hide) model component layers that cause the computer to slow down. For example, turn off all vegetation layers, and then create the scene (Fig. 14.24). Off scenes will allow you to model, pan, zoom, and orbit with ease.

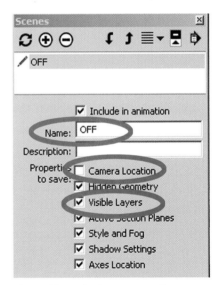

To create an Off scene, follow these steps:

1. Open the Layers menu (Window → Layers).
2. Turn off (uncheck) Component Detail Layers.
3. Open the Scenes menu (Window → Scenes).
4. Uncheck Camera Location.
5. Make sure Visible Layer is checked.
6. Create the scene.
7. Rename the scene to **OFF**.

On Scenes

On scenes, when clicked, turns on all model layers. This setting is useful for creating new saved camera views. Turn Off all of the model detailing using the OFF scene. Next, position the camera in a desired location, and (Fig. 14.25) click the On scene, assess the view and, if wanted, create a new scene saving the Camera Position.

Fig. 14.23: In the Scene menu, Camera Location is unchecked and Visible Layers (and other options) are checked, indicating that SketchUp should remember those properties when it creates a new scene.

Fig. 14.24: When you create an Off scene, all of the component detail is turned off. The highlighted (blue) layers remain visible in the model. The Off Scene tab is located at the top-left of the SketchUp screen.

Fig. 14.25: An On scene is created for the park model. All layers are toggled to visible. Clicking the On scene will toggle on all the detail in the model.

Chapter 14: Organizing the Model

To create an On scene, follow these steps:

1. Open the Layers menu (Window → Layers).
2. Turn on all layers.
3. Open the Scenes menu (Window → Scenes).
4. Uncheck Camera Location, unless you want to save the Camera Position.
5. Make sure Visible Layer is checked.
6. Create the scene.
7. Rename the scene to **ON**.

Assessment Scenes

Consider creating similar On/Off scenes to control the visibility of differing layers. For example, create scenes that turn off only the vegetation or furniture (Fig. 14.26, Fig. 14.27). Or, create any other scenes to filter different layer and component types. These filtered scenes can help you assess the model, including the placement of details, the model design, the composition for graphic views, etc.

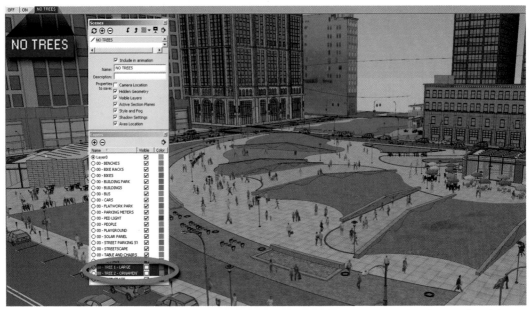

Fig. 14.26: In this assessment scene, the Tree layers are turned off (highlighted in blue and circled in red) and the scene is created. The scene is then renamed NO TREES. Selecting this scene will turn on all of the layers except the trees.

Fig. 14.27: This rendered view of the park model was created using scenes (Shaderlight). The model contains 2.7 million faces, which makes it essential to keep it organized.

Toggling Layers

There are specific times when scenes should be toggled off and on. Follow these general guidelines to help maintain your model performance, create specific camera views, and generate renderings.

Off

When you're modeling forms, adding or adjusting geometry, keep the component detail layers turned off, particularly vegetation layers. This will help maintain performance and allow you easy access to model geometry. Turn on specific component detail layers as needed.

Keep the layers off when you're panning, orbiting, zooming, and generally moving around detailed models.

In general, keep the vegetation layers turned off. Turn specific vegetation layers on when you're editing specific model areas.

Off or On as Needed

On/Off scenes provide efficiency when you're working with vegetation. Because of the large potential number of plant layers you might need, using scenes will allow all of the vegetation to be turned off or on with a single click.

Navigate around the model and generate specific camera view scenes. Pan around with Layers off. When you're trying to find a specific view, turn on Layers, save the scene, and turn the layers off again. Use the Scene tabs to quickly hide and reveal layers. Ensure the Position Camera property is checked prior to creating a saved camera scene.

On

When you're exporting an image from SketchUp or prior to rendering a scene, turn the desired layers on. Create specific camera scenes as mentioned previously to increase efficiency.

The Selection Toy Ruby Script

The Selection Toy Ruby created by ThomThom is free and it's indispensable. This Ruby Script allows components, groups, edges, and faces to be quickly selected and sorted. It not only speeds up the selection of geometry, it permits the quick placement of components onto layers.

The Selection Toy options useful for layer management are reviewed here. Explore the other options as well. You can find a link to the Ruby Script, located at www.SketchUcation.com, on this book's resources page (Fig. 14.28).

Fig. 14.28: SketchUp will be much more difficult to use if this Ruby Script ever disappears.

Selection Toys Menu

Although Selection Toys comes with its own menu button, you should use the right-click menu to select components and geometry. The right-click options are context-sensitive and change depending on the type of geometry selected.

Component Quick Select

Selecting and right-clicking a component reveals the Instances option toward the bottom of the menu. From instances, there are four selection options (Fig. 14.29). Clicking Select Active will instantly select all copies of that component (Fig. 14.30).

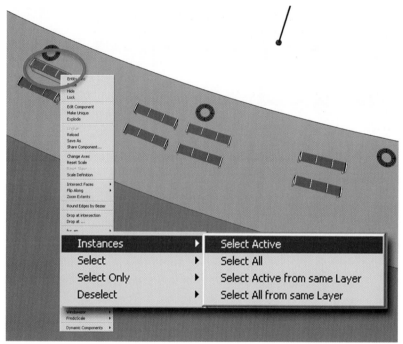

Fig. 14.29: Select a single component in the model. Right-click over it and select Instances → Select Active.

Once a specific component and all its copies are selected, you can use Entity Info to quickly place the components onto the same layer (Fig. 14.31, Fig. 14.32). This technique is useful when components are placed on the wrong layer or need to be moved to a new layer.

Other Options

The Selection Toy Ruby offers many more selection options, including the ability to quickly select edges and faces, select similar groups, and convert them into components. Explore the different option available and have fun using them.

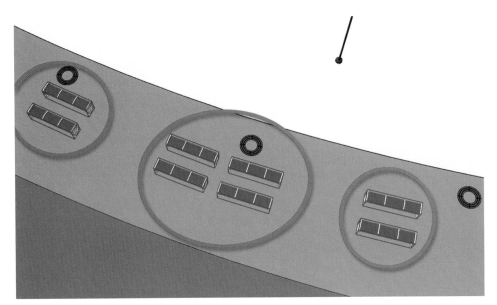

Fig. 14.30: All versions of the component will be selected.

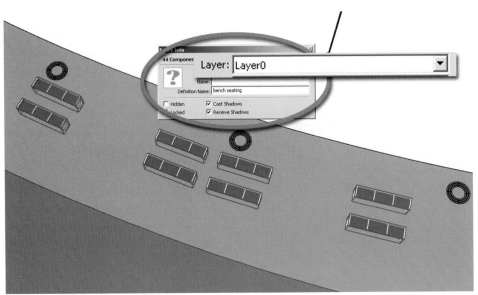

Fig. 14.31: When all the components are selected, they can be easily placed onto new layers with Entity Info. As shown, the benches are on the wrong layer (Layer 0).

Part 3: Modeling Detail

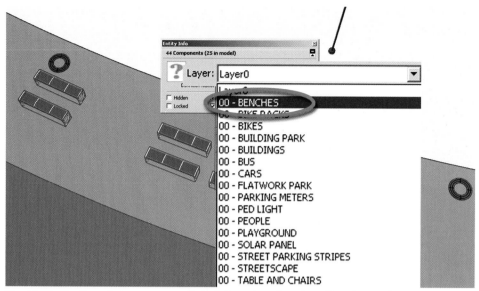

Fig. 14.32: Use the pull-down menu on Entity Info to place the selected benches on the 00 - BENCHES layer, keeping the model organized with a few simple clicks.

Warning!

If you read to the end of this chapter and then don't use layers, you will not like working with SketchUp and you will complain that it does not function properly. (Fig. 14.33). You might even buy an expensive computer hoping it will fix the problems. It won't. Use layers!

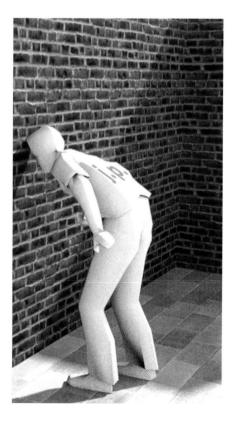

Fig. 14.33: If you ignore this chapter, you'll be banging your head (Shaderlight).

Camera Scenes, Composition, and Backdrops

D etermining and saving camera views as scenes before you render them can facilitate an efficient workflow (Fig. 15.1). You can add component detail based on a particular scene, which will save time while allowing precise object placement. Placing image backdrops and 2D components into particular scenes will help you establish both context and location while filling gaps in the model.

The process is as follows:

1. Save scenes of specific camera views.

2. Add detail and compose components based on the scenes.

3. Add backdrops to create context and hide gaps in the model.

Camera Scenes

As outlined in Chapter 12 camera scenes can be saved at any time during the modeling process and adjusted as needed. Save the scenes you want to use for rendering before you add component detail to those scenes. Use the camera tools to set eye-level and bird's-eye views (Fig. 15.2).

Create Scene

Delete Scene

Expand Menu

Rename Scene

Scene Properties

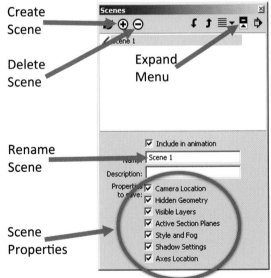

Fig. 15.1: The Scene menu

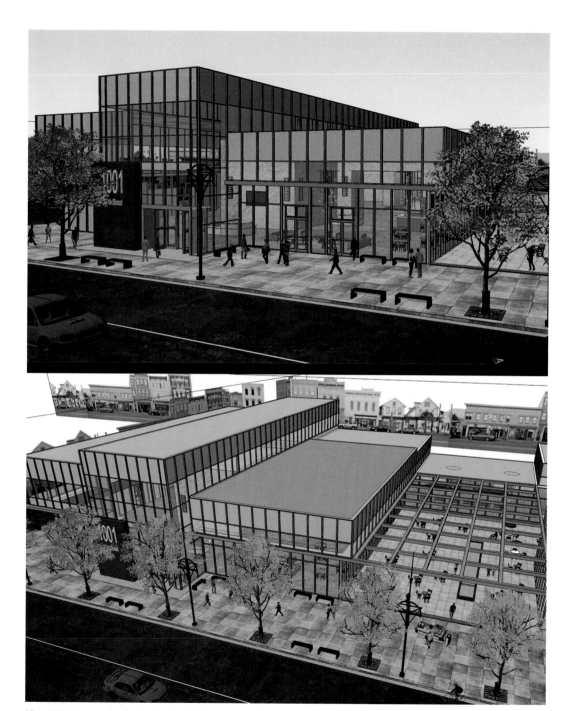

Fig. 15.2: An eye-level view (top); a bird's-eye view (bottom)

Composition

Composition refers to the placement, arrangement, and organization of visual elements in a scene. Composition, including placement of detailed components, helps determine the focus of attention in a rendering. This section deals with composition as it pertains to the placement of components and filling in a scene to make it look complete.

Composition Zones

Camera views have foregrounds, midgrounds, and backgrounds. These three zones are found in most images, including eye-level views, bird's eye views, and elevated camera scenes. For modeling purposes, components and objects should be placed in these zones to create focus. In general, the *midground* is where the render view will focus. This is usually true for architecture, interior design, and site renderings (Fig. 15.3, Fig. 15.4, Fig. 15.5, Fig. 15.6).

Foreground

The *foreground* is the front area of the scene, closest to the viewer. Model detail in the foreground is useful for drawing attention to the midground, the area where focus is usually needed (Fig. 15.7, Fig. 15.8).

Fig. 15.3: The rendering of this building and site will be analyzed to show composition zones (Su Podium).

Fig. 15.4: In this composition, blue represents the foreground, red the midground, and yellow the background.

Fig. 15.5: This interior rendering will be analyzed to show the composition zones (Twilight Render).

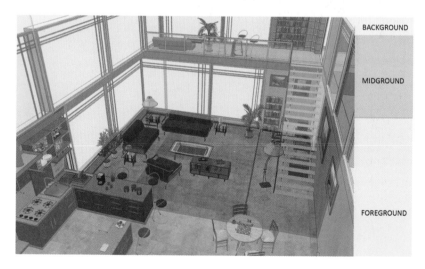

Fig. 15.6: In this composition, blue represents the foreground, red the midground, and yellow the background.

Fig. 15.7: The foreground for the building rendering includes the road and cars. These elements provide context and scale but do not command attention.

Fig. 15.8: The foreground detail of the interior frames the rest of the scene. The kitchen counters and table are off to the side, leaving the middle of the view open and leading the eye to the midground.

Consider the following tips when you are placing components in the foreground:

▶ Minimize detail, keeping the view open to the midground.

▶ Avoid views in the foreground centering on components or model detail. Detail should be on the sides, helping frame the view. If an object cannot be moved, adjust the camera view around the object.

- Hide objects on layers if the objects cannot be moved or worked around—for example, buildings, walls, roofs, trees, cars, or any obstructing component or model object. Create a special layer for the scene and place those objects on the layer. Turn the layer off and Save/Update the scene. See Chapter 14 for a refresher on working with layers and scenes.

- Ensure that textures are sharp, correctly scaled, and not pixilated.

- Avoid placing people or poorly modeled or textured objects in the foreground because they can detract from the view.

Midground

For most renderings, the *midground* is the area of focus (Fig. 15.9, Fig. 15.10). Be it a building, interior, or site, the rendering content and detail are in this general zone. A standard method for composing views is to use the Rule of Thirds. Divide the selected view into thirds, both horizontally and vertically. Try to keep the object of focus on the far left or right third or two-thirds. Consider the following tips when you're placing components in the midground:

- Most component detail will be arranged in the midground.

- Add enough detail to create a comparable view to a real-world context (see Chapter 14).

- Use the Rule of Thirds.

Fig. 15.9: The focus of the render, which is the building, is located in the midground. The various site details (trees, lights, benches, etc.) are arranged to frame the building.

Fig. 15.10: The interior scene midground is balanced with the foreground, leading the viewer's eye to capture the entire scene.

Background

The model *background* is the area off to the side or in the distance of the midground focus (Fig. 15.11, Fig. 15.12). For many site and building models, the background might be empty, which can be distracting. For interior models, the background is typically the view out of a window, doorway, or opening. Backgrounds include the area where a sky would be present in the real world.

Fig. 15.11: A sky and buildings (included as an image) are included to create the background and provide important settings for the building.

Fig. 15.12: A sky and city image is enhanced using Photoshop to help provide context for the interior scene.

The background can be filled with backdrops, such as sky or neighborhood images, 3D building models, and 2D FaceMe components such as trees. Filling in the background goes a long way in making a model appear in context and realistic.

Background also refers to parts of the model that are not directly seen. Many renderings will utilize reflective surfaces, like glass. Reflective surfaces with nothing to reflect will have reflections that are curiously blank and flat (Fig. 15.13).

Backgrounds should encircle the model's main content. This will allow reflective objects to mirror the detail of the backgrounds (Fig. 15.14, Fig. 15.15). In many cases, simply placing an image backdrop away from the camera view but facing reflective objects is enough.

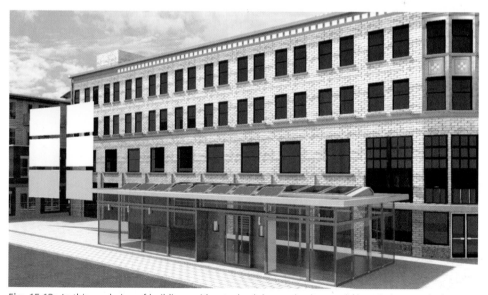

Fig. 15.13: In this rendering of buildings without a backdrop or background, the windows and other reflective surfaces (including the six surfaces set up to act as mirrors) appear flat.

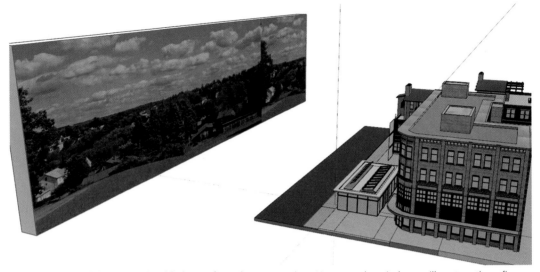

Fig. 15.14: A backdrop image is added away from the camera view. However, the windows will capture the reflection of the backdrop when rendered.

Fig. 15.15: The windows and reflective surfaces (including the six surfaces set up to act like mirrors) reflect the off-view backdrop.

Backdrops

Backdrops are images or objects placed in the SketchUp model background to provide context and fill in gaps. Backdrops range from city skylines, vegetated yards, to views outside of windows and settings specific to the model. This section describes two ways to add backdrops to a SketchUp model (Fig. 15.16, Fig. 15.17).

Fig. 15.16: The rendered interior needs a backdrop (Shaderlight).

Fig. 15.17: A backdrop is added in Photoshop.

Other methods can be used to add backdrops. No one method is superior, and the use of some backdrops will depend on the user's skill level (for example, knowing how to use Photoshop) and the desired result.

Photoshop Postproduction

Using a photo-editing program, you can add backdrop images to a rendering during the postproduction phase (Fig. 15.18, Fig. 15.19). Part 7 reviews postproduction methods you can use.

Fig. 15.18: Marina and buildings (Twilight Render)

Fig. 15.19: A backdrop is added to the rendered image in Photoshop.

IRP Backdrops

Shaderlight and Twilight IRPs allow you to insert image files into a rendering (Fig. 15.20, Fig. 15.21, Fig. 15.22). When the rendering is processed, the image will be included in the background. This technique will be explained in the IRP-specific chapters.

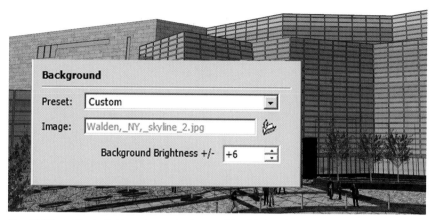

Fig. 15.20: In Shaderlight, an image background is added to the Render options.

Fig. 15.21: The selected image renders with the scene.

Fig. 15.22: The completed rendering with background image included

SketchUp Backdrops

You can create backdrops in SketchUp using two different methods: 3D model detailing or image placement (Fig. 15.23, Fig. 15.24). Both methods can be used in tandem to achieve some great effects. Interior models will benefit more from image backdrops.

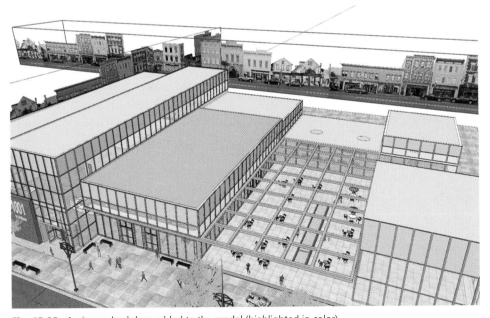

Fig. 15.23: An image backdrop added to the model (highlighted in color).

Fig. 15.24: 3D buildings used as model backdrops when rendering (highlighted in color)

Model Backdrops

3D buildings and 2D photo trees make excellent backdrops (Fig. 15.25, Fig. 15.26). Place them in the background and between model gaps. Combine them with image backdrops to add additional depth and environment. 3D Warehouse and FormFonts have both types of models, in particular buildings. FormFonts and DynaSCAPE Sketch3D have excellent 2D photo trees.

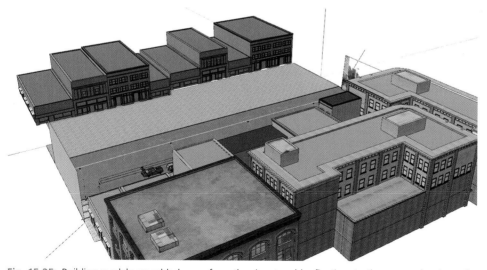

Fig. 15.25: Building models are added away from the view to add reflections to the scene when it renders.

Fig. 15.26: This streetscape rendering (SU Podium) includes building model backdrops (added in Fig. 15.23) and building models for reflections (added away from the view in Fig. 15.24).

Image Backdrops

Image backdrops are photos applied to vertical surfaces and placed around the model's background. The content of the backdrop is subjective and depends on the model. Obviously, using accurate images is ideal but not always possible.

Obtaining Backdrops

CG Textures.com (see Chapter 7) has its own set of backdrops for download. Search CG Textures using the terms "background," "city," "forest," and "sky" to obtain some useful images (Fig. 15.27). Save them into the Texture Library and even use them for postproduction. Make your own backdrops by taking photographs appropriate for the model.

Fig. 15.27: CG Textures offers backgrounds and sky images to use as image backdrops.

Inserting Image Backdrops

An image backdrop benefits from being placed onto a vertical surface in the model.

1. Make a cube and place it in the area where the backdrop image is to be located. Make the cube roughly the size of the needed backdrop (Fig. 15.28).

2. To place an image backdrop on the cube, select File → Import and navigate to the image file location. To the right of the menu, select Import as Texture. Select the image and click OK (Fig. 15.29).

3. The inserted image can be snapped onto the vertical surface of the cube and then scaled upward or downward to fit (Fig. 15.30, Fig. 15.31).

4. Once placed, make the cube into a component (select the entire cube, right-click, and select Make Component, Fig. 15.32) and place it on a layer called **00 - BACKDROP** (Fig. 15.33).

5. The background image can be further sized and positioned by scaling the cube component.

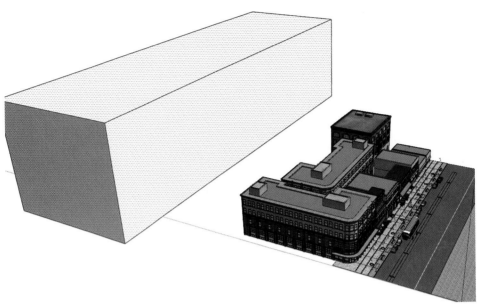

Fig. 15.28: A 3D cube is created. The background image will be placed on the cubes surface facing the model.

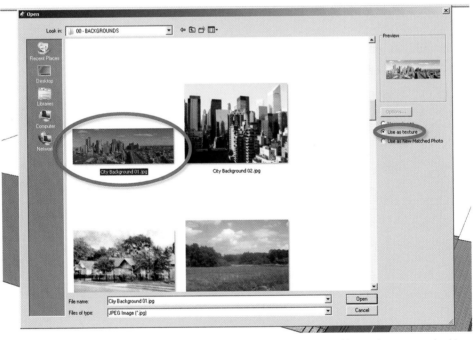

Fig. 15.29: The SketchUp Import function allows you to insert a background image (as a texture in this case).

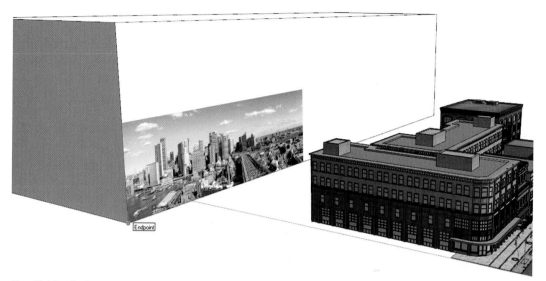

Fig. 15.30: The image is placed on the cube's surface.

Fig. 15.31: The placed image is scaled larger during the insertion process to fit the entire front of the cube face.

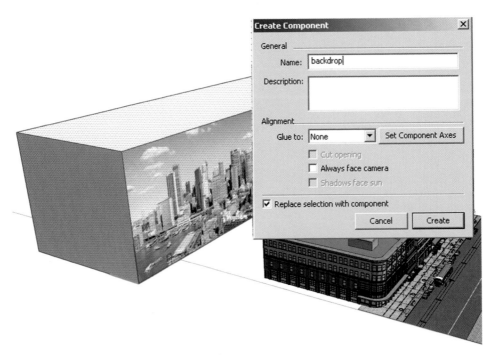

Fig. 15.32: The cube, with image, is converted into a component.

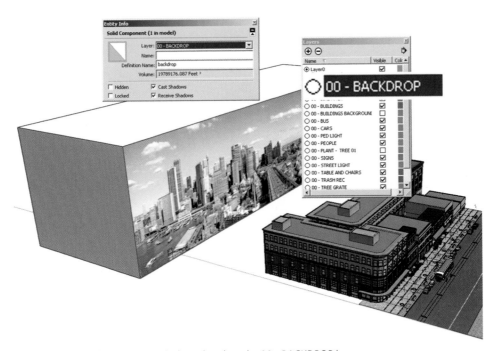

Fig. 15.33: The cube component is then placed on the 00 - BACKDROP layer.

Advanced Detailing

Advanced detailing entails taking an extra step and learning to include additional articulation to surfaces and objects before rendering them (Fig. 16.1, Fig. 16.2). Users of all levels can benefit from these methods, but they are well suited for *intermediate and advanced users.*

Fig. 16.1: The Artisan Ruby Script by Dale Martens was used to help shape the contours and apply textures to this terrain model (SketchUp).

Fig. 16.2: Rendering of terrain model (Twilight Render)

This chapter discusses several general methods of advance detailing:

▸ **Texture Modeling**: Push/pull and articulate texture image surfaces

▸ **Detailing at Transitions**: Creating realistic edges and transitions

▸ **Ruby Scripts**: Custom detailing tools

Although more methods exist, these particular ones provide an excellent place to begin improving your models.

Texture Modeling

Instead of applying a texture to imply a surface, model the applied texture character into the objects. You can create wood beams; extruded concrete and pavers; rounded roofing tile and house siding; blocks of bricks and masonry; and so on (Fig. 16.3, Fig. 16.4, Fig. 16.5, Fig. 16.6). The texture image itself is used to create the initial object.

Fig. 16.3: Instead of using a roof texture for the individual clay roof tiles, the roofing tile is modeled and placed around the roof.

Fig. 16.4: Rendering of the modeled roof tiles (Shaderlight)

Fig. 16.5: The individual paving tiles are modeled and extruded (model by John Palmer).

Fig. 16.6: The rendered version of the modeled paving is more realistic than a textured version (Shaderlight).

The following steps illustrate how this technique can be applied. Although it's specific to wood material, the method is the same for other textures.

1. Apply a texture to the model surface. Make sure that it is correctly scaled (Fig. 16.7).

2. Subdivide the surface of the wood at the wood *gaps,* the areas where a joint appears between the planks of the wood in the flooring (Fig. 16.8).

3. Copy and array the edges that subdivide the joint/gap along the surface of the texture. Align the copies with the other joints and gaps (Fig. 16.9, Fig. 16.10).

4. Select each subdivided wood face (the larger areas between the joints), right-click over it, and choose Make separate surface into a group; in the example, each plank of wood will be made into its own group (Fig. 16.11).

5. Enter each group instance and extrude the surface upward (in this case, 1″ or 2″), adding thickness and creating a wood plank. The gap between each plank will become more pronounced as it remains flat (unextruded) relative to each wood plank group (Fig. 16.12).

6. When extruding the groups, vary each group slightly in height to create a subtle, uneven look common with real-world flooring and materials (Fig. 16.13, Fig. 16.14).

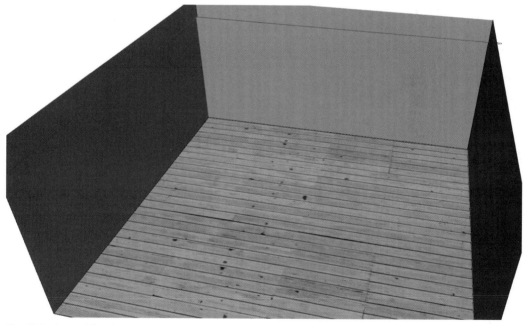

Fig. 16.7: A wood flooring texture is applied to the model surface.

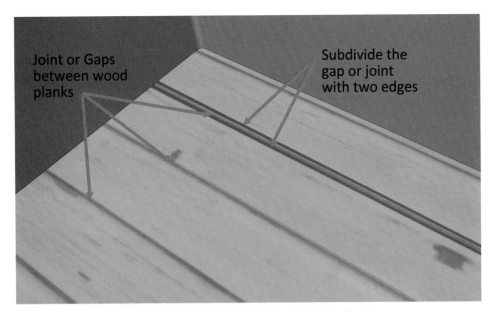

Joint or Gaps between wood planks

Subdivide the gap or joint with two edges

Fig. 16.8: Using the texture as a reference, the joint/seam is subdivided with edges.

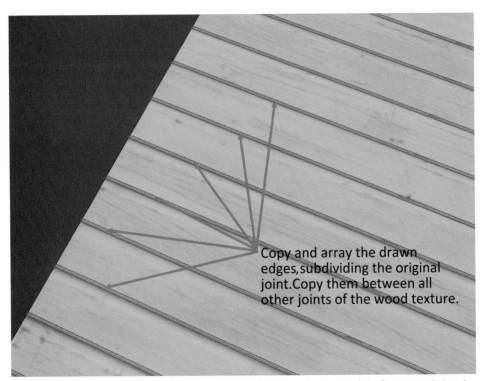

Copy and array the drawn edges, subdividing the original joint. Copy them between all other joints of the wood texture.

Fig. 16.9: The edges used to subdivide the joint are copied along the length of the flooring and placed at each seam/joint.

Fig. 16.10: The edges defining the wood joint are copied along the texture, subdividing the faces of each wood plant relative to the texture image.

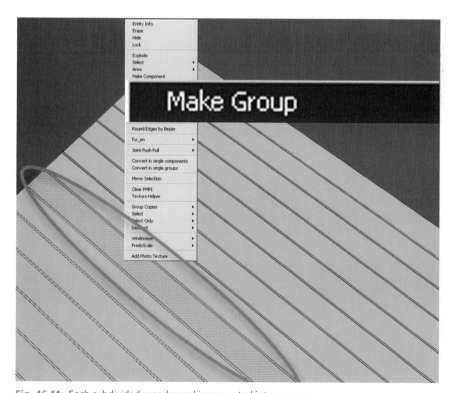

Fig. 16.11: Each subdivided wood panel is converted into a group.

Fig. 16.12: Each wood panel group is edited and the surface extruded.

Fig. 16.13: The goal is to create a slightly uneven look for the flooring by extruding each panel at a slightly different height.

Fig. 16.14: The resulting render gives the wood floor a more realistic and detailed appearance.

Detailing at Texture Edges

The term *texture edges* refers to the edge that is created where two textured surfaces meet—for example, where concrete meets a lawn or where floor tile meets carpeting or a hardwood floor.

Irregular Texture Outlines

One approach to handling texture edges is to create irregular edge outlines where the two textures meet, such as where a granite stone paving texture meets a lawn or similar ground cover (Fig. 16.15). Outline the irregular pattern of the stone texture, subdividing the texture edges (Fig. 16.16, Fig. 16.17). Next, apply the adjacent texture to the subdivided surface, creating an irregular but more realistic outline (Fig. 16.18).

Fig. 16.15: The paving edges are outlined and subdivided to give them a more irregular edge.

Fig. 16.16: The Freehand SketchUp tool is used to outline the edges of the paving.

Part 3: Modeling Detail

Fig. 16.17: The outline subdivides the surface.

Fig. 16.18: The adjacent ground-cover texture is applied to the outlined portion of the paving.

The much overlooked and little-used Freehand drawing tool is ideal for this method. Zoom in close to the texture, and make sure the starting points and endpoints of the Freehand tool edges connect to the edge boundaries of the textures in order to subdivide the surface.

Room or Surface Transitions

Transitions between areas or surfaces are usually accompanied by a slight variation in height. Such transitions include edging, such as metal, wood, or plastic banding that endcaps carpets, and places where flooring meets another surface (Fig. 16.19, Fig. 16.20, Fig. 16.21, Fig. 16.22, Fig. 16.23, Fig. 16.24, Fig. 16.25).

One approach to handling a transition is to extrude or depress one or both of the surfaces to create a small lip between the two transition areas. The exaggeration does not need to be very large, usually just inches or less. Shadows added in the scene for lighting usually will cast a small shadow based on the minor extrusion, adding nice, subtle detail.

Consider modeling or subdividing the area between the transition or seam with an actual edging surface. Extrude the edging and consider push/pulling one of the adjacent surfaces as discussed previously.

Fig. 16.19: The paving edges all run into each other.

Fig. 16.20: The edges are offset to create a subdivided band between the paving and ground cover.

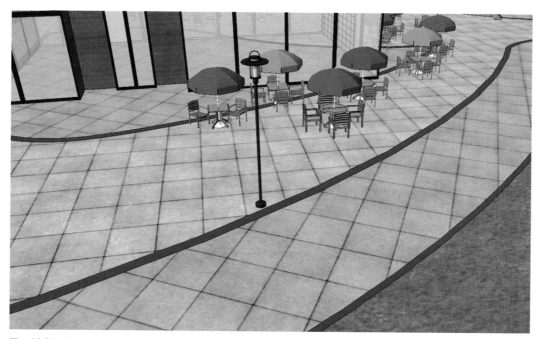

Fig. 16.21: A stone texture is added to the subdivided faces forming the transition band.

Fig. 16.22: The stone band is slightly extruded to help differentiate between the transitions.

Fig. 16.23: Rendering of the paving with transition

Fig. 16.24: A narrow but long portion of the floor is subdivided between the two flooring materials.

Fig. 16.25: To create the transition, a color (metal band) is added to the subdivided portion.

Fixing Seams

The Extrude Transition method and the Model Edging Band both work well to fix visible texture seams as described in Chapter 9. Subdivide the surface at the seam with an edge and add a transition band and/or adjust the heights of the surfaces relative to each other. Even a slight elevation or depression or narrow transition band adds a good level of realism.

That provides three options for fixing the seam:

- ▶ Extrude or depress the surface.
- ▶ Add an edging object.
- ▶ Using the right-click Texture tool, reposition one or both of the textures.

Ruby Scripts for Detailing

Several Ruby Scripts are very useful for adding detail to your model (Fig. 16.26, Fig. 16.27). All of the scripts mentioned here are excellent modeling tools that greatly expand what SketchUp can model and detail. Round Corner and Profile Builder are outlined here with some detail because these are quick and easy tools to use. Extrude Edges, Artisan, Instant Roof, and Road Ruby Scripts are mentioned but not explained in depth. Refer to their respective websites to learn more about how to use these scripts.

This book's website, www.ambit-3d.com, provides links to the various Ruby Scripts described here.

Fig. 16.26: Smustard.com is a good source for Ruby Scripts.

Fig. 16.27: SketchUcation has many amazing and free Ruby Scripts.

Rounded Edges

A common method used in renderings is adding rounded edges to corners. Street curbs, steps, table and chairs edges, and many furnishings and amenities do not have right-angled corners. In fact, it might be safe to say that in the real world, most objects with even 90-degree angles have soft, tapered edges. Most objects extrude in SketchUp with a 90-degree corner. Fortunately, adding rounded corners in SketchUp is easy.

The RoundCorner Ruby Script allows you to add a variety of soft, curved, and beveled edges to your model (Fig. 16.28, Fig. 16.29, Fig. 16.30, Fig. 16.31). RoundCorner is freely available from SketchUcation.

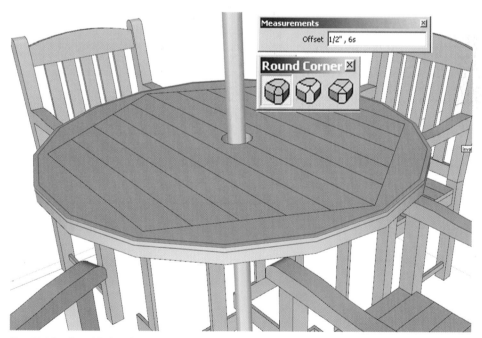

Fig. 16.28: The table has sharp 90-degree edges.

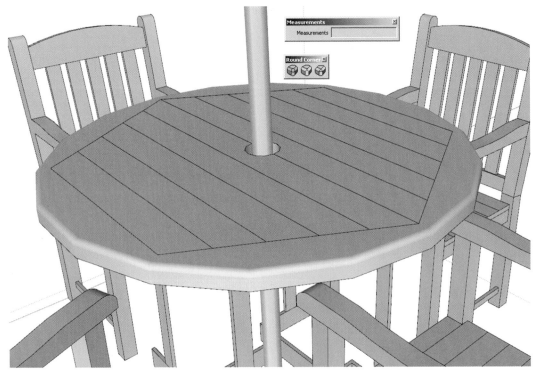

Fig. 16.29: The Rounded Edges Ruby Script is used on the table edges to simulate real-world tables.

The Ruby Script menu has three options: Rounded Corners, Sharp Corners, and Bevel Edges. The simplest way to make this method work is as follows:

1. Select one of the three options.

2. Start with Rounded Corners.

3. In the Measurements box, simply enter the amount of roundness in units, and then select the edges you want to round. Select as many edges as needed.

4. Press the Enter key and the script will run, rounding all of the selected edges.

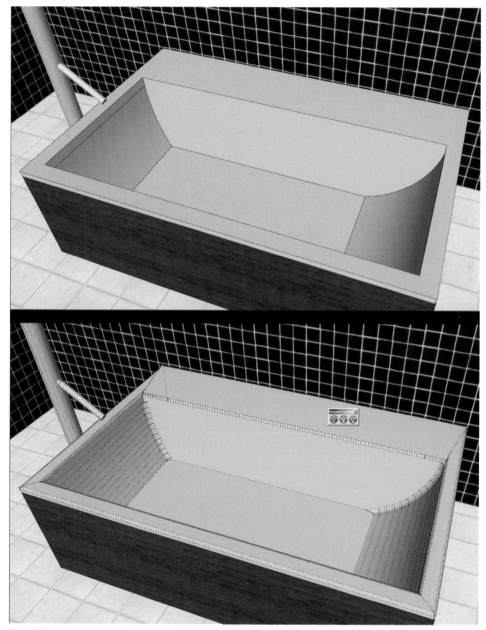

Fig. 16.30: The bath lip and some of the interior form have perpendicular edges, which are unrealistic (top). All of the edges are selected, and Rounded Edges will be applied to them (bottom).

Fig. 16.31: The edges are softened.

Profile Builder

Profile Builder, available at Smustard.com, is best described as the Follow Me tool on steroids (Fig. 16.32). The tool has multiple options.

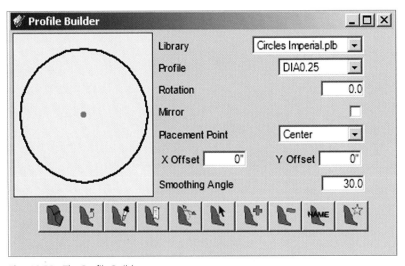

Fig. 16.32: The Profile Builder menu

Here are the basic steps to use the Profile Builder:

1. Create a 2D outline of a shape to be extruded—for example, crown molding, building columns, articulated and rounded edges, building parapets, complex furnishings, or any form or object to be extruded along a path. The surface can be any shape but it must be a single, selectable surface. It cannot have edges subdividing its parts (Fig. 16.33).

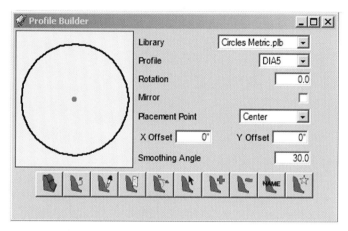

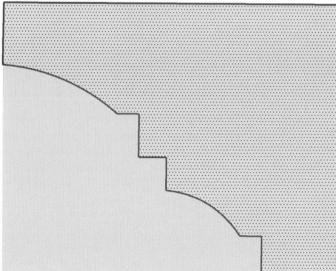

Fig. 16.33: A square surface is created and a 2D profile (highlighted) is drafted.

2. Select the surface and click the Create a New Profile button. Give the profile a name (Fig. 16.34).

3. Use the pull-down menu to the right and a red dot on the profile to adjust the Placement Point. This will indicate how the profile is placed on selected edges (Fig. 16.35). You may need to take several tries to get this correct once you apply the profile.

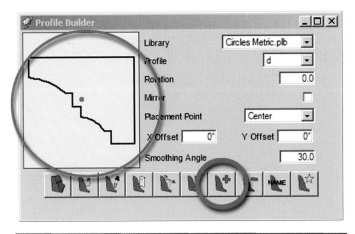

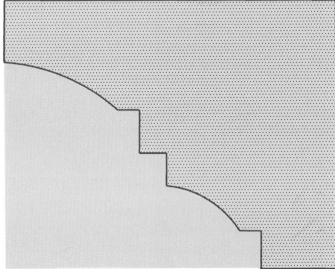

Fig. 16.34: With the profile selected (highlighted), the profile is added to Profile Builder.

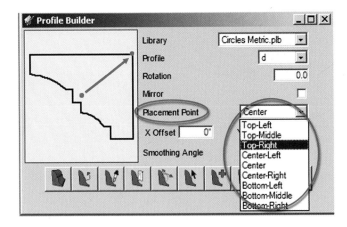

Fig. 16.35: Adjust the Placement Point.

4. There are two options for constructing the profile:

   ▶ Select the Build button. You can just build the profile and place it anywhere you like.

   ▶ Build Along Path is similar to Follow Me. Select continuous edges and then click on Build Along Path. The profile will be placed on the selected edges (Fig. 16.36, Fig. 16.37, Fig. 16.38).

5. Once the profile is constructed, an option will appear asking if you want to reverse the extrusion along the path. If the profile is not correctly positioned or you want to adjust the Placement Point, select Yes.

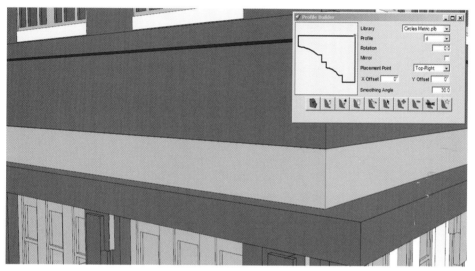

Fig. 16.36: The path to which the profile will be applied is selected. In this case, it's the edge around the building.

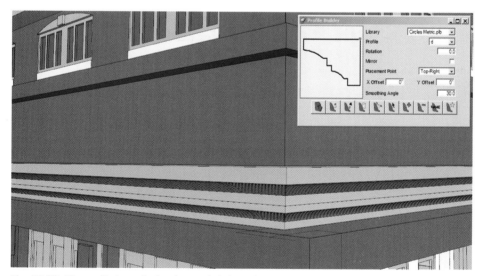

Fig. 16.37: The profile is applied and extruded along the selected building path, creating extruded building detail.

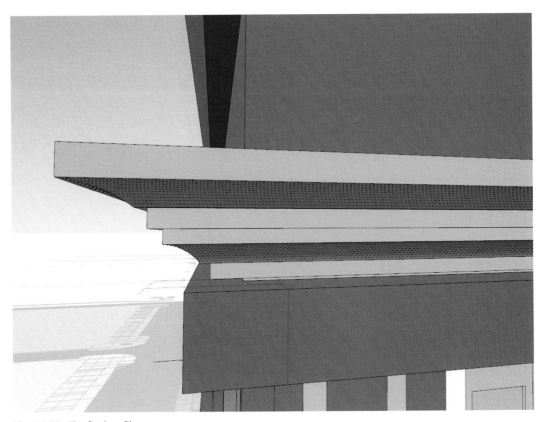

Fig. 16.38: The final profile

Chris Fulmer Tools

Chris Fulmer (landscape architect, SketchUp user, and Ruby Script writer) created an excellent Ruby Script to randomize the rotation and size of components. It is an excellent script for creating irregular planting plants filled with rotated and scaled vegetation. With the Ruby Script you can enter specific parameters to control the amount of rotation and scale for selected vegetation (Fig. 16.39, Fig. 16.40).

Extrude Edges by Rail

The Extrude Edges Ruby Script is a powerful set of free tools that allows you to generate complex, organic forms. They are ideal for creating billowing canopies, complex building structures, and fluid curvy furnishings. The Extrude Ruby allows you to create these shapes using several different tools. If you want to learn to use the scripts, check out the post on SketchUcation about the tool itself (Fig. 16.41, Fig. 16.42).

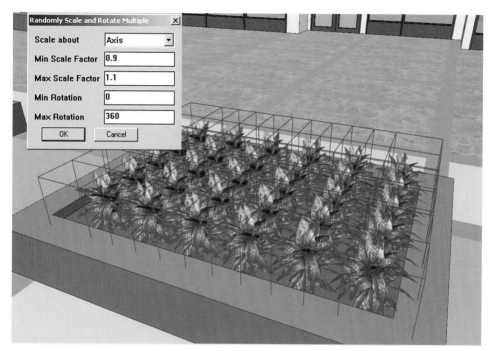

Fig. 16.39: The shrubs in the planter are all selected.

Fig. 16.40: The Scale and Rotate Multiple scripts are applied to the vegetation, randomly altering their rotations and heights to create a more natural habitat.

Fig. 16.41: The Extrude Edges Ruby Scripts can be used to create complex, organic forms—in this case, the Walt Disney Concert Hall (SketchUp).

Fig. 16.42: Rendered version of the concert hall (SU Podium)

Artisan Ruby Script

Dale Martins, a civil engineer in Canada, created a set of very powerful tools to create complex, organic shapes and to work with terrain models. The script's website includes tutorials and instructions. Understanding how these tools work and what they can do takes some practice (Fig. 16.43).

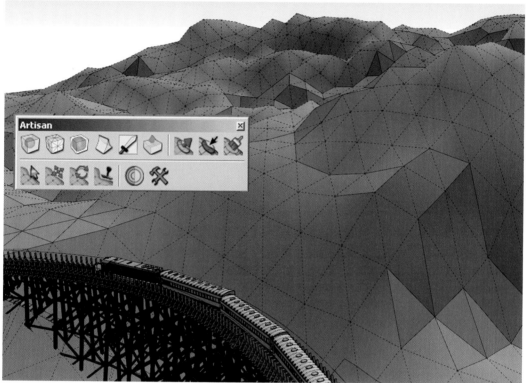

Fig. 16.43: The Artisan Ruby Scripts are another set of excellent tools for creating and modeling complex organic forms and terrain.

Instant Roof/Instant Road

From the Island of Kauai, Vali Architects have created a series of Ruby Scripts useful for terrain and building modeling. They are complex and powerful parametric Ruby Scripts that allow you to grade a road into a terrain model from a simple center line. They include a tool for creating complex, parametric roofs for buildings with many options. They also include a tool for grading objects, steps, buildings, and walls into terrain models (Fig. 16.44, Fig. 16.45, Fig. 16.46).

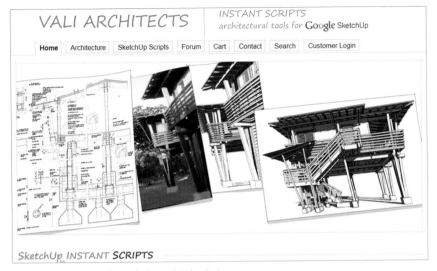

Fig. 16.44: Chuck Vali's website and Ruby Scripts

Fig. 16.45: The top, flat surface of the building is selected.

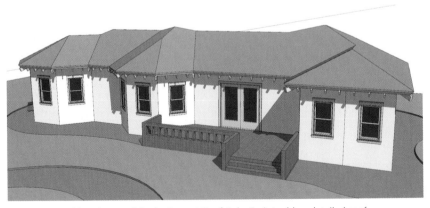

Fig. 16.46: With only one click, the Instant Roof Ruby Script adds a detailed roof.

Setting Light with Shadows

The Shadow Menu

Adding shadows to a model creates depth and contrast, and it adds a nice aesthetic value. Although no visible light source is available in SketchUp, objects will cast and receive shadows. IRPs cast light into a rendering using values entered into SketchUp's Shadow menu to determine the quality of light (Fig. 17.1)

Fig. 17.1: The USDA building model render (Twilight Render)

At minimum, you should learn how to use the Shadow menu to set basic lighting for your renderings. This chapter reviews the basics of working with shadows and related tools. Chapter 18 further explores ways to use light to accentuate a rendering.

The SketchUp Shadow Menu

Turning on the Shadows tool in SketchUp will cast simulated light into the model. The simulated shadows are based on real-world values, including time, day, month, and direction of exterior light, which can be easily adjusted. Adjusting the values alters the length, contrast, and direction of the shadows.

To find the SketchUp Shadow menu, select Window → Shadows. Click the arrow at the top-right of the menu to expand the menu if any options are missing (Fig. 17.2).

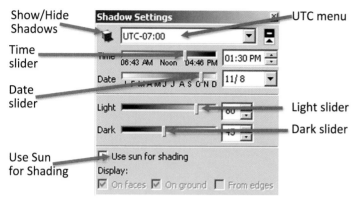

Fig. 17.2: The SketchUp Shadow menu and features

Show/Hide Shadows

Click the Show/Hide button to turn Shadows on and off. When they are turned on, you can adjust the Shadows settings.

The UTC Menu

This pull-down menu provides options for setting Coordinated Universal Time (UTC). Generally, do not use this menu unless you need to set a specific time and date for shadows for a particular location. Adjusting the UTC can distort and create inaccurate shadows. At the end of the chapter, you'll learn how to set custom locations and shadows in SketchUp.

The Time and Date Sliders

The Time slider modifies the time of day (Fig. 17.3, Fig. 17.4, Fig. 17.5). It moves the light source east to west, simulating a typical day from sunrise to sunset. The time of day affects the color and amount of light. Early morning and afternoon times provide less light and longer shadows. Setting the time around noon gives the most light with the shortest shadows. Setting a time when there is normally no light (for example, 3:00 AM) will cause the model to appear dark with Shadows on.

The Date slider adjusts the day and month of the year, replicating sun angles associated with seasons. You can enter specific dates to customize the length and quality of shadows. Winter shadows (December 21 to March 21) will be longer and darker. Summer shadows will be shorter and brighter.

Fig. 17.3: The Time and Date sliders affect the direction of shadows (SketchUp).

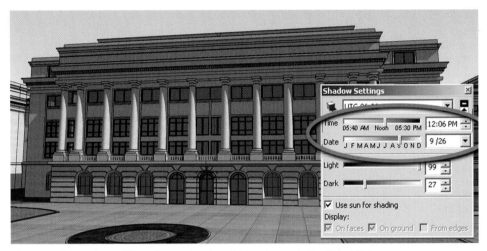

Fig. 17.4: The settings will be referenced and applied to the rendering (SketchUp).

The Light and Dark Sliders

These contrast settings affect the light and dark values of surfaces and shadows. The Light slider causes faces to be lighter or darker. The Dark slider causes shadows to be lighter or darker. In tandem, they alter how dark or light the model appears when Shadows are on or when Use Sun for Shading is checked (Fig. 17.6, Fig. 17.7). Most IRPs ignore these settings; however, they are useful for assessing the quality and direction of the shadows in a model prior to rendering.

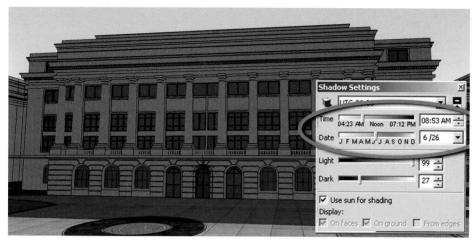

Fig. 17.5: You can set specific dates and times (SketchUp).

Fig. 17.6: The effects of the Light slider on Shadows. Top shows a low setting causing faces to shade darker. The bottom shows a higher setting resulting in lighter face shading.

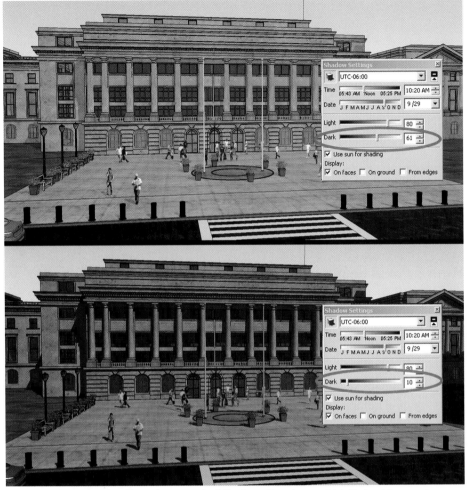

Fig. 17.7: The Dark slider affects the strength of Shadows. Top shows a high Dark setting causing shadows to be flat. Bottom: A lower Dark setting creates greater shadow contrast.

Use Sun for Shading

Check the Use Sun for Shading box to simulate the shading of surfaces as if Shadows were on. Use the Time, Date, Light, and Dark values to adjust the way surfaces appear, again, as if a shadow were being cast in the model. Checking this box provides a quick demonstration of how the shadows will cast in your model, without eating up the computer resources used by Shadows (Fig. 17.8, Fig. 17.9).

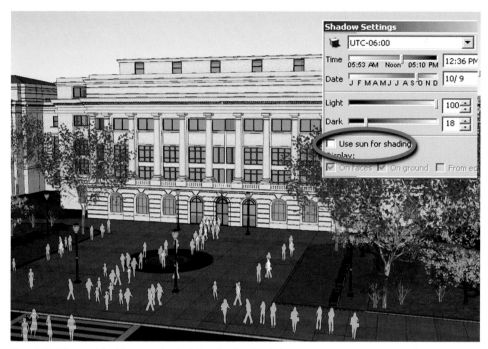

Fig. 17.8: The model with an unchecked Use Sun for Shade box

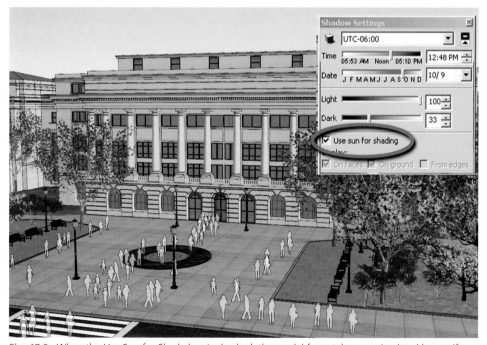

Fig. 17.9: When the Use Sun for Shade box is checked, the model faces take on a simulated hue as if Shadows were turned on.

Solar North

The Solar North option is available only in SketchUp Pro. The Solar North menu displays and adjusts the direction of north in the model. Adjusting Solar North alters the direction of cast shadows. To find Solar North, select View → Toolbars → Solar North. The Solar North tool has three options:

- Toggle North Arrow
- Set North Tool
- Enter North Angle

The North tool and Enter North Angle tool are useful when you're composing good light for renderings, as discussed in Chapter 18.

Toggle North Arrow

Clicking this option on will display an orange arrow indicating the direction of north in the model.

Set North Tool

The tool allows you to manually set the direction of north in your model, either by using your mouse or entering a value in Measurements.

Enter North Angle

Entering a value into this menu will rotate solar north. The values are entered in degrees (Fig. 17.10, Fig. 17.11).

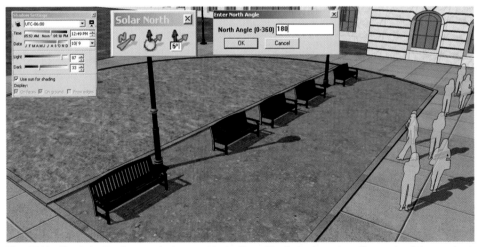

Fig. 17.10: The Solar North menu is shown with the Enter North Angle option. The angle of the sun is at 180 degrees.

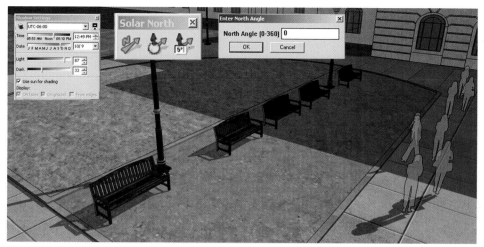

Fig. 17.11: The Enter North Angle option is used to adjust the angle of the sun to 0. This flips the direction of light and shadows in comparison to direction in Fig. 17.10.

Working with Shadows

Displaying shadows in SketchUp is fun. Doing so makes even simple models come to life. However, the Shadows tool has some downsides. Detailed or large models, particularly models with 3D vegetation, can experience extreme performance degradation. There are specific times and ways to use Shadows to maintain computer performance and model efficiency. Here are some general rules you can follow when you're using shadows for normal modeling and setting light for rendering.

Shadows Off

Do not work with Shadows turned on. Do not model, insert components, or take similar actions with Shadows on. Performing tasks with Shadows on will slow performance even with small models, and working is almost impossible with large ones.

Don't Move

Once Shadows are turned on, especially in large models and particularly those with 3D vegetation, don't move. Once you pan, orbit, or zoom, SketchUp will turn off the Shadows, move to the new location, and have to reprocess the shadows again to make them visible.

Don't Save

Do not save your models with Shadows turned on. Doing so makes it take exponentially longer for the model to open; doing so for large models can cause crashes.

Don't Multitask

When waiting for Shadows to turn on or when they are on, switching to other programs, tasks, or browsers will cause SketchUp to reprocess the Shadows when switching back.

Using Shadows

The Shadows tool should be treated as a precision instrument. Timing is everything! Use Shadows only when you're assessing or exporting views. Follow the previous rules when you're performing either task.

Turn Shadows on to assess light for renderings and images when you have a specific camera view set. Assess the quality and the direction of the shadows; if needed, save it as a scene.

Turn Shadows on to export images when the view is set and you are exporting images from SketchUp. Turn the Shadows off before you move to the next scene or camera view.

Chapter 18 expands on the process of assessing light and shadow.

Troubleshooting Shadows

Some computers have issues with the Shadows tool. When Shadows won't turn on, there are several possible causes. Two of them are probable. Either the video card does not support SketchUp Shadows or SketchUp needs to be run in compatibility mode, depending on your operating system. Be methodical as you to try to track the cause of your conflicts.

Video Card Open GL

First, confirm that the video card is set to display shadows and that it can display shadows. Go to Window → Preferences (PC) or Option → Preferences (Mac) and select OpenGL. Confirm that the Use Hardware Acceleration option is checked. If it's not, check the box, close SketchUp, restart it, and see if that fixes the problem. If you cannot check the box, your computer does not support this option, which can cause trouble when you're using SketchUp. Consider upgrading your computer if you want to pursue serious SketchUp modeling and rendering.

Next, under Capabilities, ensure that the highlighted setting says "Yes" under Shadows. If it does not, select a setting that does by clicking on it and selecting OK. If you do not have a Yes option, you will not be able to display shadows.

Compatibility Mode

SketchUp might have problems running on some Microsoft Windows systems. Windows 7 and beyond can be set to fix this problem if the Shadows tool does not work. The following fix is completed outside of SketchUp; you might need to have Administrator privileges on your computer to perform these steps:

1. Find the SketchUp icon on the computer's desktop.
2. Select the icon and right-click it. Select Properties.

3. Select the Compatibility tab.

4. Check the box for Run This Program in Compatibility Mode.

5. Under Privilege Level, select Run This Program As Administrator.

When you launch SketchUp in the future, you will need to click OK when Windows asks if it's OK to run the software.

Shadow String Fix

A notable problem with previous versions of SketchUp was turning on Shadows and having an object cast a shadow on the camera location/view. This would cause the shadows to distort and look wrong. The Shadow String Fix, which is available in SketchUp 8 and presumably later editions, corrects the issue.

When this occurs, keep the shadows turned on. Go to View → Toolbars and Select Shadows String Fix. A small Menu button will appear on the screen. Press the button and SketchUp will recalculate the shadows and fix the distortion.

UTC and Accurate Shadows

Follow these steps to ensure that shadows display correctly in the model and simulate reality appropriately.

Solar North

Using the Solar North tools, make sure the model is oriented the correct way. If it's not, adjust Solar North to the correct direction as described previously.

Latitude and Longitude

You can enter the exact latitude and longitude of your model location into SketchUp. Go to Window → Model Info → Geo-Location and enter the latitude and longitude. If necessary, go to http://www.findlatitudeandlongitude.com/ to find latitude and longitude for the model.

UTC Value

The UTC value is the difference between local time and the Coordinated Universal Time standard. You can adjust the UTC at the top of the Shadow menu. You need to this to set the correct time for shadows relative to latitude and longitude. To find UTC, go to http://www.timeanddate.com/.

Composing Light

L ight in a rendering sets the mood and focus. It helps accentuate the appearance of materi- als and contrast surfaces. Exterior light achieving good focus and contrast produces better renderings (Fig. 18.1). Compose light before you render so that your lighting is deliberate and well-directed.

Most IRPs use a setting called Physical Sky that references the SketchUp Shadow menu to generate daylight/exterior lighting (Fig. 18.1, Fig.18.2, Fig. 18.3). For many IRPs, using the Shadow menu is the default and only option for day lighting.

Fig. 18.1: Twilight Render (v1) Lighting menu with the Physical Sky option

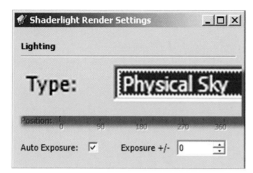

Fig. 18.2: Shaderlight Lighting menu with the Physical Sky option

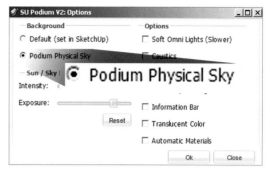

Fig. 18.3: SU Podium (v2) Lighting menu with Physical Sky option

This chapter has three sections covering the overall process of setting light:

▶ **Composing Light Tools**: Tools and suggestions for adjusting light

▶ **Composing Light Strategies:** Guides for setting light based on model types

▶ **Composing the Light:** A step-by-step outline of the process

Using the SketchUp Shadow menu to set lighting is essential for most exterior renderings (Fig. 18.4). Although some IRPs have image-based lighting options, light based on the Shadow menu is easy to set and yields good results (Fig. 18.5).

Fig. 18.4: Setting light with the SketchUp Shadow menu in the model prior to rendering

Fig. 18.5: Duplicating the shadows as they were set in SketchUp (SU Podium)

Many interior scenes and exterior night models rely on simulated light sources, such as point lights, instead of exterior lighting (Fig. 18.6). However, in the case of interiors, the Shadow menu can cast light through windows and portals, rendering daylight scenes without needing simulated light. Similarly, exterior lighting can be combined with interior simulated light to duplicate real-world conditions.

Fig. 18.6: Nighttime exterior rendering using simulated lights (Shaderlight)

Composing Light Tools

When setting light, aim for surfaces to have a balance of brightness and shade. Good contrast helps create depth and focus, adding a realistic quality to the rendering (Fig. 18.7). Use these tools in conjunction with "Composing Light Strategies."

Fig. 18.7: A rendering with good contrast and balance between light and shadows (SU Podium)

Redirecting Light

Light composition involves altering the direction of light and shadows in the model. Light in SketchUp comes from an invisible sun source. Imagine the SketchUp model surrounded by a giant dome. The light source runs east-west across the dome, depending on the direction of North in the model, imitating the sun's path (Fig. 18.8). As you learned in Chapter 17, the Time and Date sliders are the primary tools used to modify the direction of light and shadows (Fig. 18.9).

However, achieving the desired lighting direction is not always possible using just the Time and Date options. You can also alter the direction of North in SketchUp Pro by rotating the light source around the dome. The rotation changes the sun angle, casting light from different directions. Rotate Solar North by 45-degree increments (45, 90, 135, 180, 225, 270) until you are happy with the light effect (Fig. 18.10).

Fig. 18.8: The sky dome illustrates how light runs east-west in SketchUp, simulating sun positions and angles.

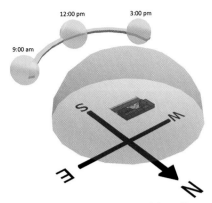

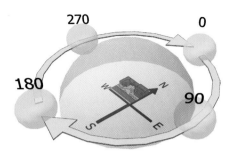

Fig. 18.9: The Time and Date sliders affect the sun and direction of light in a SketchUp model.

Fig. 18.10: The SketchUp Solar North tool can adjust the overall rotation of the sun from 0 to 360 degrees.

Shadow Settings

The following Shadow menu settings are a good starting point for those new to rendering. They will yield good, consistent results. For most exterior renderings (buildings and site plans), set Time between 10:00 AM and 2:30 AM and set the Date to September 9. Set the Light slider to 80 and the Dark slider to 35. Adjust Solar North as needed.

Keeping Shadows off, save the scene once the camera view and lighting are set. Move to another camera position, reset the light (keeping the Shadows off), and save another scene. Repeat the process for as many views as you want for rendering.

Use the Scene Properties options and confirm that layers, shadow settings, and camera views are selected. The scene tools and methods are reviewed in Chapter 12 and Chapter 15.

Shadow Boxes

A *shadow box* is a grouped 3D cube. It can be positioned anywhere in the model and casts shade into a scene. When positioned off camera and placed on layers, shadow boxes provide flexibility when you're composing light (Fig. 18.11). Use Shadow Boxes to cast shade into a scene's foreground and onto building facades (Fig. 18.12, Fig. 18.13). You can learn about other uses in the next section. To create a shadow box, use the following procedure.

1. Create a 3D cube and make it into a component.
2. Place it on a layer: SHADOW BOX 01, etc. (Fig. 18.14).
3. Position the bird's eye view to the model (see Chapter 15).
4. Position the cube so that it casts a shadow into the scene.
5. Turn on the Shadows tool, making sure that the detailed layers are off (Fig. 18.15).
6. Assess the shadow box cast. Scale and reposition the cube to achieve your desired results (Fig. 18.16).
7. Create additional boxes as needed. Place each shadow box on its own individual layer.

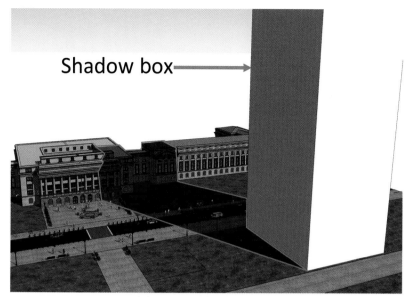

Shadow box

Fig. 18.11: A shadow box, the big white cube, is created and positioned off camera to cast shadow onto the USDA building and site.

Fig. 18.12: The rendering shows the USDA building without a shadow box casting light onto the scene.

Fig. 18.13: The added shadow box (shown in Fig. 18.11) adds contrast and shade to the right side of the render, covering the building facade and site.

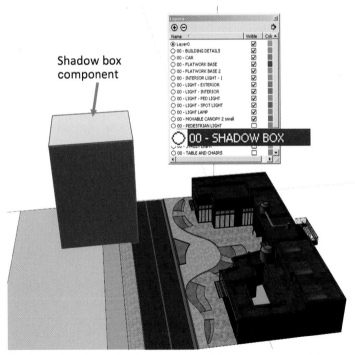

Shadow box
component

Name	Visible	Col
⦿ Layer0	☑	
○ 00 - BUILDING DETAILS	☑	
○ 00 - CAR	☑	
○ 00 - FLATWORK BASE	☑	
○ 00 - FLATWORK BASE 2	☑	
○ 00 - INTERIOR LIGHT - 1	☑	
○ 00 - LIGHT - EXTERIOR	☑	
○ 00 - LIGHT - INTERIOR	☑	
○ 00 - LIGHT - PED LIGHT	☑	
○ 00 - LIGHT - SPOT LIGHT	☑	
○ 00 - LIGHT LAMP	☑	
○ 00 - MOVABLE CANOPY 2 small	☑	
○ 00 - PEDESTRIAN LIGHT	☐	
○ **00 - SHADOW BOX**		
○ 00 - STREET LIGHT	☐	
○ 00 - TABLE AND CHAIRS	☐	

Fig. 18.14: The shadow box is created, made into a component, and then placed on its own layer.

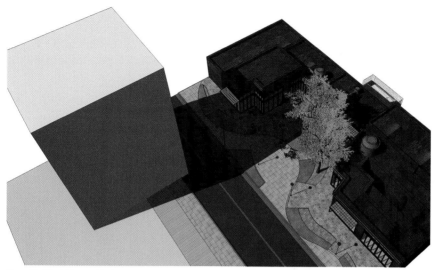

Fig. 18.15: Using a bird's eye view camera, the shadow box is positioned and the Shadows are turned on to the cast shadows into the scene.

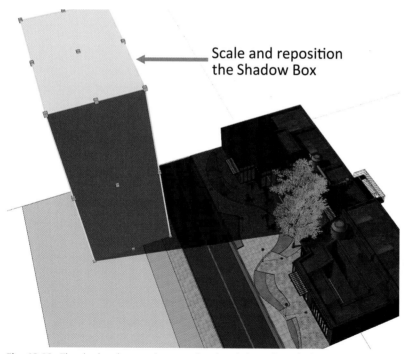

Scale and reposition the Shadow Box

Fig. 18.16: The shadow box can be moved and scaled to adjust the length and direction of the shadow being cast into the scene. The resulting shadow can be seen in the render in Fig. 18.5.

Composing Light Strategies

Set the lighting based on model type and camera view. Architecture, interiors, and sites have different focuses and lighting needs. Some general strategies for each model type are discussed here. These guidelines are not intended to be comprehensive. Only you know what type of focus and light your model requires.

Architecture

Set light to provide depth to building fenestrations and facade volumes. Extruded sills, mullions, columns, etc. should cast and receive light. Create an even balance of shaded and exposed facade surfaces. The resulting depth gives focus to a building. Generally, SketchUp shadows should run slightly parallel to the facade face that is the focus of the rendering (Fig. 18.17, Fig. 18.18).

Fig. 18.17: The sun is set behind the building causing a shadow to be cast on the building facades facing the view. This creates excess darkness and obscures the building facades and details (Twilight Render).

Fig. 18.18: The shadow direction is adjusted to highlight the facade details, creating good contrast and depth (Twilight Render).

Use adjacent building faces, other buildings, and shadow boxes to accentuate the contrast of light and dark throughout a rendering. Cast shadows onto the foreground, between buildings, and onto building facades. Use a shadow box and cast shade onto the main building side or focus. If a building has two visible facades, choose one to have an exposed focus. The other side should cast or receive shadow (Fig. 18.19, Fig. 18.20).

Fig. 18.19: The shadows are set so the building facades highlighted in blue will cast shadow and be darker compared to the adjacent facades.

Fig. 18.20: The resulting render has a good level of contrast and depth.

Illuminate the interior of a building by casting light directly at the facade. The lower the angle (winter months on the date slider), the more light will enter through windows, doors, and other portals. The intent is to light up the facade and the building interior (Fig. 18.21). Ensure that the interior contains furnishings and other features. Glass materials should be set with IRP values, allowing light to pass through and not just reflect off the glass windows (Fig. 18.22).

Fig. 18.21: SketchUp model with Shadows set to cast into and through the windows, lighting up the interior of the model

Fig. 18.22: The resulting render has a good level of depth, context, and interest.

Interior

Exterior lighting can illuminate an interior. Casting light in an interior space is identical to casting light into a building interior. The difference is that the view is set inside. Cast light through portals like doors, windows, and other openings. The portal must be open or utilize a transparent material such a glass. Once SketchUp Shadows are on, shadow direction will stream through the portals.

To cast daylight through a ceiling, convert that interior ceiling into a group. Next, place it on a layer and turn the layer off, hiding the ceiling. In essence, you are removing the interior "lid" allowing daylight into the scene (Fig. 18.23, Fig. 18.24, Fig. 18.25, Fig. 18.26).

This is an excellent and quick way to assess an interior model prior to adding simulated lighting.

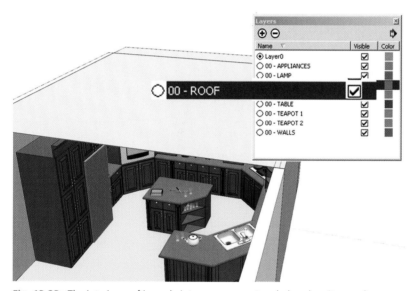

Fig. 18.23: The interior roof is made into a component and placed on its own layer.

Site Plans

You can spread contrast throughout a scene to enhance your site plan renderings. Site elements and vegetation should possess offset and dark shadows but be surrounded by exposed surfaces reflecting light (Fig. 18.27, Fig. 18.28).

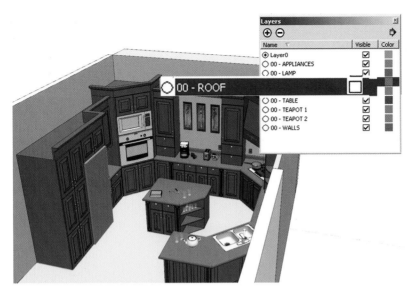

Fig. 18.24: The roof layer is turned off so the roof is hidden from view.

Fig. 18.25: Without the roof, SketchUp shadows can be cast into the scene and rendered.

Fig. 18.26: The rendered version of the interior scene using SketchUp shadows for lighting (Twilight Render)

Fig. 18.27: Shadows and light are set parallel to the view (Shaderlight).

Fig. 18.28: Shadows are cast toward the camera, creating an overly dark render with poor contrast (Shaderlight).

To create this type of contrast, use the following guidelines:

▶ Set light to cast relatively parallel to the camera view.

▶ Cast light away from the camera view. Light pointed at the camera causes a scene to look flat and muted because the shaded surfaces will dominate. The brighter, forward-facing surfaces will be contrasted by the longer, darker shadows cast behind them.

▶ Use Shadow Boxes to cast longer, darker shadows into part of the foreground and midground. Use any building mass for the same effect. Shadows should be visible and long, but not long enough to meld into each other.

Composing the Light

The various steps and settings outlined here will help ensure that your composing process is efficient and quick. The process requires using layers and scenes to maintain performance, as outlined in Part 3. These steps will enable you to save scenes that simulate a rendered appearance, thus mimicking rendering contrast.

1. Pick a camera view. Pan, orbit, zoom, and use Position Camera to achieve your desired view (Fig. 18.29).

2. Turn off the detail layers. Toggle off the component detail, especially vegetation. Hiding the detail will make it easier to turn on and adjust Shadows. Use an Off scene, as discussed in Chapter 14, to quickly hide detail.

3. Hide the edges and make the textures visible. Do so by selecting View → Edge Styles and uncheck all the edges. Make textures visible by going to View → Toolbars → Styles and clicking Shaded with Textures (Fig. 18.29).

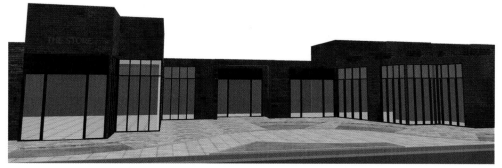

Fig. 18.29: Select a camera view, turn off component details, and hide the model edges. Make sure the textures are visible.

4. Set the Light and Dark settings. Open the Shadow menu and set the Light slider to 75 and the Dark slider to 30 (Fig. 18.30).

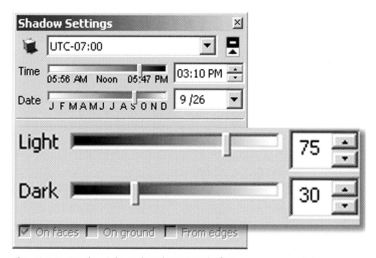

Fig. 18.30: Set the Light and Dark settings before you compose light.

5. Compose light. Turn on the Shadows tool. Move the Time and Date sliders to modify the direction, length, and strength of shadows. Once you're happy with the results, turn the shadows off and go the next step (Fig. 18.31, Fig. 18.32, Fig. 18.33).

6. Adjust the Solar North setting only if you're working with SketchUp Pro and you're not happy with your results. Alter the angle of Solar North to rotate the source of light for a better vantage point.

Fig. 18.31: Compose light by adjusting the Time and Date sliders on the SketchUp Shadow menu.

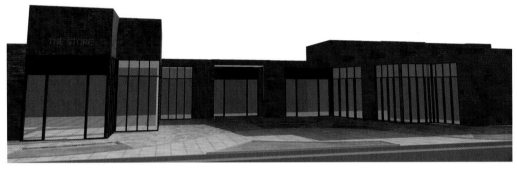

Fig. 18.32: Continue tweaking the settings.

Fig. 18.33: The final result

7. Turn on the Detail layers you want for the rendered view. Create and use an On scene, as reviewed in Chapter 15, to quickly toggle on the detail (Fig. 18.34).

8. Save the scene. With the shadows set (but not on) and the appropriate detail visible, create your scene. The scene will retain the shadow settings and detail. Return to this scene prior to rendering (Fig. 18.35).

9. Save multiple scenes. Repeat the process of setting up multiple rendering views.

Fig. 18.34: Once the shadows are set, turn on the component detail and update or create a new scene saving all the settings (Layer Visibility, Camera View, and Shadows).

Fig. 18.35: The completed rendering (SU Podium)

Assessing vegetation and light can be tricky. With large amounts of 3D vegetation, even the process of turning on the Shadows tool can take a while. However, you can master the process, and the technique can be useful for assessing light. Refer back to Chapter 17 for working and troubleshooting shadows. Here are some quick tips:

▶ Make sure the view is set and in position.

▶ Turn on the vegetation layers.

▶ Turn on Shadows. Wait.

▶ Do not rotate the view (or do anything else!).

▶ Assess the lighting. Adjusting the shadow settings will cause the shadows to reprocess.

▶ Once the lighting results are acceptable, turn Shadows off and update the scene.

The Iterative Rendering Process

A Rendering Overview

The reality of rendering is that the majority of the work is completed in SketchUp by applying textures, setting light with the Shadow menu, and choosing appropriate camera views. This means that the same steps described in previous chapters are used to prepare a model for rendering in any IRP.

Also, while the tools, menu names, and appearances vary among the IRPs, they all function in the same manner. Each IRP will process textures, lighting, and camera views placed in a model to create a render. These similarities will allow you to take a universal rendering approach, making it easy to experiment with the different IRPs.

If you understand the methods described in Part 5 you will be able to use IRPs in tandem with SketchUp.

- ▶ Chapter 19 describes the universal system and common tools of integrated rendering programs.

- ▶ Chapter 20 outlines the complete iterative rendering process, describing how to go from the SketchUp model to rendered view.

- ▶ Chapters 21 through 24 provide specific instructions for using IRPs to prepare the textures, exterior lighting, simulated lighting, and output resolution that create the rendering.

IRP Universal Features

The following general tool descriptions are common to most, if not all, IRPs. These tools are used to apply values and are part of the typical iterative rendering process described in this part.

Texture/Material Editor

Every IRP includes a Material Editor (Fig. 19.1). The Material Editor allows you to assign rendering values to textures. These values dictate how the IRP bounces light off the material surfaces to create photorealism. Typical settings include Bump (3D Contrast), Shininess, and Reflection. These values are reviewed in Chapter 21.

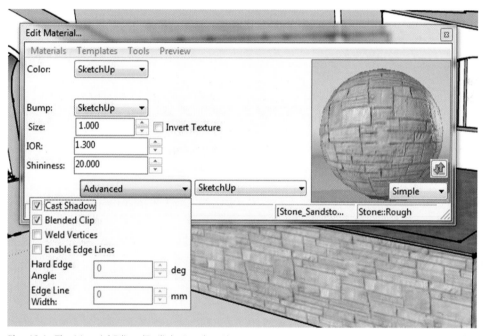

Fig. 19.1: The Material Editor (Twilight Render v2)

Exterior Lighting

All IRPs reference the SketchUp Shadow menu to generate light. Many IRPs also have additional lighting features. Chapter 23 reviews lighting options.

Simulated Lighting

All IRPs allow you to place artificial lights into the model for rendering. Chapter 24 reviews simulated light options (Fig. 19.2, Fig. 19.3).

Point Lights for
Simulated Lighting

Fig. 19.2: Point lights placed in SketchUp model

Fig. 19.3: Rendered simulated lighting image (Shaderlight)

Resolution

The IRPs allow you to select or enter image output resolution. *Resolution* dictates the size (width and height) of a render. All resolution is measured in pixels, which can be converted into imperial units like inches. Many IRPs have preset resolutions and allow custom resolutions (Fig. 19.4). Chapter 22 reviews output resolution.

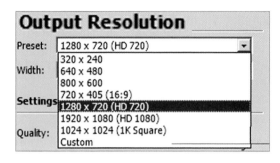

Fig. 19.4: Preset resolution options (Shaderlight)

Render Quality

All IRPs include a menu that sets render quality (Fig. 19.5). The better the quality, the more refined the final render will appear and the longer the render will take to process.

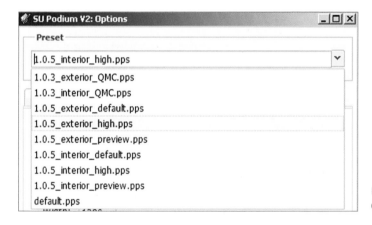

Fig. 19.5: Render quality options (Su Podium v2)

Starting/Stopping/Saving Renderings

Each IRP provides options for starting, stopping, and saving a render. Some IRPs allow the rendering to be saved while it's being processed but not yet finished.

Preview Screen

The IRPs provide a window showing the progress of the rendering as it's being created. The window appears after the rendering is started (Fig. 19.6, Fig. 19.7, Fig. 19.8).

Fig. 19.6: Preview screen with render being processed (Twilight Render v1)

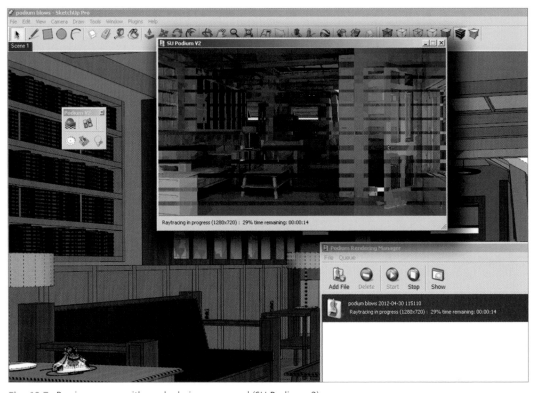

Fig. 19.7: Preview screen with render being processed (SU Podium v2)

Fig. 19.8: Preview screen with render being processed (Shaderlight)

Custom Features

Some integrated rendering programs have unique features that are not available in other IRPs. Certain features are advanced or require the use of high-powered computers. Others features allow the inclusion of background images or the use of image-based lighting (see Chapter 23) to create different lighting effects. The following set of features is by no means complete, but it highlights the more significant options. These and other features are reviewed within the IRP-specific chapters.

Animation

Using SketchUp scenes, an IRP can generate an animation. Animating a render can take a great deal of time to process due to the number of images that need to be produced.

Backgrounds

This option allows the insertion of an image that becomes a visible backdrop once the model is rendered. Using backgrounds is a great way to add sky, city, and other backdrops to a rendering.

Clay Rendering

IRPs can produce renderings without displaying textures. These *clay renderings* have a similar appearance to physically built models (Fig. 19.9, Fig. 19.10, Fig. 19.11). They can be overlaid on a rendering in the postproduction process to create contrast and provide additional depth.

Fig. 19.9: Clay model render (Shaderlight)

Fig. 19.10: Clay model render (SU Podium v2)

Fig. 19.11: Clay model render (Twilight Render v1)

Dynamic Rendering

Dynamic rendering allows you to adjust the camera view, lighting, and texture *during* the rendering process. It allows you to make changes on the fly and create multiple rendered images.

IBL/HDRI Lighting

IBL is image-based lighting. HDRI stands for High Dynamic Range Images and is considered an IBL. Photographs created in HDRI contain lighting information that is inserted and referenced by the IRP. The IRP samples the light in the photo using it to generate the render.

IES Lighting Profile

IES profiles are specific metrics used to simulate real-world light sources and fixtures. IES profiles can be inserted into the IRP, which will then render simulated light based on the IES profile.

Instanced Rendering

Instancing refers to how the IRP's rendering engine treats components. Instead of processing every single component in a SketchUp file, the IRP looks for identical components and processes only one of them.

Instancing allows you to create very large renders that include forests of trees and objects. Because only one of the trees is processed, the IRP can easily process and render the rest (Fig. 19.12, Fig. 19.13).

Fig. 19.12: Each vertical line represents a tree that will be instanced and replaced with a 3D detailed tree component when rendered (SketchUp model).

Fig. 19.13: The vertical lines are replaced and rendered with a 3D tree. Twilight instances the tree, allowing very large models to be rendered (Twilight Render).

Proxy Rendering

Proxy rendering allows you to place a component into the model as a placeholder. The placeholder is then linked to another component *not* in the model. The linked component is rendered, not the component in the model.

The feature is ideal when you're working with 3D vegetation. You can place 2D Face Me vegetation components in the model and then link the 2D components to 3D versions. When rendered, the 3D vegetation will be displayed, replacing the 2D vegetation. This helps maintain SketchUp and computer performance (Fig. 19.14, Fig. 19.15).

Instancing and Proxy Rendering

Instancing and proxy rendering are very different. When you're *proxy rendering*, each vegetation component must still be processed. For example, if there are ten trees in the model, the 3D versions of those ten trees must still be processed by the IRP. This means that face-count limitations and the amount of RAM will affect the length of time the IRP takes to render. With many proxy models of vegetation, the IRP can run out of RAM before the rendering is finished.

In contrast, *instancing* can have just as many trees; however, the IRP will process only one of the 3D trees. Any identical components will be instanced and not processed by the IRP. Thus, the instanced tree does not max out the RAM limitations or affect rendering times.

Fig. 19.14: Model with 2D trees (SketchUp)

Fig. 19.15: Use the Replace Me feature to swap out the 2D trees with 3D detailed versions (Shaderlight).

Steps of the Iterative Rendering Process

No initial rendering will ever look correct. By following the iterative rendering process, you will be able to produce rendered images in a coherent and speedy fashion. You will need to refine the model and the associated texture and lighting values to achieve the best possible output. The iterative rendering process entails two general steps:

1. Values are applied to textures, lighting, render quality, and render resolution.

2. A series of draft image renders are generated, steadily leading to the final image.

Rendering can be a time-consuming process. You'll spend lots of time waiting for the computer to complete an image. Understanding the factors that affect rendering times will help you determine the best iterative rendering process for your specific needs. You can control such factors to shorten the duration of a rendering. Quickly produced renders serve as *drafts* that allow users to evaluate textures, adjust lighting and cameras, make modifications, and run additional draft renderings.

The following factors affect the length of time it takes to render an image. All of these factors can be controlled, shortening or lengthening render times.

- **Exterior versus Simulated Light**: Exterior light produced from SketchUp Shadow menu lighting or image-based lighting will render faster than simulated lights such as area, point, spot, and IES profile lights. Models with simulated lights should use exterior lighting for the initial draft.

- **Model Size**: The more detail that is visible in a model, the longer it will take to render. This is why model organization is paramount. Turning off layers with detailed components makes faster render times.

- **Render Quality**: Every IRP includes quality settings that affect the render output. These settings are intended to create draft renders for assessment. The lower the quality, the faster the render will be. The highest settings take time and are intended for final graphics.

- ▶ **Resolution**: Resolution is the measure of the width and height of the render. The higher the resolution, the longer the render time will be. To speed up the process, set lower resolutions for draft renders.
- ▶ **Computer Hardware**: Computation ability and computer hardware will also affect the time it takes for an image to render.

Add Initial Values

The first step prepares the model for rendering by applying values defining texture appearance, lighting, resolution, and quality (Fig. 20.1). Each of these values must be set prior to rendering. Applying all these values leads to step 2. During step 2, these values will be adjusted based on the render evaluation.

Texture Values

The IRP's Material menu is used to assign a rendering value to all visible textures (Fig. 20.2). The applied values set how dull, glossy, shiny, reflective, smooth, or coarse the materials will render. Chapter 21 reviews texture values in detail.

Lighting Settings

Lighting can be set in multiple fashions. The most common method is to use the SketchUp Shadow menu to set exterior light as outlined in Part 4 (Fig. 20.3). IRPs can substitute SketchUp light using image-based lighting, which is discussed in Chapter 23. Simulated lights, such as point, spot, or IES profile lighting, are common for interiors and some exteriors and are reviewed in Chapter 24.

Resolution

Resolution determines the output size of the graphic, quality of detail, and render times. The initial resolution setting is low to accommodate the first-draft renders (Fig. 20.4, Fig. 20.5). Resolution is examined in Chapter 22.

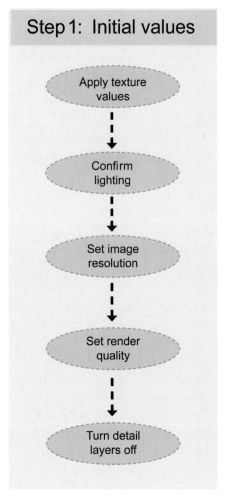

Fig. 20.1: Step 1 flowchart

Fig. 20.2: Texture values are added to all of the model textures (Shaderlight Material menu).

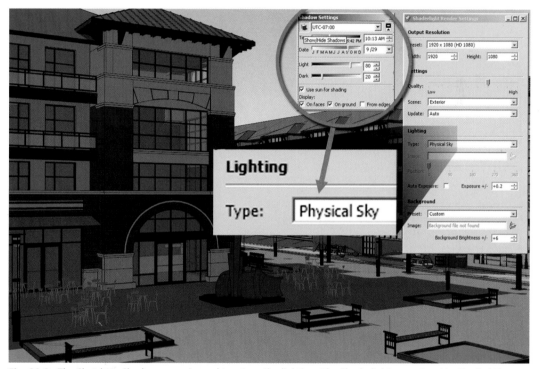

Fig. 20.3: The SketchUp Shadow menu is used to set up the lighting. The Shaderlight menu is set to Physical Sky so that it references the SketchUp Shadow menu to cast light for the rendering.

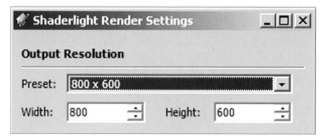

Fig. 20.4: Resolution settings (Shaderlight)

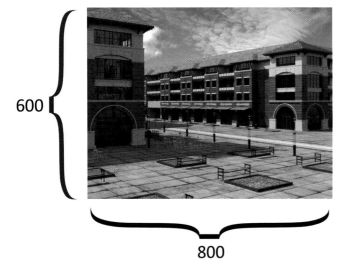

600

800

Fig. 20.5: Initial draft render at 800 x 600 resolution

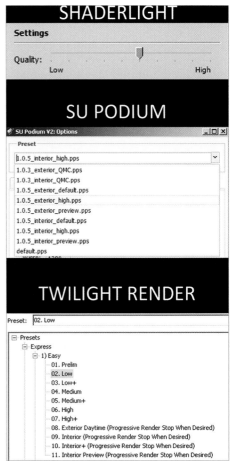

Fig. 20.6: Quality Settings menus for Shaderlight (top), SU Podium v2 (middle), and Twilight Render v1 (bottom)

Quality

Quality determines how refined the image will appear once it's rendered (Fig. 20.6). Low quality settings produce grainy and sometimes hazy renderings. The higher quality settings produce crisp clear images. Like resolution, quality is initially set to a low value for the first draft rendering, as outlined in step 2.

Draft to Final Render

The underlying principle of the draft-to-final-render process is to make image creation efficient (Fig. 20.7). The initial and subsequent render will usually reveal flaws with textures, lighting, camera angles, and model detail. These values and details will need to be adjusted and another draft will need to be run and evaluated. Starting with high quality settings with full-model detail visible is inefficient due to long render times.

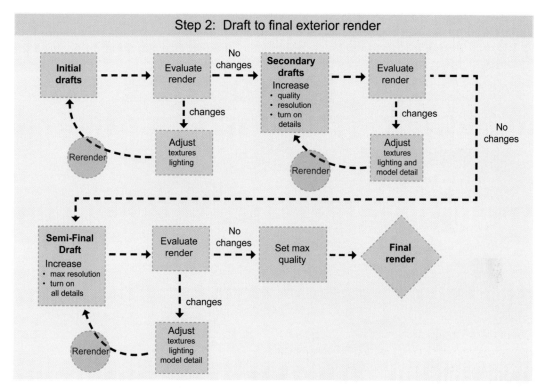

Fig. 20.7: Draft-to-final-render flowchart

Number of Drafts

There is no set number of drafts that should be run. You make that subjective determination based on your goals and what is acceptable as a final rendering. However, experience has shown that for most models, five to ten drafts are usually needed to get the settings and values correct for the final graphic (Fig. 20.8).

Completing and Saving Draft Renders

It is not always necessary to let a draft render processes to completion. The IRP preview window allows you to watch the render progress. Usually, you can catch the flaws in a render from the onset when the image begins to coalesce. The more experienced you become with the process, the easier it will be to catch flaws and changes in the image.

Regardless of whether the draft render is complete, save the draft image. Most IRPs can save a render while it's processing or after it's been stopped. Having a visual record of the draft will help you review while you make updates and changes to the model. Keep notes about the settings like exposure, texture values, and other things for reference.

Fig. 20.8: Eight draft renders were generated for the exterior building and site model.

Evaluating Drafts

Evaluate the draft render textures, lighting, model detail, and camera view. Also, evaluate the renders based on which sets are being run (initial, secondary, or semifinal) as each set will reveal different aspects of the render. Make any necessary adjustments and move onto the next draft render (Fig. 20.9).

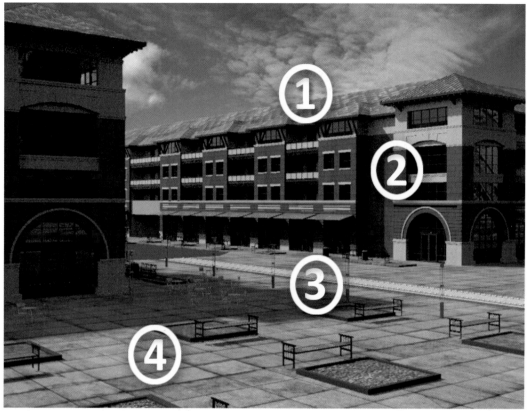

Fig. 20.9: In this example of an initial draft render, (1) the roof texture needs to be adjusted; (2) the window reflections rendered incorrectly (no reflections); (3) the pedestrian lighting is obscured due to its blue color; and (4) the paving is incorrectly scaled and positioned.

The actions for step 2, the simulated light drafts-to-final process, differ depending on whether the render relies on exterior or simulated lighting. The process outlined later in this chapter is modified for simulated lighting renderings.

Draft Sets

The process leading to a final render relies on leveraging the ability to control rendering times. This results in the process being divided into three sets of drafts: initial, secondary, and semifinal. Each set steadily increases the quality, resolution, and amount of detail visible in the model.

The IRP-specific chapters provide details about draft-to-final quality, resolution, and lighting settings. The following approach generally describes how the draft settings work, incrementally increasing toward the final image.

Initial Drafts

The *initial drafts* are used to evaluate textures and lighting (Fig. 20.10). These drafts will be run at low render quality, at small resolution (typically, 800 × 600), and with minimal detail visible (Fig. 20.11). The quickly outputted image is then evaluated, adjustments are made, and the draft is rerun and reevaluated. Once the results are satisfactory, you can move onto the secondary draft set.

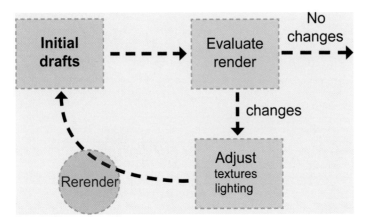

Fig. 20.10: The initial draft process

Fig. 20.11: 800 x 600 initial draft render

Initial drafts will appear grainy; objects will be indistinct and small (due to the resolution); the lighting can be dull; and the overall appearance can be less than realistic. Expect these conditions (Fig. 20.12).

Fig. 20.12: Grainy, low-quality initial draft render

You need to look for the quality of the textures, determine if they'll render with good character, and check to see that the texture values applied in step 1 are appropriate. Adjustments to textures are the most common changes made during this phase. Evaluate the lighting based on the direction and desired contrast in the scene and adjust as needed.

Secondary Drafts

Increase the render quality to medium, increase the resolution (typically, 1280×720) close to final, and turn on all of the detail in the model, except vegetation if used (Fig. 20.13).

The renderings in this phase will still appear grainy, but they will be considerably sharper. Evaluate the model detail, reassess the texture characters and texture values, and assess the camera view (Fig. 20.14). Lighting will be brighter with deeper shadows and brightness, providing a clearer perspective of the final render lighting (Fig. 20.15).

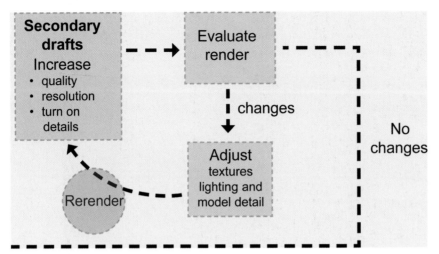

Fig. 20.13: The secondary draft process

Fig. 20.14: In this evaluation of a secondary draft render, (1) the camera view should be adjusted for a better angle; (2) the white stucco texture is too dull and should be brighter and more reflective; and (3) the glass facade of the balcony rails is not set to reflect.

Fig. 20.15: Final secondary draft render with adjustments made to items 1, 2, and 3.

Keep running secondary drafts until you are satisfied with the results and then move onto the semifinal draft.

Semifinal Drafts

It's typical to run only a single semifinal draft and usually not to completion (Fig. 20.16). The goal is to make sure that no last-minute changes are needed and nothing was missed during the secondary drafts phase. For the semifinal rendering, keep the quality at Medium, but increase the resolution to the final output (typically, 1920 × 1080), and turn on all of the detail (Fig. 20.17).

Final Render

Run the final render when you have no more changes that need to be made to the model, textures, lighting, or camera views. Expect the final rendering to take some time, particularly if the model is large and loaded with details.

Run the final render using the maximum settings. This means using the highest quality, full-resolution settings with all of the details layers turned on (Fig. 20.18).

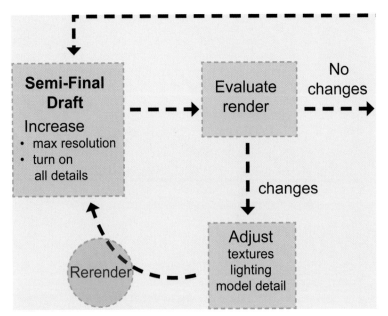

Fig. 20.16: The semifinal render process

Fig. 20.17: The semifinal render was not completed. It was stopped and saved midway through its process because the in-process evaluation showed the model was ready for the final rendering.

Fig. 20.18: The resolution and quality were adjusted to final settings to produce the final rendering.

Simulated Light Drafts-to-Final Process

Using point, area, spot, and IES profile lighting, *simulated light* illuminates a model similarly to real-world illumination with lamps, bulbs, and fixtures. Even when using lower settings, models with simulated lights take longer to render. Also, the more lights there are, the longer the render takes. Trying to evaluate a model's textures during the initial draft set with simulated lights would take much longer than necessary. Using exterior lighting is far more efficient.

In this section, you'll learn a modified approach to the draft render sets intended for simulated light renders (Fig. 20.19). Refer back to the corresponding descriptions when you use these modified settings.

Initial Draft Renders for Simulated Lighting

For the initial drafts, do not add any simulated lights to the model. In fact, make sure that none are present. If any are, the method won't work (Fig. 20.20). Instead, use exterior lighting (SketchUp Shadow menu) to provide light. For interior models, ensure that the roof is on its own layer and keep that layer turned off. This will allow light to be cast into the scene. Using the SketchUp Shadow menu, set the light. Make sure the model has good contrast and abundant light hitting surfaces (Fig. 20.21).

Run the draft renders and evaluate the texture character and surfaces. Adjust the textures, and rerun the drafts until the textures are the way you want them (Fig. 20.22).

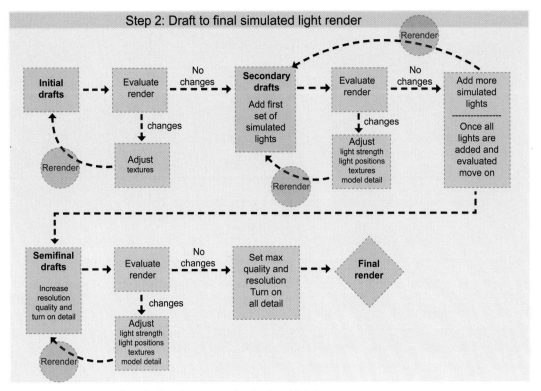

Fig. 20.19: Modified draft-to-final render process for simulated lighting

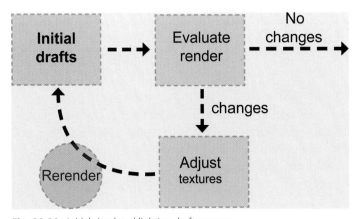

Fig. 20.20: Initial simulated lighting draft process

Fig. 20.21: Turn off the interior roof and use the SketchUp Shadow menu to set the initial lighting for these drafts.

Fig. 20.22: Interior rendering with exterior lighting (Twilight Render)

Secondary Draft Renders for Simulated Lighting

The secondary draft process is when most of the work is done with simulated lighting (Fig. 20.23). During the secondary phase, start adding the simulated lights. Do not add all the lights you want to the render. Start by adding the first set of lights into lighting fixture components—or if you aren't using fixture components, start with individual lights (Fig. 20.24). You'll learn more about placing simulated lighting in a model in Chapter 24. With the first lights in place, run the secondary draft (Fig. 20.25). Start by keeping the model detail off or at a minimum.

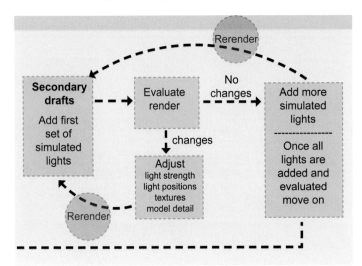

Fig. 20.23: Secondary-draft flowchart for simulated lighting

The render settings to process the image will be very different than the ones you used for the exterior lighting. The IRP must be set to process the simulated lighting. This means turning off the exterior light source coming from the SketchUp Shadow settings. Each IRP handles this differently and is reviewed in the IRP settings chapters.

Secondary Simulated Lighting Draft Evaluation

In addition to appraising the model's textures and detail, you'll need to evaluate the simulated lights. The position, light strength, light color, and exposure represent typical adjustments. Rerun the render and evaluate the lights again. Make more adjustments to the first set of lights and repeat the process.

Adding lights singularly or by component sets does not overburden the model or negatively affect render times. Adding them makes it easier to assess and edit the light settings.

Fig. 20.24: Add the first set of lights to the model. In this example, Twilight point lights are inserted into a fixture component.

Fig. 20.25: The first simulated light render is run.

Add More Lights

Once the first set of lights are satisfactorily rendered, add more lights as needed (Fig. 20.26, Fig. 20.27). Repeat the evaluation process until all of the desired light sources are inserted into the model (Fig. 20.28).

Fig. 20.26: Another set of lights is added to the rendering.

Fig. 20.27: After the second set of lights is added, another draft render is completed and evaluated.

Fig. 20.28: More lights are added to the model and another draft render is completed.

Turn On All Detail

Once all the lights are placed and the settings are refined, turn on all the model detail and rerun the render at the same quality and resolution settings. Run one last draft before running the semifinal draft sets.

Semifinal Draft Renders for Simulated Lighting

During this phase, increase the resolution to maximum and make sure that all of the detail is visible. Quality should not be set to maximum. You shouldn't run this render to completion because it can take quite a bit of time. Evaluate the render as it's being processed. If everything looks acceptable, stop the render and proceed to the final render.

Final Render for Simulated Lighting

Run the render with all of the lights and detail and use maximum resolution and quality. Be warned: these renders can take a considerable amount of time to complete (Fig. 20.29).

Fig. 20.29: Once all of the lights are added and evaluated, run the final rendering.

Texture Values

When you're using an IRP's Material Editor, assign a value to the textures. Once rendered, these values will accentuate the textures so that they take on realistic qualities. This chapter provides a general description of texture values and explains how to troubleshoot textures that are rendering incorrectly.

IRPs and Texture Values

Every IRP has a Material Editor. To apply a value, select the texture and choose a value from the IRP Material Editor. A value needs to be applied only once. After a value is applied to a texture or solid surface, *all* versions of that texture or solid surface will receive the applied value (Fig. 21.1). When you're applying values using the IRP texture tools, appearances in the underlying SketchUp model will not change (Fig. 21.2). The texture values and how they affect the appearance of a material become apparent only when the model is rendered (Fig. 21.3).

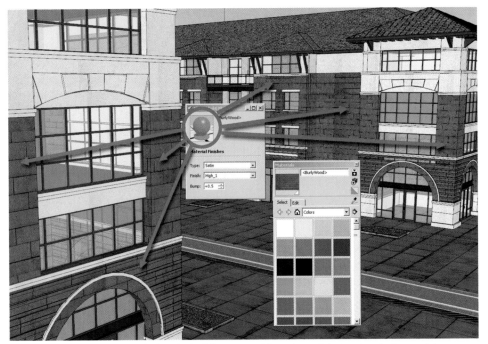

Fig. 21.1: Texture value is applied to the building stone. All versions of that texture in the model now have that same value.

Fig. 21.2: The values applied to materials do not affect the materials' appearances in SketchUp itself.

Fig. 21.3: Texture values are visible only once the model is rendered (Shaderlight).

Shaderlight, SU Podium, and many other IRPs use the Eye Dropper in the SketchUp Material menu to select textures and apply values (see Chapter 8). Twilight Render has its own Eye Dropper as part of the Material menu.

Presets

Most IRPs use *presets* with predetermined values that are applied to textures. With names like Satin, Metal, Glossy, Shiny, Plastic, and Stone, these presets are logically named to remove some of the guesswork for their uses. Shaderlight and Twilight both use presets; SU Podium (v1 and v2) relies on numeric values (Fig. 21.4, Fig. 21.5).

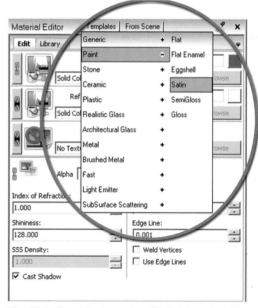

Fig. 21.4: Preset texture values (Twilight Render v1)

Value Types

Each IRP uses different names and methods for applying values. However, they all reference four values. Almost every material will have at least two of these four values applied prior to rendering. The values are

- ▶ **Bump**: How smooth or coarse the texture renders
- ▶ **Surface Condition**: How much reflection a surface can possess
- ▶ **Surface Reflection**: How visible surroundings appear on a surface
- ▶ **Transparency**: A material's opacity

Bump Values

Bump can be described as 3D contrast. It controls how smooth or coarse a material appears. Bump is a universal value found in all IRPs and is never applied with preset values—at least for now.

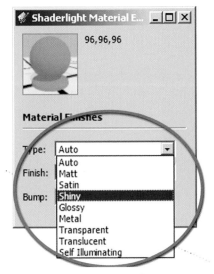

Fig. 21.5: Preset texture values (Shaderlight)

The higher the bump value, the coarser or more contrasted the surface will render, allowing some materials to take on a 3D appearance. For example, bump will allow materials like concrete with scoring, house siding, fabrics, or countertops to possess a 3D relief (Fig. 21.6, Fig. 21.7). Bump can make individual brick patterns appear extruded or provide soft indentations to painted walls and surfaces (Fig. 21.8, Fig. 21.9). Bump can cause lawn and similar groundcovers to have a rough character, and it can provide subtle relief to brushed metals.

Fig. 21.6: A bump value will be applied to the concrete texture in SketchUp.

Fig. 21.7: The same concrete surface as it appears rendered with a bump value for greater surface contrast and depth.

Fig. 21.8: The brick texture viewed in SketchUp

Fig. 21.9: The brick surface after it's rendered with a bump value applied

Value Range

A little bit of bump can go a long way. Bump values range from 0.1 to 10 for Shaderlight and Twilight and from 1 to 100 in SU Podium (Fig. 21.10, Fig. 21.11, Fig. 2.12, Fig. 21.13). Smooth surfaces like porcelain, plastics, and glass will not have a bump value. When Shaderlight and Twilight are used, *most* texture bump values will range from .1 to 2.5. For example, a wood texture in Shaderlight will have a bump value of .3. Setting the bump value too high can cause textures to have a dimpled, distorted appearance when rendered.

Fig. 21.10: When applied and rendered to concrete cubes, bump values of +1 and +2 create a small but noticeably coarse appearance and depth. Most textures do not require a bump value greater than +1.

Fig. 21.11: Bump values of +3 and +4 are applied and rendered to the concrete cubes.

Fig. 21.12: Bump values of +5 and +6 are applied and rendered to the concrete cubes.

Fig. 21.13: Bump values of +7 and +8 are applied and rendered to the concrete cubes. The high bump values create a very coarse texture.

Inverse Values

Bump values can be inverted, causing the "3D contrast" to reverse across the surface. For example, a negative bump value on concrete with scoring will cause the scoring to rise and the concrete character to appear depressed (Fig. 21.14, Fig. 21.15). Inversing bump depends on the IRP and how it provides and applies these values.

Fig. 21.14: Paving with positive bump value

Fig. 21.15: The inverted bump value reverses the extruded appearance of the texture, as compared to Fig. 21.15.

Surface Condition and Surface Reflection

Surface condition and reflection define the most predominant values applied to model textures. The concepts behind these terms are described here.

Surface Condition

Surface condition defines how reflective, diffuse, bright, or muted a surface is. The smoother the surface, the more it reflects light and its environment. Uneven surfaces diffuse more light along their surface, providing little to no reflection (Fig. 21.16).

For example, painted surfaces possess an irregular, coarse condition. Thus, painted surfaces reflect little if any of their surroundings (Fig. 21.17) in contrast to porcelain or plastic surfaces, which have smoother conditions and reflect more of the environment (Fig. 21.18, Fig. 21.19).

Fig. 21.16: Different surfaces and surface conditions

Fig. 21.17: Rendered image highlighting the painted wall with no reflections and a coarse appearance

Fig. 21.18: The porcelain has a subtle but visible reflection in this rendered image highlighting the porcelain on the Utah teapot.

Fig. 21.19: The wood on the table has a limited but noticeable reflection.

Many surfaces can have a wide range of conditions. For example, wood can be rough like bark, coarse like wood cabinets, or glossy as found in wood flooring (Fig. 21.20). The same is true for painted surfaces, which can range from satin (nonreflective) to semiglossy to glossy. The increase in the painted surface smoothness allows more reflections (Fig. 21.21).

Fig. 21.20: The wood flooring is the most reflective; the wood cabinets are bright but much less reflective; and the tree bark is set to appear rough.

Fig. 21.21: When IRP texture values are used, the painted surface can appear anywhere from flat to a reflective glossy.

In contrast, most concrete and hardscape surfaces benefit from coarse surface conditions (Fig. 21.22). In these situations, they do not reflect their surroundings and tend to diffuse light.

Fig. 21.22: Nonreflective and coarse values are typically used for paved and stone surfaces.

Surface Reflection

Surface reflection value refers to the range of reflectivity a surface can possess. This reflectivity can range from no reflection, to indistinct and hazy reflection, all the way to 100-percent reflection, as in a mirror or chrome surface (Fig. 21.23).

Fig. 21.23: Material reflection values can range from none to little, and all the way to highly reflective like a mirror.

IRP Surface Condition and Reflection

Surface reflection is contingent on surface condition. The smoother the surface, the greater the range of reflection will be. IRPs allow users to choose the surface condition for textures. Once the surface condition is chosen, a secondary value representing the range of reflection can be set.

For example, Shaderlight provides a Satin option for surface condition: the Satin setting indicates an irregular surface, meaning that it reflects less light. The Satin option's secondary settings provide a range of reflectivity that ranges from Low, which is no reflection, to High, which allows the surface to reflect more light. However, due to the coarse nature of the Satin setting, even a High reflection value does not act as a mirror; instead, it makes the surface appear brighter without reflecting the surroundings (Fig. 21.24).

In contrast, Shaderlight has a Shiny surface condition value, indicating that the surface is very smooth and can reflect a good amount of its environment. The secondary Shiny reflective values range from Dull to Polished to Mirrored. The Dull secondary value provides a hazy reflection of the environment, a Polished value generates a more distinct reflection, and Mirrored reflects 100 percent of its environment (Fig. 21.25).

Fig. 21.24: The surface conditions and secondary values range from Low to Medium to High (Shaderlight Material Editor).

Fig. 21.25: The Shiny option for the surface condition and secondary values range from Dull, Smooth, Polished, to Mirror (Shaderlight).

IRP Range

Integrated rendering programs provide a large range of surface conditions and secondary values representing reflection. For example, Shaderlight has five overarching surface condition types. Each condition then has nine to eleven subsettings representing reflection. Similarly, Twilight Render has at least six surface conditions, each with five to six subsettings for reflection. The wide range makes it possible to simulate real-world variations found in model textures (Fig. 21.26).

Fig. 21.26: Low reflective values are applied to all surfaces (top). Shiny and reflective values are applied to all surfaces (bottom). IRPs allow a wide range of surface conditions and secondary reflections for each condition.

Reflection Character

Reflections are affected by additional factors within the model. These factors include:

Reflections and Environment   Surface reflections, in particular for smooth surface conditions with high reflective values, render more consistently when objects are placed around it that can be reflected. The absence of objects to reflect can cause reflections to look flat or just plain wrong. Having a good amount of component detail in a model ensures that reflective surfaces have a complete environment for reflective surface to echo.

Many models, in particular buildings with reflective glass windows, benefit from having backdrops and objects placed away from the camera view. The backdrops can be positioned parallel to a reflective surface, causing the surface to mirror the backdrop. See Chapter 15.

Texture Character and Reflection   High reflective values affect the appearance of texture character. The higher the reflective value of a surface, the less visible the texture character will be. The reflected surroundings dominate the texture image.

Fig. 21.27: The color of a material affects its reflectivity. The hovering balls in SketchUp range in color from white to black (top). When rendered, the color affects the rendered material (bottom).

Texture Color and Reflections Reflection can be affected by how light or dark the surface color is. In real-world terms, darker colors absorb more light than they reflect. This real-world aspect holds true for rendering. Darker surfaces, even with shiny conditions and high reflection values, will reflect less of their surroundings in comparison to lighter textures and colors (Fig. 21.27).

Transparency

Transparent materials have a range of opacity and reflection. The more transparent a material, the less reflective it will be (Fig. 21.28, Fig. 21.29). IRPs also allow transparent materials to refract light: light passing through a see-through surface bends and distorts, depending on the type of surface. For example, when you look through a glass of water, the world becomes distorted and warped due to refraction.

Fig. 21.28: The glass is set with a higher opacity that allows more light to pass through and illuminate the interior.

Fig. 21.29: The glass is set to be less transparent, causing it to be more reflective.

Texture Categories

The textures categorized in Fig. 21.30, Fig. 21.31, and Fig. 21.32 are present in most models. Although the lists are not comprehensive, many different materials will easily fit into these categories. Use these categories as a starting point to understanding and organizing the textures you use. This reference provides a basic approach to and an explanation of the nature of textures as they relate to the real world and how those textures correlate to integrated rendering program values. Although the concepts are abstract, consider these categories as a loose formula when you start thinking about texture values in your models.

Each IRP texture chapter (for example, Chapter 27) references the same categories of real-world materials, except the materials are listed with the corresponding values that can be applied with the specific IRP. The goal is to create a link between the conceptual definitions of surface conditions and reflections and how they relate to IRP-specific values.

Each material is defined by its condition, reflection, bump, and transparency. These four top-level values correspond to the definitions provided earlier, and they directly correlate to the number of IRP texture values that can be applied. Materials can possess from one to a large range of conditions, reflections, and bumps.

Each value is further defined by additional secondary values:

▶ **Condition**: Condition ranges from coarse, uneven, smooth, to polished, and it indicates how reflective the material can be.

▶ **Reflection**: Reflection is defined by how clearly the surface can mirror its environment. These characteristics range from none, hazy, indistinct, clear, to mirrored.

▶ **Bump**: Bump values range from none, smooth, coarse, to jagged.

▶ **Transparency:** This is a yes or no condition. Yes means the texture contains some opacity. Most materials have no transparency in real-world or IRP values.

	Brushed metal	Ceramics	Glass	Groundcover
Condition:	Uneven to smooth	Uneven to polished	Uneven to polished	Coarse
Reflection:	Hazy to clear	Hazy to clear	Indistinct to mirrored	None
Bump:	Smooth to coarse	Smooth	None	Coarse to Jagged
Transparent:	No	No	Yes	No
	Metal	**Paint**	**Plastics**	**Polished surfaces**
Condition:	Uneven to polished	Coarse to smooth	Smooth	Polished
Reflection:	Indistinct to mirrored	None to indistinct	Hazy to mirrored	Indistinct to mirrored
Bump:	None to smooth	Smooth to coarse	None to smooth	None to smooth
Transparent:	No	No	No	No
	Porcelain	**Paving**	**Rubber**	**Stone and brick**
Condition:	Uneven to polished	Coarse	Uneven	Coarse
Reflection:	Indistinct to mirrored	None to indistinct	None	None to indistinct
Bump:	None to smooth	Coarse to jagged	Smooth to coarse	Coarse to jagged
Transparent:	No	No	No	No
	Vegetation bark	**Vegetation leaves**	**Water**	**Wood**
Condition::	Uneven	Uneven to smooth	Coarse to polished	Coarse to polished
Reflection:	None	None to indistinct	None to mirrored	None to indistinct
Bump:	Jagged	Smooth to coarse	None to coarse	None to Jagged
Transparent:	No	No	Yes	No

Fig. 21.30: General texture values and descriptions

Builidng blocks
Condition: coarse
Reflection: none
Bump: jagged

Windows
Condition: smooth
Reflection: mirrored
Bump: none

Leaves
Condition: smooth
Reflection: indistinct
Bump: smooth

Bench wood seating
Condition: smooth
Reflection: none
Bump: none

Metal poles
Condition: smooth
Reflection: hazy
Bump: none

Light rail panel
Condition: smooth
Reflection: hazy
Bump: none

Concrete paving
Condition: coarse
Reflection: none
Bump: jagged

Fig. 21.31: Common exterior textures and descriptive values

Glass
Condition: smooth
Reflection: mirrored
Bump: yes

Brushed metal
Condition: uneven
Reflection: hazy
Bump: smooth

Counter top
Condition: polished
Reflection: hazy
Bump: smooth

Porcelain tea pot
Condition: polished
Reflection: indistinct
Bump: no

Wood
Condition: uneven
Reflection: hazy
Bump: coarse

Coffee maker plastic
Condition: smooth
Reflection: hazy
Bump: no

Paint
Condition: uneven
Reflection: none
Bump: coarse

Fig. 21.32: Common interior textures and descriptive values

Troubleshooting Textures

On occasion, some textures will not render. This failure manifests on surfaces in one of three appearances: black, no color (gray or white), or displayed as a different texture already applied in the model. Fixing these problems is part of the evaluation process.

Apply to Both Sides of Surface   SketchUp faces have two sides. The first approach is to apply the texture to the other side of the incorrect surface. This might require maneuvering underneath or through the model surfaces.

Apply a New Texture/Reapply the Texture   You might need to apply a new texture to the surface. Do not swap the texture. Apply a new color and link the appropriate texture file as outlined in Chapter 8.

Components and Groups   Colors and textures applied to the *outside* of a component group can dominate other textures. In this case, select the component or group with the SketchUp Material Eye Dropper and apply the default/noncolor. This might cause some surfaces in the component or group to lose their color or texture. Enter the component/group instance and reapply the texture to blank surfaces as needed.

Image Resolution

Resolution is a key part of the rendering process. Image resolution determines the size and view of the rendering. Resolutions can be set for digital presentation (online or PowerPoint) or printed output, such as 8-½″ × 11″, 11″ × 14″, and 11″ × 17″. You can also set custom and larger sizes.

Resolution has a direct effect on the rendering process: higher resolutions provide more clarity but take longer to render, as discussed in Chapter 20. This chapter explains how to determine resolution for your renderings.

What Is Resolution?

Resolution is the measurement of a graphic calculated in pixels. For example, 800 × 600 resolution means the render has 800 pixels across its width and 600 pixels in height (Fig. 22.1). Pixels translate into dots per inch (DPI). One pixel equals one dot. Dots per inch can be translated as pixels per inch. DPI is a standard measure for online and printed media (Fig. 22.2). Typical screen images are 72 DPI or 72 pixels per inch. Typical print media output is 150 DPI to 300 DPI and higher (600, 1200, etc.) (Fig. 22.3, Fig. 22.4).

Fig. 22.1: Resolution refers to the height and width of the rendered image.

Height

Width

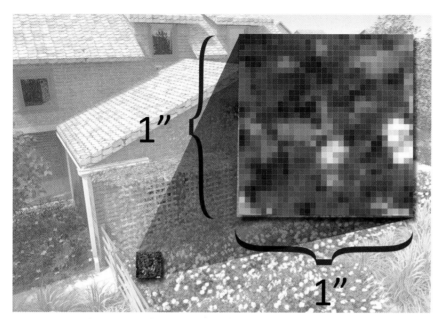

Fig. 22.2: An enlarged view of pixels from the rendering

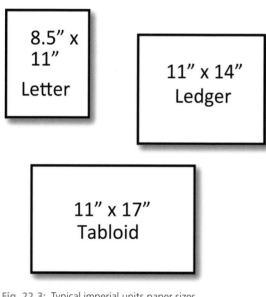

8.5" x 11"
Letter

11" x 14"
Ledger

11" x 17"
Tabloid

Fig. 22.3: Typical imperial units paper sizes

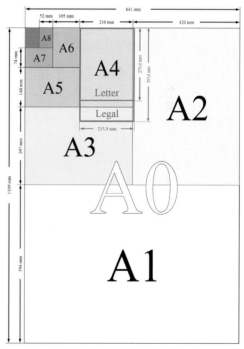

Fig. 22.4: Typical metric paper sizes with imperial sizes for comparison

Calculating Pixels to DPI to Paper Size

Because the resolution in IRPs is set as pixels, you'll need to know how to convert pixels to DPI and to actual paper size. The formula is simple. It is determined by the final desired print size.

- ▶ **Resolution Width**: Sheet width × DPI = Width pixel resolution
- ▶ **Resolution Height**: Sheet height × DPI = Height pixel resolution

For example, the size of a typical letter, 8-½″ × 11″ (Fig. 22.5, Fig. 22.6), can be calculated as:

Width of 8-½″ × 72 DPI = 612 pixels

Height of 11″ × 72 DPI = 792 pixels

8-½″ × 11″ = 612 × 792 (frequently rounded to 600 × 800)

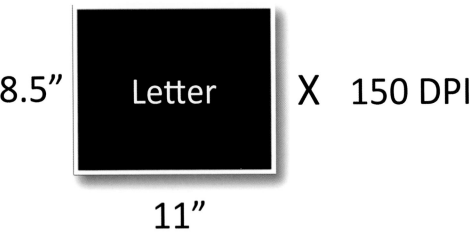

Fig. 22.5: Conversely, letter size can be calculated at 150 DPI.

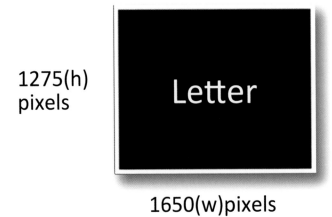

Fig. 22.6: Letter pixel resolution at 150 DPI

You may be able to better understand the relationships between paper size and resolution by seeing them in a chart form (Fig. 22.7).

Sheet size (")	72 DPI	150 DPI	300 DPI
Letter: 8.5(h) x 11(w)	612(h) x 792(w)	1275 (h) x 1650 (w)	2550(h) x 3300(w)
Legal: 11(h) x 14(w)	792(w) x 1008(w)	1650(h) x 2100(w)	3300(h) x 4200(w)
Tabloid: 11 (h) x 17 (w)	792(h) x 1224 (w)	1650 (h) x 2550 (w)	3300 (h) x 5100 (w)

Fig. 22.7: Letter, legal, and tabloid resolution values in pixels

Viewport Size

Viewport size refers to the height and width of the visible SketchUp screen and is measured in pixels (Fig. 22.8). Rendering resolution will usually differ from the viewport resolution unless you set them to match. A difference between rending resolution and viewport resolution will cause the height and width of the draft or final to appear smaller or larger compared to the scene in the viewport (Fig. 22.9). Some IRPs provide the option to match the viewport size for the render.

916 Viewport pixel width

1916 Viewport pixel width

Fig. 22.8: SketchUp viewport resolution can differ from the final render output. In this example, SketchUp's viewport is set to 1916 x 916.

1280
Pixel
height

1280 Pixel width

Fig. 22.9: The outputted IRP render resolution differs from SketchUp's viewport resolution, creating a narrow, more-focused view.

Aspect Ratio

Aspect ratio refers to the proportional relationship between an image's width and its height. Adjusting one value will alter the other, maintaining the proportionate relationship. This feature is useful for draft renderings. Just enter the final resolution render size (if you know it), make sure aspect ratio is selected, and lower the resolution to at least half the size. This ensures that the view in the draft renders is the same as the final resolution.

For example, if the final render size is 1920 × 1080 (HD), the draft renders can be set to 960 × 540. Adjusting one value, such as 1920, will cause the aspect ratio to automatically adjust the second value, doing the math for you.

Atypical Sizes

The aspect ratio can be unlinked, allowing differing focuses and atypical sizes. Unlinking the height and width allows disproportionate values. Various render sizes can be set with this method, including narrow views or wide panoramics (Fig. 22.10, Fig. 22.11).

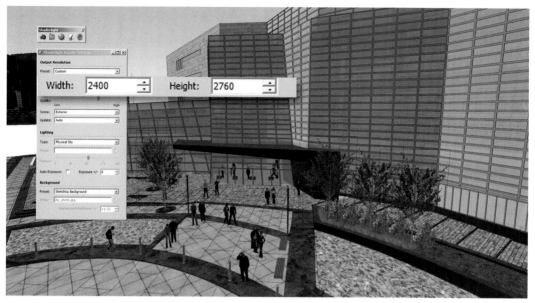

Fig. 22.10: The settings are set for a narrow viewport when rendered (Shaderlight).

2750
Pixel
height

2400 Pixel width

Fig. 22.11: The resulting render is a typical resolution size (Shaderlight).

IRP Custom and Presets Resolution

Most IRPs offer resolution presets. Various sizes can be selected from a pull-down menu. All IRPs offer custom options, allowing the resolution to be set manually.

Determining DPI

DPI is determined based on two factors:

- ▶ The size of the final render
- ▶ The draft-to-final iterative process

The final render size is subjective and depends on what you need to convey in the image.

As outlined in Chapter 20, resolution affects render times: higher resolutions equal longer times. Start with low resolutions, using IRP presets or setting custom small sizes. Here are some useful initial resolutions for first and second drafts:

- ▶ 640 (width) × 480 (height)
- ▶ 800 (width) × 600 (height)

Useful resolutions for third and fourth drafts can range from these initial values to 1280 (width) × 720 (height). Final typical resolutions can be set between 1280 × 720 and 1920 × 1080.

Large Resolutions

Larger resolutions greater than 1920 × 1080 can be set using the custom option under the IRP resolution menu. Large resolution images take longer to render and might require additional RAM (memory) to complete. This is especially true for models filled with a good amount of vegetation components.

When calculating custom pixel width and heights for large resolution images, use the 150 DPI value when multiplying the measured (imperial or metric) values.

Exterior Light

Exterior lighting uses sunlight to illuminate a rendering. For exterior lighting, there are two general options: you can use the SketchUp Shadow menu or image-based lighting (IBL/HDRI). All IRPs support the SketchUp Shadow menu to set lighting; the Shadow menu is also referred to as the Physical Sky setting in the IRP. Some IRPs allow you to insert image-based lighting photos to generate light.

This chapter reviews the various lighting settings found in the different IRPs. Specific lighting options are detailed in the IRP-specific exterior lighting chapters.

First Lighting Steps

When first you're learning to render, use the SketchUp Shadow menu (Physical Sky) to set the lighting (Fig. 23.1, Fig. 23.2). Make sure you understand how to compose light for different scenes and settings as outlined in Chapter 17. Once you are familiar with the settings, experiment with HDRI images if they are available in the IRP you are using.

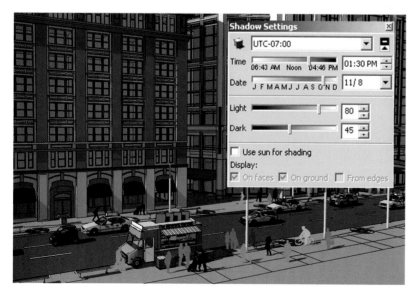

Fig. 23.1: Shadows settings in a SketchUp model determine the lighting for the exterior rendering.

Fig. 23.2: This model rendered in Twilight Render duplicates the light settings from the SketchUp (model by John Palmer and Daniel Tal).

SketchUp Shadows

Most IRPs use the default Physical Sky setting of the SketchUp Shadow menu. For some IRPs, this is the only option. To learn how to best compose a scene using Physical Sky, make sure you've read Chapter 17 and Chapter 18 in Part 4.

Some IRPs have a setting called SketchUp Sky. It is identical to Physical Sky as it references the SketchUp Shadow menu. Using this setting, the render engine will cast equal light throughout the render. It will not alter the color or amount of light based on the time and date. It references only the direction of sunlight in the scene.

Image-Based Lighting

Using and mastering IBL concepts takes some practice. If you are new to rendering, you should start using Physical Sky as your primary exterior lighting option because it is so easy to use and set up.

Image-based lighting offers unique exterior lighting options based on real-world locations and light. Using special cameras, photographers can capture the metrics of light (strength, quality, and color) in a real-world scene (Fig. 23.3). These specially captured images can be inserted into IRPs that offer this option. Once they are inserted, the IRP references the light data in the image to simulate the exact lighting in the rendering (Fig. 23.4, Fig. 23.5, Fig. 23.6).

Fig. 23.3: A high-dynamic range of images used for rendering

Fig. 23.4: Model rendered with noontime HDRI

Fig. 23.5: Model rendered with late afternoon HDRI

Fig. 23.6: Model rendered with early morning HDRI

The IBL format typically used for these types of photographs is called high dynamic range images (HDRI). Compared to Physical Sky settings, HDRI images can generate more realistic lighting in a scene.

HDRIs are delinked from the SketchUp Shadow menu (Fig. 23.7). The direction and exposure of light are adjusted through the IRP menu only.

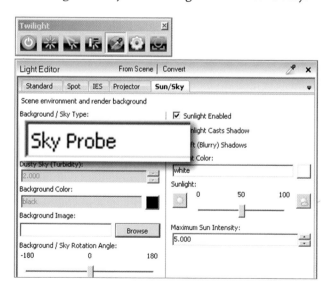

Fig. 23.7: Twilight Render v1 provides the options to insert HDRI images to use for rendering.

HDRI images are inserted into a model with the IRP's Lighting menu. Simply browse to locate the image and insert it into the rendering. Once it is inserted, the IRP will use the HDRI for lighting.

IBLs/HDRIs *are* images. When inserted, the associated image will appear in the image background. Shaderlight has the option to hide the image content while still referencing the lighting metrics of the HDRI.

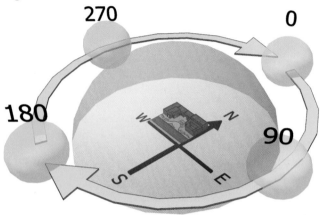

Fig. 23.8: HDRI light sources can be rotated around the model to provide the best result. The light direction can be rotated 360 degrees.

Unlike when you're using SketchUp Shadows, HDRI lighting is not visible in a SketchUp model. You will need to assess and maybe adjust HDRI lighting by running draft renders. You can use them to adjust the direction of the HDRI lighting if necessary.

You can adjust the direction of light coming from an HDRI image. IRPs with IBL options include a slider that ranges from 0 to 360 degrees (Fig. 23.8). Adjusting the slider rotates the image and its direction of light in the model (Fig. 23.9). This method is identical to how light is rotated around a model, as outlined in Chapter 17.

A quick Internet search of HDRI images will yield many results. Check the IRP website forums and review their resource pages to see if they have available images. One such site is **www.moofe.com**, which provides preset HDRI images to Shaderlight. Moofe offers commercial and free HDRI images useful with any IRP that allows IBL inserts for rendering.

Shaderlight includes several preset HDRI images under its Lighting options (Fig. 23.10). Instead of inserting the HDRI image into the IRP and model, you can select them under the Lighting options (see Chapter 28).

Fig. 23.9: The HDRI Rotation tool (Twilight Render v1)

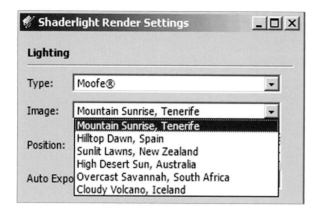

Fig. 23.10: Shaderlight comes with prepackaged HDRI image options.

Exposure/Gamma/Intensity

IRPs have additional lighting options that affect the strength and tone of light. The three most common options are Exposure, Gamma, and Intensity (Fig. 23.11). Of the three, Exposure is the most common and important one to set (Fig. 23.12, Fig. 2313, Fig. 23.14).

Exposure plays an important role during the rendering process. Make sure you adjust the exposure to obtain the best results. The IRP-specific lighting chapters review these settings.

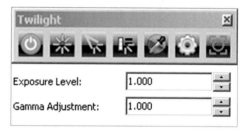

Fig. 23.11: The Exposure and Gamma options (Twilight Render v1)

Fig. 23.12: The rendering Exposure and Gamma options are adjusted.

Fig. 23.13: The options are adjusted again.

Fig. 23.14: The options are adjusted again for the final image.

Simulated Lighting

S imulated light illuminates a model using light sources similar to real-world lamps, bulbs, and fixtures (Fig. 24.1, Fig. 24.2). Typically used for interior renderings, simulated light is created by inserting and placing light sources throughout a model (Fig. 24.3). The light sources can be directed, set to specific lighting outputs, and adjusted to produce different color outputs (Fig. 24.4).

Fig. 24.1: Simulated lighting is typically used for interior renderings.

Fig. 24.2: Easter Seals SketchUp-a-Space Competition 2012, winning entry (model by Kala Letts, Twilight Render v1)

Fig. 24.3: Simulated lights are used to illuminate the scene (Shaderlight).

Fig. 24.4: Exterior rendering with simulated lights (SU Podium)

Simulated lighting is a complex topic in terms of rendering. The many options and almost infinite combinations of lighting found in the real world result in a higher learning curve when compared to other rendering methods and topics. To help you achieve a general understanding of how to create and use simulated light, this chapter reviews the following:

▶ Universal approaches

▶ Types of lighting

▶ Placing and editing lights

▶ Render times

▶ General simulated lighting strategies

Every IRP will let you incorporate point lights, spotlights, and IES profiles. The IRPs approach insertion, placement, and light settings in a nearly identical fashion. Each IRP includes one or more lighting menus to control light settings. The simulated lighting settings for particular IRPs are reviewed in the IRP-specific simulated lighting chapters.

Types of Lighting

Point lights, spotlights, light-emitting materials (LEMs), and IES profile lighting comprise the backbone of simulated light in renderings. Collectively, these lighting elements are called *emitters*. As strange as it seems, none of these lights is self-illuminating (Fig. 24.5, Fig. 24.6). They cast light and make visible their surroundings—i.e., surfaces that are reflecting the light back. They are not visible themselves, as is a typical lightbulb.

Light Source ⟶ lighting showroom

Fig. 24.5: The point light at the center of this SketchUp model will illuminate the entire scene.

lighting showroom

Fig. 24.6: The point light lights up the rendering. However, there is no visible light source.

Point Lights

A *point light,* also called an area light, is a single point of light that casts light in all directions. Point lights can be placed behind shades, glass, and similar transparent surfaces to cast light through them. A point light is the simplest form of simulated lighting used in IRPs (Fig. 24.7, Fig. 24.8, Fig. 24.9).

Spotlights

Spotlights, also called directional lights, are emitters that cast light in a specific direction. Spotlights can be used to direct a light in a specific line of sight over long distances (Fig. 24.10, Fig. 24.11, Fig. 24.12).

Fig. 24.7: SketchUp view of point light placed inside the lamp

Fig. 24.8: SketchUp view of point lights, highlighted in blue, placed in all the fixtures

Fig. 24.9: Rendered lights (Shaderlight)

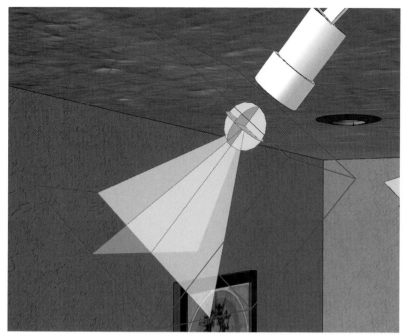

Fig. 24.10: Most spotlights share the same configuration: a pyramidal shape. The pyramid indicates the direction of the light to be emitted.

Fig. 24.11: A series of spotlights are placed around the SketchUp model directed at each painting.

Fig. 24.12: Each spotlight illuminates the painting at which it's directed. Three lamps on the corners of the room use point lights to illuminate the rest of the room.

IES Profiles

IES (Illuminating Engineering Society) profiles are standard data files that include photometric data of actual lights—i.e., a digital profile of real-world lights. IES lights are always spotlights. The light's characteristics depend completely on the profile itself.

IES profiles are available from most lighting manufacturer's websites (Fig. 24.13). You can download the light profiles and import them into an IRP to use actual data to simulate a specific light output based on the photometric for the product or light type (Fig. 24.14, Fig. 24.15).

Photometric **IES Files** - Eclipse Lighting Inc.™
www.eclipselightinginc.com/pages/.../photometric-ies-files.php
You are here: Download > Photometric **IES Files**. Photometrics Download Section.
Download IES Photometric Viewer Program (Compressed Zip File) ...

Philips Color Kinetics **IES Files**
www.colorkinetics.com/support/ies/
Philips evaluates and tests all fixtures during development for optical performance but when it comes to the finished product, we use independent, third party ...

IES / Photometric **Files** - Find and Download - GE Commercial ...
www.gelighting.com/na/business_lighting/.../iesna_downloads.htm
Find and download **IES** / photometric **files** for GE lighting products.

IES Files
www.americanelectriclighting.com/Library/Photometry/
Key: = View list of files | = Download Zip archive of files in category | = View *.**ies** file details | = Download individual *.**ies file**.

Photometric (**IES**) **Files** | SiteLighting.com - Architectural Outdoor ...
sitelighting.com/photometry.cfm
IES files are of little use without lighting software like Footprints™, our new iso-illuminance template generator. The data contained in **IES files** is formatted for ...

IES Files | Amerlux
www.amerlux.com/en/resources/ies-files
Product, **IES Files**. 2.9" EVOKE ROUND ADJUSTABLE · E2.9RA-20-MM-CL / E2.9RA-SDW 0° · E2.9RA-20-MM-CL / E2.9RA-SDW 30° · E2.9RA-20-MM-NF ...

CGArena : Understanding **IES** Lights
www.cgarena.com/freestuff/tutorials/max/ieslights/
An **IES file** is basically the measurement of distribution of light (intensity) stored in ASCII format. You can think of it as a digital profile of a real world light. In 3d ... You've visited this page 3 times. Last visit: 5/14/12

Fig. 24.13: A quick search yields many results for downloadable IES profiles.

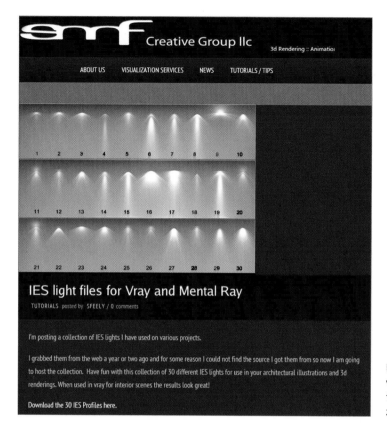

Fig. 24.14: SMF Creative Group's website (see www.ambit-3d.com for link) offers a downloadable zipfile of 30 IES profiles.

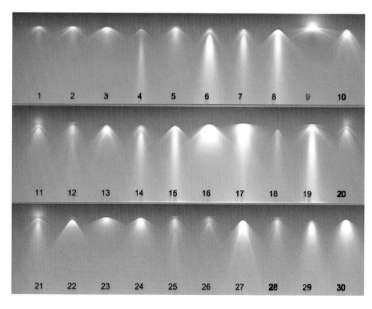

Fig. 24.15: Rendering of the 30 IES lights from SMF Creative Group

Light-Emitting Materials

Selected textures can be transformed into light-emitting materials (LEMs). Usually, this will cause all versions of the material to cast light. Some IRPs cause the material to glow without casting light. LEMs are usually set as texture values, not through a Lighting menu (Fig. 26.16, Fig. 26.17, Fig. 26.18).

Fig. 24.16: Gray solid color material placed under cabinets and above counter.

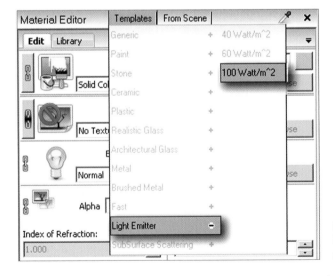

Fig. 24.17: In this LEM menu in Twilight Render v1, the gray color will be set to emit at 100 watts.

Fig. 24.18: The LEM renders the counter.

IRP Light Fixture Libraries

Many IRPs—including Shaderlight, SU Podium, and Twilight Render—have stock lighting fixtures that can be downloaded from their websites or from 3D Warehouse. Stock lights are ready to render. Simply download and place them into your model for use (Fig. 24.19).

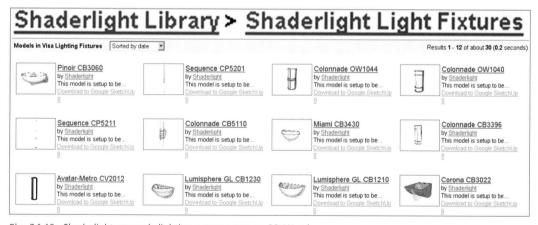

Fig. 24.19: Shaderlight premade lighting components on 3D Warehouse

Placing and Editing Lights

With some variation, the approach to inserting and placing each simulated light type is similar in the different IRPs. Inserted lights appear as small balls or object groups that can be moved around the model (Fig. 24.20).

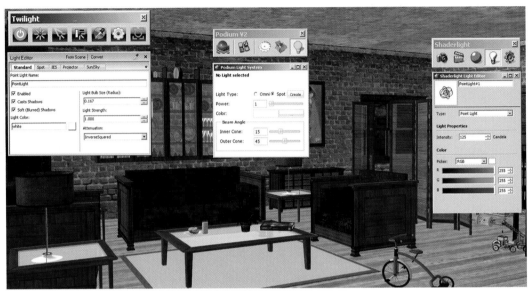

Fig. 24.20: Simulated lighting menus for Twilight Render v1, SU Podium v2, and Shaderlight

Placing Lights on Layers

Before you add any lights to the model, create a new layer called "Lights" and make it the active layer (see Chapter 14). Make sure that lights are inserted onto that layer (Twilight does this automatically). Using layers will make it easier for you to locate lighting in the model and make adjustments (Fig. 24.21).

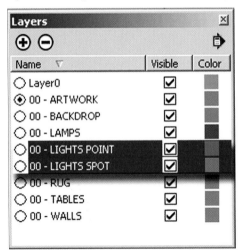

Editing Simulated Lights

Each IRP comes with a menu that allows you to edit the simulated light settings (Fig. 24.20). Simply select the placed light, and adjust the light strength and color from the IRP Properties menu. Adjusting a light inserted into a component will adjust all versions of that light in similar components.

Fig. 24.21: Create layers for the lights before you insert them into the model. Insert the lights onto those layers.

Referencing Geometry

Due to SketchUp's inference system, placing lights into a scene can be tricky: the lights will try to snap to wherever your mouse is pointing. This can make things especially difficult when you're trying to place a light inside a fixture: the light emitter will snap to whatever geometry you are pointing at in the model.

One solution is to draw reference edges with the Line tool, and then snap the light to the edges' endpoints or midpoints. For example, draw a line dissecting a fixture opening. Insert the light by snapping to the edge midpoint. Then, with the light selected, move it upward into the fixture (Fig. 24.22, Fig. 24.23).

Fig. 24.22: A spotlight component is shown in SketchUp (left). Draw an edge across the front of the light (middle). Snap the midpoint of the drawn line (right).

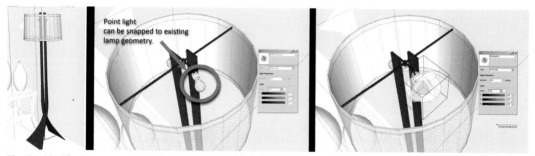

Fig. 24.23: The lamp component includes modeled lightbulbs. Snap the emitter lights to the existing bulb model surfaces (Shaderlight Lighting menu).

Placing In Components

You can also place lights in component fixtures and objects. This works if you have multiple fixtures of the same type in your model, such as pedestrian, street, wall, ceiling, or track lighting. Once the point light is inserted into one component, every copied version of the component will have a point light. This is a quick way to populate a scene with lights.

Place the light directly *into* the component instance as if you were placing a lightbulb into the light. Next, simply copy the component around the model as needed. The light emitter will copy with the component (Fig. 24.24, Fig. 24.25).

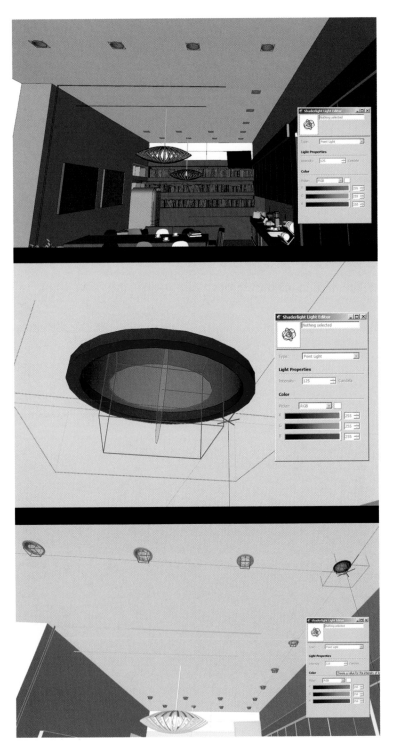

Fig. 24.24: Ceiling fixture components are placed on the ceiling (top). Each ceiling light is a component. The point light is placed into one of these components (middle). Each ceiling component now has a point light (bottom).

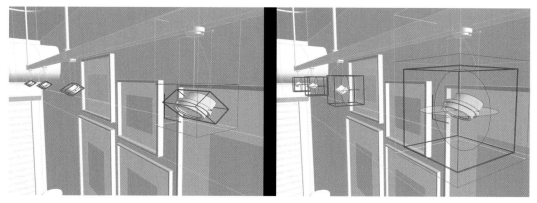

Fig. 24.25: A light is inserted into one of the track light components. Each light now includes a point light.

Placing Point Lights

When you click the Point Light button, you will be prompted to place the light. In Shaderlight and SU Podium, the center of the light will be placed at the point where you left-click. Twilight requires two points of input: the general light location and the location of the actual light.

Placing Spotlights

Spotlights require two points of input. The first input sets the light's location, and the second input sets the light's direction (Fig. 24.26). Spotlights can be tricky to place: be patient. Remember to move and zoom your camera and use the SketchUp inference system (snap-to-points) to maneuver the spotlight in the right direction.

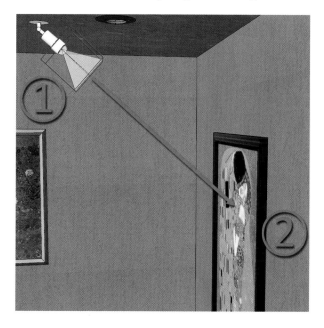

Fig. 24.26: The first point is the insertion point of the spotlight (1). The second point indicates the direction of the light (2). It's best to snap onto an object or surface that the light will illuminate.

Placing IES Lights

Before you place any IES lights, you'll need to download the IES light profile. When you have the profile you want, you can insert into the model (Fig. 24.27). The IRP Lighting menu will include a Browse button you can use to insert the light into the scene. Then the light must be placed similarly to the way you place point or spotlights, depending on the profile.

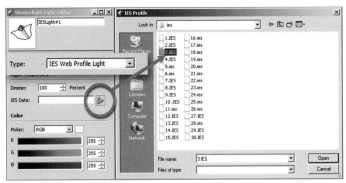

Fig. 24.27: IRPs that support IES profiles will provide an option to browse to the file location.

Placing Light-Emitting Materials

Select a texture just as you normally do to apply a texture render value. From the IRP Material menu, select LEM. For most IRPs, the strength of the LEM can be set as a secondary value.

Render Times

Having multiple simulated light sources in a model is common. Simulated lighting takes time to render, and rendering times for simulated light sources are relatively higher than they are for exterior lighting. In addition, rendering simulated lighting in large models requires robust computers with a lot of RAM to ensure the render completes (see Chapter 4). In general, the following rules of thumb apply when you're working with simulated lighting:

▶ The greater the number of simulated lights, the longer the render times will be.

▶ Larger models (higher face counts) have longer render times. This is particularly true for models filled with 3D vegetation (Fig. 24.28).

▶ Simulated lighting renders require higher quality settings and presets. The higher the quality, the better the results will be. However, higher settings cause longer render times.

Fig. 24.28: The park model render has many lights and large amounts of 3D trees.

General Simulated Light Strategies

This section reviews some general strategies for rendering with simulated lighting. The goal is to achieve faster and more efficient renderings.

Exposure

The Light Exposure settings found in all of the IRP lighting menus are very important when you're working with simulated lighting. You will need to increase or decrease the exposure during the iterative rendering process to achieve the best results from the placed simulated lightings. There is no set value that can define the best settings. Each scene will contain a differing number of lights and light types, and will have lights placed in different positions.

Before adding or removing lights, try to adjust the exposure settings first to see if this improves the lighting in the scene. If the scene appears overlay bright, decrease the exposure. Conversely, if a scene appears too dark, increase the exposure to bring out more of the model detail. These settings are reviewed in the IRP chapters.

Placing Lights Realistically

Add the light sources as you would in the real world (Fig. 24.29, Fig. 24.30). Place a light emitter wherever a light might be needed in a room, interior scene, or exterior scene (Fig. 24.31, Fig. 24.32). These light sources will usually be associated with some sort of fixture:

ceiling light, wall lights, lamps, bulbs, florescent lights, etc. For most models, these fixtures are part of the design, so placing the light sources will depend on the amount and locations of model features (Fig. 24.33, Fig. 24.34).

Fig. 24.29: Lights are placed in outlined blue components for the hanging light fixtures (1). An LEM is placed above the counter (2). A point light is inserted into the ceiling component (3).

Fig. 24.30: The rendered scene

Fig. 24.31: Lights are placed in the outlined blue components: hanging lights (1), track lighting (2), hanging bulbs (3), and a light inserted into the lamp (4).

Fig. 24.32: The model is rendered (model by Kala Letts and Daniel Tal; render by Daniel Tal).

Fig. 24.33: Lights are placed in the outlined blue components: ceiling light (1), hanging ceiling lights (2), lamp components (3), and lamp (4).

Fig. 24.34: The rendered scene

Placing Fixtures

Place your light sources inside light fixtures. Place the light source as if you were inserting or screwing a bulb into the fixture. For open fixtures, this process can be simple. As with a lamp with a shade, the lamp provides simple access so that you can place the point light. For enclosed fixtures, this procedure can be tricky but you can complete it as follows (Fig. 24.35):

1. Make the outsides of enclosed fixtures into components.

2. Next, hide the component. Select the component, right-click over it, and select Hide. The fixture encasement will now be invisible.

3. Make sure that View → Hidden Geometry is not checked. Place the desired light into the center of where the fixture will be located when visible.

4. Go to View → Hidden Geometry and turn on the hidden geometry. The fixture will be visible again.

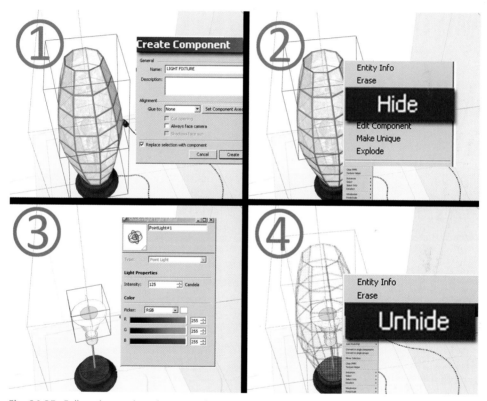

Fig. 24.35: Follow the numbered steps to place an enclosed fixture.

5. Select the dashed lines representing the hidden fixture, right-click over the fixture and select Unhide (Fig. 24.36). Make sure the fixture has transparent materials, which will allow the light to pass through the surface.

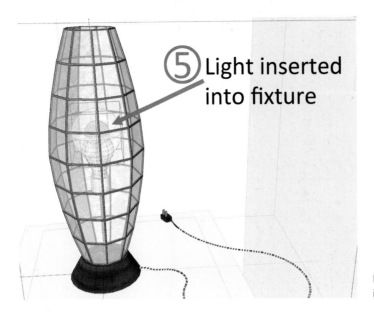

⑤ Light inserted into fixture

Fig. 24.36: Fixture with light inserted into center

Illuminating Fixtures and Light Sources

It is possible to create the illusion of a light source inside a fixture (Fig. 24.37). This works when the fixture has an opening, like ceiling lights, enclosed with an encasement or behind a see-through material like a lamp shade. When you're working, consider taking advantage of SketchUp's ability to apply two different materials to a face. A SketchUp face has two sides; each side can receive a different material and each material can have a different texture rendering value.

For the inside material (the one facing the light source) provide some level of IRP reflection value; doing so will cause the light source to illuminate and reflect, creating the illusion of a light source or bulb (Fig. 24.38, Fig. 24.39).

Transparent Fixtures

Simulated lights will cast through transparent surfaces such as glass fixtures and light shades. In these instances, the transparent enclosure will be illuminated. The lower the material opacity, the brighter the surface illumination of the fixture will be. Light passing through the material will take on the color of the surface. To achieve this effect, ensure the surface encasement of the fixture has some transparency (Fig. 24.40, Fig. 24.41).

Fig. 24.37: Ceiling fixtures with point lights, while housing the light emitters, do not illuminate.

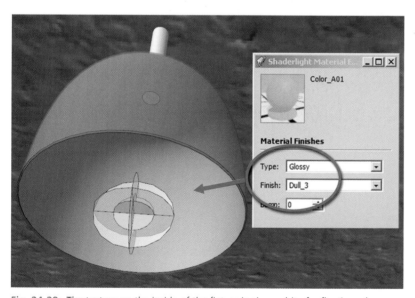

Fig. 24.38: The texture on the inside of the fixture is given a bit of reflective value.

Fig. 24.39: The fixtures now render as light sources.

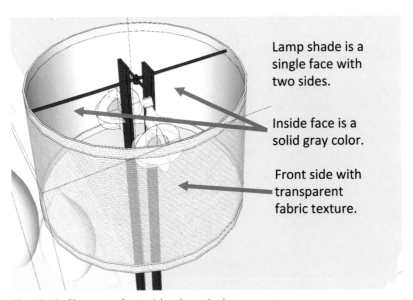

Lamp shade is a single face with two sides.

Inside face is a solid gray color.

Front side with transparent fabric texture.

Fig. 24.40: Placement of material on lamp shade

Fig. 24.41: Rendering of lamp with transparent lamp shade

As previously mentioned, the opposite side of the transparent material should be a different color, usually solid. This will not prevent the other side of the material from being transparent. Give the inside material a reflection value. This will cause the light to pass through the transparent (outside-facing) surface, while illuminating the inside creating the illusion of a light source.

Solid Fixtures

Solid surfaces surrounding a fixture will block the light being cast. Light will only spill out of fixture openings. This is typical for spotlights, in-ceiling lights, and track lighting. Simply place the light sources in the encasing (Fig. 24.42).

Fig. 24.42: Rendering of lamp with solid enclosure with a point light

Hot Spots

Hot spots occur when a light emitter oversaturates an adjacent surface with light. The result is a bright spot on the surface. These hot spots occur when the emitter is too strong or too close to the adjacent surface. Because you want to place emitters near surfaces, hot spots can be hard to avoid (Fig. 24.43). Here are suggested remedies:

- ▶ Move the emitters away from the surface so they avoid the hot spot but still cast the desired light into the scene (Fig. 24.44, Fig. 24.45).

- ▶ Fix the hot spots with photo-editing software (see Chapter 32 for more details).

Fig. 24.43: Light placement can cause lights to render with hot spots.

Fig. 24.44: The positions of the point lights are adjusted.

Fig. 24.45: The scene renders without hot spots.

Separating the Models

If your goal is to render a model to show exterior and simulated lights separately, create two individual models for each condition. Simulated lights used in a model rendering with exterior lighting can cause the render to take longer.

Rendering by Scene

Turning off layers and associated details will speed up render times, as outlined in the Chapter 20. When you're using simulated light, go a step further. After placing the lights, save a new version of the model based on a specific camera view. Then, open up the saved models and *delete* all of the geometry and detail that is not visible in the scene. This will help you further reduce render times.

Adjusting Postproduction

Using Photoshop or similar photo-editing software, you can adjust any simulated light renderings during the postproduction process. The method outlined in Part 7 adds light sources that lend flares to create the illusion of lightbulbs.

Shaderlight
by ArtVPS

Introduction to Shaderlight

Part 6 details how to use the IRP Shaderlight IRP by ArtVPS (Fig. 25.1). You can download Mac and Windows versions of the software at www.artvps.com (Fig. 25.2). Read and refer to this part when you're working with Shaderlight. Menu and tool descriptions, directions for getting started with Shaderlight, and the exact settings you'll need for drafting to final renderings, textures, lighting, and unique features (Fig. 25.3, Fig. 25.4) are covered in these chapters as follows:

- ▶ **Chapter 25:** Menu and tool overviews
- ▶ **Chapter 26:** Shaderlight iterative rendering process and settings
- ▶ **Chapter 27:** Texture menus and category settings
- ▶ **Chapter 28:** Exterior lighting and backdrops
- ▶ **Chapter 29:** Simulated lighting, including point, spot, IES profiles, and other lighting options
- ▶ **Chapter 30:** Special features

Fig. 25.1: Shaderlight rendering of 1970 Chevelle SS

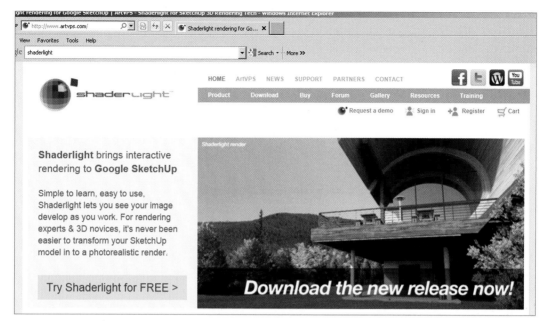

Fig. 25.2: ArtVPS's website where you can download Shaderlight

Fig. 25.3: Rendering with simulated lights completed in Shaderlight

However, this section is not a software manual, detailing every tool and aspect of the program. In some instances, the settings are provided without an explanation of the specific options. For the software manual and other resources, visit Shaderlight's website (www .artvps.com).

Due to the changing nature of many rendering plug-ins, including Shaderlight, some of the specifications in this book could become out of date. Visit the author's website (www.ambit-3d .com) to check for updated content reflecting future updates to the software.

Fig. 25.4: Exterior park rendering completed in Shaderlight

The settings outlined in these chapters are for the full version of Shaderlight. They can be used in tandem with the demo version; however, the demo version has limited settings and does not include all of the features and options available.

Menu Overview

Once Shaderlight is installed, go to View → Toolbars and look for Shaderlight in the list. In most cases, the toolbar will already be active within SketchUp space. The Shaderlight toolbar contains five buttons. They are, from left to right (Fig. 25.5):

- ▶ **Shaderlight Rendering**: Clicking this button will launch the render of the current view.
- ▶ **Shaderlight Animation**: This option will launch a menu for creating animated sequences from preexisting SketchUp scenes.
- ▶ **Material Editor**: This option opens a menu for editing textures and materials so they will render.
- ▶ **Shaderlight Light Tool:** This option opens a menu to place and set artificial lights.
- ▶ **Shaderlight Settings**: This option opens a robust menu where you can set render presets, resolution, lighting, and backgrounds.

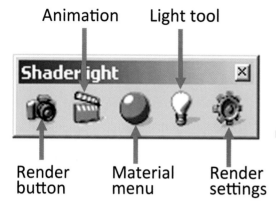

Animation   Light tool

Render
button

Material
menu

Render
settings

Fig. 25.5: The Shaderlight main menu

Secondary Menu

Shaderlight includes additional options that are not located in the main menu. Go to Window →
Plugins and hover over Shaderlight to reveal the same menu options with one additional
feature: ReplaceMe Creator, which is discussed in Chapter 30 (Fig. 25.6). The secondary menu
includes the option to activate Shaderlight if you purchase a license.

Fig. 25.6: The Shaderlight secondary menu under Plugins

Special Features

Shaderlight includes some extra features you'll enjoy using. Chapter 30 describes how to use
some of them.

Dynamic and Batch Rendering

Shaderlight allows you to adjust camera views, lighting, exposure, and texture values while
an image is being rendered. You can save your work anytime during the rendering process.

You can even use SketchUp scenes to move the camera around and allow each scene to render. When you also use the Animation menu, you can render multiple images in one sitting (or even while you sleep). This is a very powerful and effective tool for creating a series of images from one model that depicts many views.

Animation

The Animation tool allows you to harness SketchUp's ability to animate scenes to create still (batch rendering) or moving media.

Clay/Chalk Renders

Using the Chalk Render option under the Shaderlight presets, Shaderlight can produce clay renders (Fig. 25.7). As you learned earlier, clay renders have similar appearances to physical models. See Chapter 30 for specifics about using this feature.

Fig. 25.7: Chalk (clay) render in Shaderlight

Image-Based Lighting (HDRI)

Shaderlight includes several HDRI images. These images offer different lighting options so you won't have to obtain or insert your own HDRI/IBL images. These settings are excellent alternatives to the Physical Sky lighting options in Shaderlight.

ReplaceMe

The ReplaceMe feature allows *proxy object* rendering. ReplaceMe enables you to link components in the model to components outside the model. For example, you can link a 2D tree component in your model to a 3D tree in your Component Library. Shaderlight will render the linked 3D tree instead of the 2D version. This ability allows you to populate your model with simple, low-face-count objects and render them outside of SketchUp with high-face-count versions. This technique is ideal when you're working with vegetation (Fig. 25.8, Fig. 25.9).

Fig. 25.8: Using the ReplaceMe feature, you can exchange the 2D trees shown in SketchUp with 3D trees for the rendering.

Fig. 25.9: Rendering in Shaderlight showing the 3D trees replacing the 2D versions in the model

Shaderlight Iterative Rendering Settings

This chapter reviews settings related to the iterative rendering process outlined in Chapter 20 and includes exacting resolution, quality, and draft-to-final-render options.

The Render Settings Menu

The Render Settings menu is where you set the values for resolution, render quality, and lighting (Fig. 26.1). Correctly using these settings is paramount for the draft-to-final iterative rendering process.

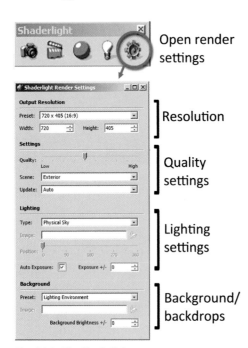

Open render settings

Resolution

Quality settings

Lighting settings

Background/ backdrops

Fig. 26.1: The Shaderlight Render Settings menu

Resolution

From the Output Resolution pull-down menu, you can access presets and custom options (Fig. 26.2, Fig. 26.3). Select Custom to enter values under Width and Height. When you're entering custom resolution settings, double-check the entered values. The menu will sometimes ignore custom entries and they'll need to be reentered.

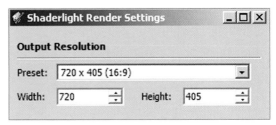

Fig. 26.2: The Output Resolution window

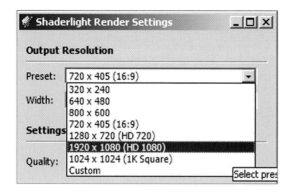

Fig. 26.3: The Output Resolution pull-down menu with preset resolution options

Quality

The Quality slider is found under Settings; its values range from Low (left) to High (right). The higher the slider setting, the better the render quality will be. The slider has a total of 10 notches (Fig. 26.4). It cannot be set between notches, meaning that Shaderlight render quality ranges from 1 to 10. These increments can be easily interpreted to correspond to a Quality percentage (%). For example, the first notch is 10 percent, notch 2 is 20 percent, notch 3 is 30 percent, all the way to 10 equaling 100 percent (Fig. 26.5).

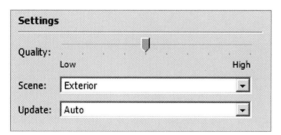

Fig. 26.4: In the Quality Settings menu, the slider bar settings range in increments from 1 to 10 to specify the quality of the rendering.

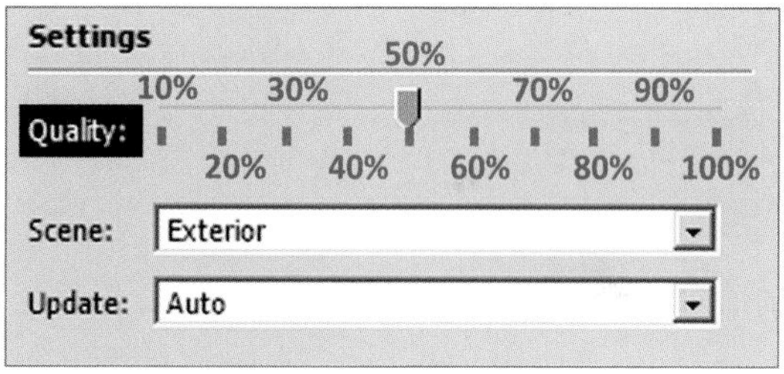

Fig. 26.5: The quality increments can be thought of as percentages, with 10 percent as the lowest and 100 percent as the highest.

Setting the Quality slider to 7, 8, 9, or 10 (maximum quality) will automatically set Shaderlight into Tile mode under Update. These higher settings turn off the Dynamic rendering abil-

ity. Higher settings are required for simulated lighting renders. Exterior renderings benefit less from higher quality. You'll learn more about these settings soon.

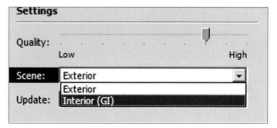

Scene

You can find the Scene pull-down menu under Quality (Fig. 26.6). It contains two settings that correspond to the type of light used

Fig. 26.6: The Scene option under Settings is used to determine the type of overall lighting for the model: Exterior or Interior (GI).

for the render: Exterior and Interior (GI). Exterior is used for Physical Sky and image-based lighting. Interior is used for simulated lighting (Fig. 26.7).

Fig. 26.7: To render this simulated light scene, Interior (GI) was selected from the Scene option under Settings.

Update

The Update pull-down menu determines the way Shaderlight processes a render. The default setting is Auto. When set to Auto, Shaderlight will simultaneously process the entire image (Fig. 26.8). Tile mode causes Shaderlight to process the image one tile at a time.

These settings work in conjunction with the level of quality set for the rendering. Lower quality settings work best with Auto, while the highest settings (70 percent to 100 percent) are intended to work with Tile. In fact, when the quality is set to 70 percent or greater, Shaderlight will automatically set Update to Single (Tiled).

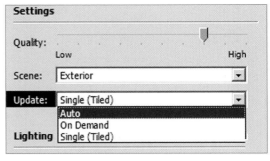

Fig. 26.8: Update determines how the rendering will be processed. The Auto setting is useful for drafts, and Single (Tiled) is used for high-quality final renderings.

Lighting

The Lighting menu includes many lighting options (Fig. 26.9). The specific options you'll use for a particular render will depend on the type of rendering (exterior or interior) and desired lighting. These options are discussed in more detailed in Chapter 28 and Chapter 29.

Relevant lighting options include (Fig. 26.10):

▶ **Physical Sky:** Uses the SketchUp Shadow menu to set lighting. See Chapter 18.

▶ **Moofe**: These preset image-based lighting (HDRI) options offered by Moofe are useful for exterior renderings. The menu includes a slider to adjust sun angle.

▶ **Custom:** The Custom settings allow you to insert your own HDRI for lighting.

▶ **Artificial Lights Only**: This setting will render only simulated lights in the model.

▶ **Chalk**: This clay render setting is covered in Chapter 30.

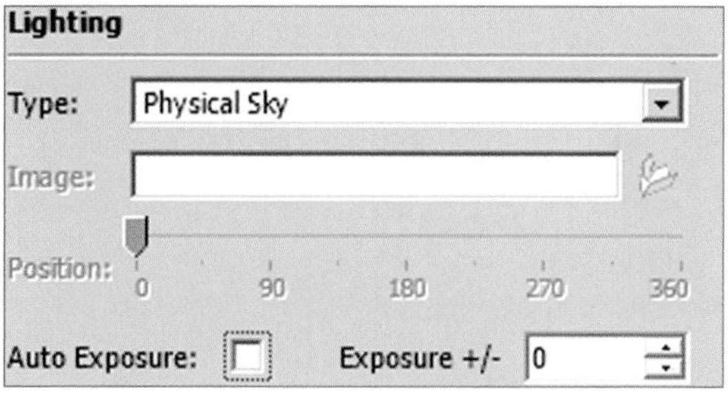

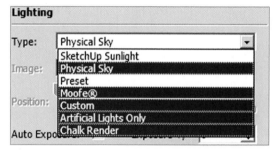

Fig. 26.9: The Shaderlight Lighting options in the Render Settings menu

Fig. 26.10: The Lighting pull-down menu with various lighting options

Auto Exposure and Exposure

The Lighting menu includes exposure settings. Regardless of which lighting option is used, you should *not* use Auto Exposure. Instead, you should learn to set and adjust Exposure manually (Fig. 26.11, Fig. 26.12).

You'll learn more about Exposure settings for different lighting types in Chapter 29 and Chapter 30.

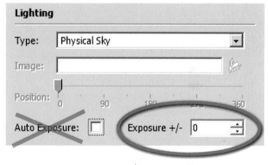

Fig. 26.11: Enter Exposure values manually.

Fig. 26.12: Adjusting the Exposure values will alter the appearance of the render, making it lighter or darker.

Below are some basic sets of exposures to get you started. You should tweak the exposure level as you create draft renders. These are not set values but are intended to be adjusted up or down to achieve the best result. Each render will differ based on model type and the lighting option used.

- ▶ **Physical Sky**: Set Exposure to 0.
- ▶ **Moofe**: Exposure will range from 3.0 to 5.5.
- ▶ **Simulated (artificial) lighting**: Exposure will range from 4.5 to 7.5.

Dynamic Preview and Saving

To initiate the rendering process, click the Render button in the Shaderlight main menu. A new resizable screen will appear, serving as the Render preview window. The render will first upload and then start to coalesce and become visible in the preview window. The render progress will be displayed at the bottom left of the menu (Fig. 26.13).

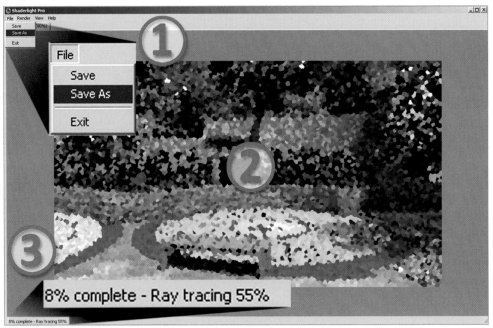

Fig. 26.13: From the Rendering preview window at the top left of the menu, you can save the rendering (1). The progress of the render can be seen in this part of the window (2). The bottom left of the preview window indicates the progress of the rendering in terms of percentage (%) complete (3).

Saving

To save the render at any time during the process, go to the top-left drop-down menu, and select File → Save As.

Dynamic Rendering

In the Render Settings menu, select Update → Auto to enable Dynamic rendering. Once the render process has started, just go back to SketchUp and perform any needed work. Adjusting the camera view, textures, and lighting will cause the preview window to update and reflect these changes when Update is set to Auto (Fig. 26.14). This does not work when Update is set to Tile.

Fig. 26.14: The left side of this dynamic rendering shows the SketchUp model; the right side shows the renderings in the Shaderlight preview window. The rendering is completed and then saved (1). The camera view in SketchUp is adjusted to a different vantage point. Shaderlight starts to render this new view (2). The view is completed and can be saved (3).

The dynamic-rendering system allows you to conduct batch renderings, which are reviewed in Chapter 30.

Draft-to-Final Settings

The following settings are based on the iterative rendering process outlined in Chapter 20. They include specific settings for exterior and interior renders, starting with the initial and subsequent draft iterations and leading to the final graphic. Settings that change from each step are highlighted in the figures.

Exterior Draft to Final

Exterior renders can use the following settings for draft-to-final images (Fig. 26.15, Fig. 26.16, Fig. 26.17, Fig. 26.18). For most final renders, a Quality setting of 60 percent is usually (but not always) sufficient. A higher setting will cause Update to reset to Tile, increasing both render time and quality. HDRI and Moofe settings are reviewed in Chapter 29.

Initial Draft

▶ **Low Resolution**: Use Preset of 800 x 600 or one third of final resolution Aspect.

▶ **Quality**: 30 percent (three notches from the left).

▶ **Scene (under Quality)**: Set to Exterior.

▶ **Update (under Quality)**: Auto.

▶ **Lighting Type**: Physical Sky/Exposure set to 0 (Auto Exposure unchecked).

▶ **Detail Layers**: Off.

Fig. 26.15: The Exterior initial draft

Fig. 26.16: The Exterior secondary draft

Secondary Draft

▶ **Increase Resolution**: Use preset of 1280 × 720 or one half of final resolution Aspect.

▶ **Quality**: 50 percent (five notches from the left).

▶ **Scene (under Quality)**: Set to Exterior.

▶ **Update (under Quality)**: Auto.

▶ **Lighting Type**: Physical Sky.

▶ **Exposure**: 0 (Auto Exposure unchecked).

▶ **Detail Layers**: Turn on some layers that contain detail.

Semifinal Render

▶ **Keep Resolution**: Use preset of 1280 × 720 or one half of final resolution aspect.

▶ **Quality**: 60 percent (six notches from the left).

▶ **Scene (under Quality)**: to Exterior.

▶ **Update (under Quality)**: Auto.

▶ **Lighting Type**: Physical Sky.

▶ **Exposure**: 0 (Auto Exposure unchecked).

▶ **Detail Layers**: On.

Fig. 26.17: The Exterior semifinal draft

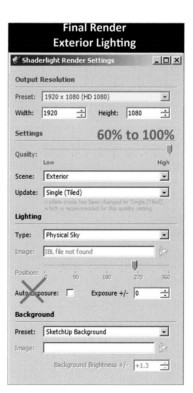

Fig. 26.18: The Exterior final render

Final Render

- ▶ **Set Final Resolution**: 1980 × 1020 and higher.
- ▶ **Quality**: Set to 60 percent or higher, but render will take longer; 100 percent is recommended.
- ▶ **Scene (under Quality)**: Set to Exterior.
- ▶ **Update (under Quality)**: Auto if at 60 percent; Tile from 70 to 100 percent.
- ▶ **Lighting Type**: Physical Sky.
- ▶ **Exposure**: 0 (Auto Exposure unchecked).
- ▶ **Detail Layers**: On.

Interior/Simulated Lighting Draft to Final

For renders with simulated lighting, use the following settings (Fig. 26.19, Fig. 26.20, Fig. 26.21, Fig. 26.22, Fig. 26.23). The Quality for simulated lighting needs to be set to 100 percent for final renders: the additional quality ensures that the final image is the best possible quality.

Initial Draft

- ▶ **Exposure**: Exposure settings for simulated lighting can be a moving target. The range starts with 4.0 and ranges to 7.5. Start with 4.0; if the scene appears dim or dark, increase by increments of 0.5—for example, use increments ranging from 4.0, 4.4, 5.0, 5.5, 6.0, 6.5, 7.0, and 7.5. The number of lights and the strength of the emitters will affect the exposure settings as well. You can adjust Exposure dynamically during the rendering process.
- ▶ **Option**: As outlined in Chapter 20, run the initial drafts using Physical Sky cast into the interior. This is a quick way to evaluate and adjust textures prior to adding simulated lighting.
- ▶ **Low Resolution**: Use preset of 800 × 600 or one third of final resolution Aspect.
- ▶ **Quality**: 30 percent (three notches from the left).
- ▶ **Scene (under Quality)**: Set to Exterior
- ▶ **Update (under Quality)**: Auto.
- ▶ **Lighting Type**: Physical Sky/Exposure - 0 (Auto Exposure unchecked).
- ▶ **Detail Layers**: Off.

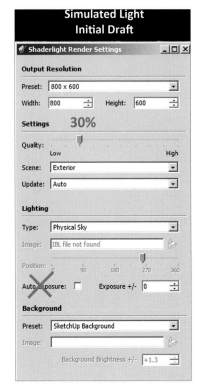

Fig. 26.19: Simulated Light initial draft of exterior lighting

Secondary Draft1

- ▶ **Low Resolution**: Use preset 800 × 600 or one third of final resolution Aspect.
- ▶ **Quality**: 50 percent (five notches from the left).
- ▶ **Scene (under Quality)**: Set to Interior (GI).
- ▶ **Update (under Quality)**: Auto.
- ▶ **Lighting Type**: Artificial Lighting only.
- ▶ **Exposure**: Start with 4.5 and adjust the exposure during the rendering process.
- ▶ **Background**: Lighting Environment.
- ▶ **Detail**: Layers Off.

Secondary Draft2

- ▶ **Increase Resolution**: Use preset of 1280 × 720 or one third of final resolution Aspect.
- ▶ **Quality**: 50 percent (five notches from the left).
- ▶ **Scene (under Quality)**: Set to Interior (GI).
- ▶ **Update (under Quality)**: Auto.
- ▶ **Lighting Type**: Artificial Lighting Only.

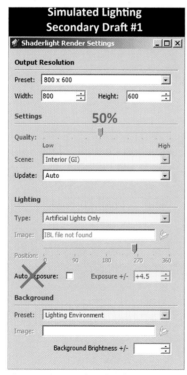

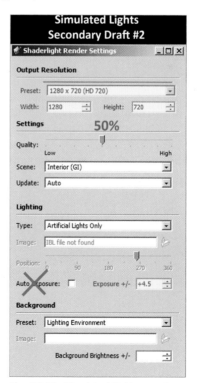

Fig. 26.20: Simulated Light secondary draft #1 (includes simulated lighting)

Fig. 26.21: Simulated Light secondary draft #2

- ▶ **Exposure**: Use setting established during initial draft.
- ▶ **Detail**: Layers On.

Semifinal Render

- ▶ **Increase Resolution**: Use preset of 1280×720 or 1/2 of final resolution Aspect.
- ▶ **Quality**: 70 percent, which is Tile mode.
- ▶ **Scene (under Quality)**: Set to Interior (GI).
- ▶ **Update (under Quality):** Tile set automatically.
- ▶ **Lighting Type**: Artificial Lighting Only.
- ▶ **Exposure**: Use setting established during initial draft.
- ▶ **Background**: Lighting Environment.
- ▶ **Detail Layers**: On.

Final Render

- ▶ **Final Resolution**: 1980×1020 and higher.
- ▶ **Quality**:100 percent, which is Tile mode.

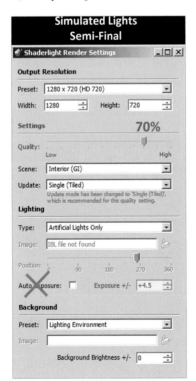

Fig. 26.22: Simulated Light semifinal draft

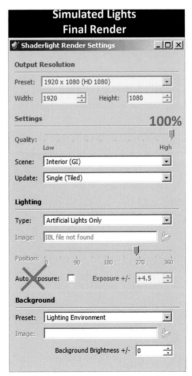

Fig. 26.23: Simulated Light final settings

- ▶ **Scene (under Quality)**: Set to Interior (GI).
- ▶ **Update (under Quality)**: Tile set automatically.
- ▶ **Lighting Type**: Artificial Lighting Only.
- ▶ **Exposure**: Use setting established during initial draft.
- ▶ **Background**: Lighting Environment.
- ▶ **Detail Layers**: On.

Shaderlight Texture Settings

S haderlight uses preset values for its texture settings. The presets use easy-to-remember names to describe their values. This chapter correlates these presets with the texture values described in Chapter 21. In this chapter, you will learn the following:

▶ How to apply Shaderlight textures values

▶ The descriptions of texture values

▶ The Texture settings by category

▶ How to set glass and water textures

Apply Texture Values

Values are applied to textures using the Shaderlight Material menu. Materials are picked with the SketchUp Paint Bucket Eye Dropper (Fig. 27.1). The chosen textures will appear in a preview window at the top left of the Material menu. Once a preset is applied, the Texture preview will update, displaying how the texture will appear once rendered. An applied value affects all versions of a texture.

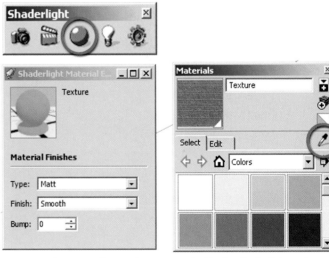

Fig. 27.1: The Material Menu button is circled in the Shaderlight main menu (at top). On the left is the Shaderlight Material menu; the SketchUp Paint Bucket is on the right. The SketchUp Eye Dropper is used to select materials that are then made active in the Shaderlight Material menu.

Shaderlight had preprogrammed values for native SketchUp textures. These materials come preloaded into the SketchUp Paint Bucket (Fig. 27.2). SketchUp native textures have pre-arranged rendering values. They do not need to be adjusted, and no additional values need to be applied. Simply apply them to surfaces and render (Fig. 27.3)

Using the native textures is an excellent way to create quick renderings. The native materials will still need to be scaled for best appearance. The SketchUp Material menu can be used to adjust the color and scale of these native textures. If you adjust the textures values in the Shaderlight Material menu (select options other than Auto) or edit the native texture in an external photo editor, the prearranged values will be removed from the native texture (but only in that model).

Fig. 27.2: SketchUp native textures in the SketchUp Paint Bucket

Fig. 27.3: Rendering created with SketchUp native textures and Shaderlight

Texture Value Descriptions

Specific values based on categories are listed under Texture Settings by category. The following descriptions expound on the explanations for reference texture values outlined in Chapter 21.

Bump

In Shaderlight, the bump values range from 0 to 10 with 1/10 increments (Fig. 27.4). Most textures will have a bump value ranging from 0.01 to 2.00. For example, many stone or paving textures will range from 0.5 to 1.5 and everything in-between (Fig. 27.5). Metallic or shiny surfaces might have zero (0) bump or a slight bump ranging from .01 to .5. Higher values are useful for rough or course surfaces such as groundcover, fabrics, lawn, and stone (Fig. 27.6, Fig. 27.7). Setting the bump value to high will result in a dimpled and distracting surface character.

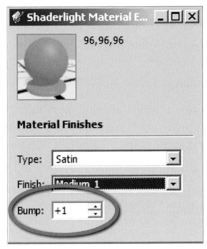

Fig. 27.4: The bump value is circled in the Shaderlight Material menu.

Type and Finish

The Type and Finish settings determine how bright and reflective surfaces will render.

Fig. 27.5: Different bump values applied to the same concrete surface

Fig. 27.6: A high bump value is applied to the ground cover in the planter, creating a rough, extruded appearance.

Fig. 27.7: A high bump value is applied to the fabric on the sofa.

Type

Type represents the possible range of reflection a texture can possess when rendered (Fig. 27.8). It corresponds to surface condition as outlined in Chapter 21. Types range from Matt, Satin, Shiny, and Glossy to Metal.

Finish

Finish is determined by type. Each type has its own range of finishes (Fig. 27.9). Ranging from flat to mirror, finishes determine how reflective a material will appear. The brighter the type, the more reflective the finish will be.

Type and Finish

The chart represents how these values work to produce surface condition and surface reflection (Fig. 27.10). The types are arranged in order from little/no reflection all the way to full reflections (mirror). The types are not in the same order as they appear in the Shaderlight Material menu.

Fig. 27.8: The Shaderlight Material menu pull-down option with the available texture types

Fig. 27.9: Each type has a range of finishes. In this example, Shiny is selected and all the finishes associated with Shiny display in the pull-down menu.

Level of reflection	Type	Finish									
		<------------------ Less - Amount - More ------------------>									
		of reflection									
None	Matt	Smooth	Rough	Chalky							
Little	Satin	Low_1	Low_2	Low_3	Medium_1	Medium_2	Medium_3	High_1	High_2	High_3	
Hazy	Glossy	Dull_1	Dull_2	Dull_3	Satin_1	Satin_2	Satin_3	Reflective_1	Reflective_2	Reflective_3	Mirror
Indistinct	Metal	Brushed_1	Brushed_2	Brushed_3	Satin_1	Satin_2	Satin_3	Polished_1	Polished_2	Polished_3	Chrome
Clear	Shiny	Dull_1	Dull_2	Dull_3	Satin_1	Satin_2	Satin_3	Reflective_1	Reflective_2	Reflective_3	Mirror

Fig. 27.10: How Type and Finish compare to Surface Conditions and Reflections (Shaderlight)

As you know, *surface condition* refers to the roughness or smoothness of a surface (Fig. 27.11, Fig. 27.12). Matt and Satin types have a rougher surface condition, and the corresponding finishes produce little to no actual reflections. Similarly, a Glossy type is much smoother, and something set with Mirror Finish will have distinct/blurry reflections. In comparison, a Shiny type with Mirror Finish will produce a 100 percent mirrored reflection.

Fig. 27.11: Shaderlight types applied to materials.

Fig. 27.12: A finish is assigned to each type, but the Finish settings are not shown.

Transparent, Translucent, and Self-Illuminating

The three additional types (Transparent, Translucent, and Self-Illuminating) have their own uses and finishes.

Transparent

The Transparent type is used to create transparent surfaces such as water and glass (Fig. 27.13). It includes several finishes: Thin_Glass, Thick_Glass, Thick_Frosted_Glass, Liquid, Diamond, and others (Fig. 27.14).

The finishes determine the level of refraction. Thin_Glass is the least refractive, and Diamond is the most. The higher the finish level, the greater the refraction will be, causing light to bend as it passes through the material. This will cause objects on the other side of the material to appear distorted, as a real-world transparent material would.

Fig. 27.13: Transparent is selected in the Shaderlight Material menu. The pull-down menu displays the available finishes.

Translucent

This type and its related finishes are similar to Transparent, except they have greater refraction values. They are useful for thick, opaque materials similar to gem stones and thick transparent plastics or glass. For most renderings, Transparent settings are usually sufficient for opaque surfaces.

Self-Illuminating

Self-illuminating types are Shaderlight's version of light-emitting materials (LEMs), except they do not emit light. They are useful for televisons, computer screens, and similar devices. See the Shaderlight Software manual for more information on these settings.

Fig. 27.14: The various transparent finishes

Texture Settings Categories

The texture categories can be paired with specific Shaderlight texture types and finishes. In these charts, Surface Condition has been replaced with Type, and Reflection with Finish. Bump remains the same. These comparisons should give you a reference point for using common materials. Use these settings when you're first applying values to textures (Fig. 27.15, Fig. 27.16).

	Appliances #1	Appliances #2	Brick	Brushed Metal
Type:	Glossy	Metal	Satin	Metal
Finish:	Dull_2 to Reflective_1	Brushed_1 to Polished_2	Low_1 to Medium_2	Brushed_1 to Satin_1
Bump:	None	None	.1 to 1	.01 to 1.0
	Ceramics#1	**Ceramics#2**	**Chrome**	**Counter Tops - Granite**
Type:	Satin	Glossy	Metal	Glossy
Finish:	High_1 to High_3	Dull_1 to Reflective_1	Chrome	Dull_3 to Reflective_3
Bump:	None	None	None	None to 1.2
	Fabric	**Groundcover**	**Leaves#1 - Dull**	**Leaves#2 - Bright**
Type:	Matt	Matt	Glossy	Shiny
Finish:	Rough	Rough or Chalky	Satin_1 to Refletive_1	Dull_1 to Dull_3
Bump:	+2 to +6	+4 to +7	None to +3	None to +3
	Metal - Dull	**Metal - Bright**	**Mirror**	**Paving**
Type:	Metal	Metal	Shiny	Satin
Finish:	Dull_1 to Satin_3	Polished_1 to Chrome	Mirror	Low_1 to Medium_2
Bump:	None to .5	None	None	.2 to 2

Fig. 27.15: Shaderlight texture values

	Paint#1 - Dull	Paint#2 - Glossy	Plastics - Dull	Plastics - Bright
Type:	Satin	Glossy	Glossy	Shiny
Finish:	Medium_2 to High_3	Dull_1 to Satin_1	Satin_2 to Reflective_2	Dull_1 to Reflective_1
Bump:	None to .3	None to .3	None	None
	Porcelain	**Polished surfaces#1 - Soft**	**Polished surfaces#2 - Reflective**	**Rubber**
Type:	Glossy	Glossy	Shiny	Satin
Finish:	ALL	Dull_3 to Reflective_3	Dull_1 to Satin_2	Medium_1 to High_3
Bump:	None	.5 to 1.2	.5 to 1.2	None to .3
	Stone	**Stucco**	**Tile**	**Wood - Rough**
Type:	Satin	Satin	Glossy	Matt
Finish:	Low_1 to Medium_2	Medium_1 to High_3	Dull_2 to Reflective_3	Smooth to Rough
Bump:	.2 to 1.5	.1 to 1.5	None to .9	.5 to 2.0
	Wood - Dull	**Wood - Reflective**		
Type:	Satin	Glossy		
Finish:	Low_2 to High_3	Dull_2 to Reflective_2		
Bump:	.5 to 2.0	.5 to 2.0		

Fig. 27.16: The charts loosely parallel the texture chart in Fig. 21.30.

Although written descriptions are helpful, you should study the figures (Fig. 27.17, Fig. 27.18, Fig. 27.19, Fig. 27.20, Fig. 27.21, Fig. 27.22, Fig. 27.23, Fig. 27.24) for the specific texture settings used in the rendered images. Chapter 39 and Chapter 40 list additional categories of Shaderlight texture value settings similar to these figures.

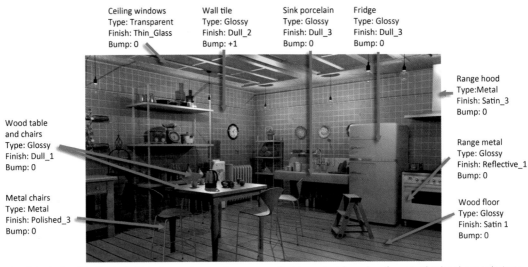

Ceiling windows
Type: Transparent
Finish: Thin_Glass
Bump: 0

Wall tile
Type: Glossy
Finish: Dull_2
Bump: +1

Sink porcelain
Type: Glossy
Finish: Dull_3
Bump: 0

Fridge
Type: Glossy
Finish: Dull_3
Bump: 0

Range hood
Type:Metal
Finish: Satin_3
Bump: 0

Wood table
and chairs
Type: Glossy
Finish: Dull_1
Bump: 0

Range metal
Type: Glossy
Finish: Reflective_1
Bump: 0

Metal chairs
Type: Metal
Finish: Polished_3
Bump: 0

Wood floor
Type: Glossy
Finish: Satin 1
Bump: 0

Fig. 27.17: Specific Shaderlight texture values as they are applied to materials and surfaces in this book's renderings; kitchen render from image in Chapter 1

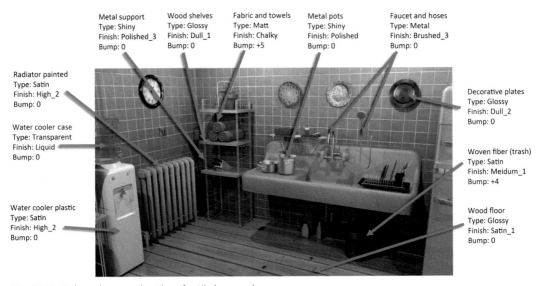

Metal support
Type: Shiny
Finish: Polished_3
Bump: 0

Wood shelves
Type: Glossy
Finish: Dull_1
Bump: 0

Fabric and towels
Type: Matt
Finish: Chalky
Bump: +5

Metal pots
Type: Shiny
Finish: Polished
Bump: 0

Faucet and hoses
Type: Metal
Finish: Brushed_3
Bump: 0

Radiator painted
Type: Satin
Finish: High_2
Bump: 0

Decorative plates
Type: Glossy
Finish: Dull_2
Bump: 0

Water cooler case
Type: Transparent
Finish: Liquid
Bump: 0

Woven fiber (trash)
Type: Satin
Finish: Meidum_1
Bump: +4

Water cooler plastic
Type: Satin
Finish: High_2
Bump: 0

Wood floor
Type: Glossy
Finish: Satin_1
Bump: 0

Fig. 27.18: Enlarged area and settings for Kitchen render

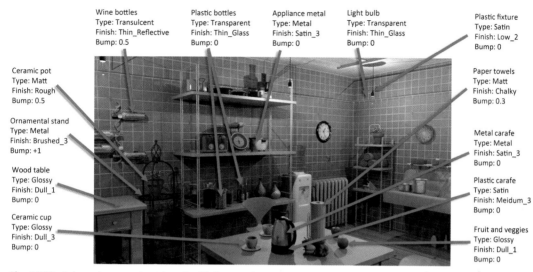

Wine bottles
Type: Translucent
Finish: Thin_Reflective
Bump: 0.5

Plastic bottles
Type: Transparent
Finish: Thin_Glass
Bump: 0

Appliance metal
Type: Metal
Finish: Satin_3
Bump: 0

Light bulb
Type: Transparent
Finish: Thin_Glass
Bump: 0

Plastic fixture
Type: Satin
Finish: Low_2
Bump: 0

Ceramic pot
Type: Matt
Finish: Rough
Bump: 0.5

Paper towels
Type: Matt
Finish: Chalky
Bump: 0.3

Ornamental stand
Type: Metal
Finish: Brushed_3
Bump: +1

Metal carafe
Type: Metal
Finish: Satin_3
Bump: 0

Wood table
Type: Glossy
Finish: Dull_1
Bump: 0

Plastic carafe
Type: Satin
Finish: Meidum_3
Bump: 0

Ceramic cup
Type: Glossy
Finish: Dull_3
Bump: 0

Fruit and veggies
Type: Glossy
Finish: Dull_1
Bump: 0

Fig. 27.19: Enlarged area and settings for Kitchen render

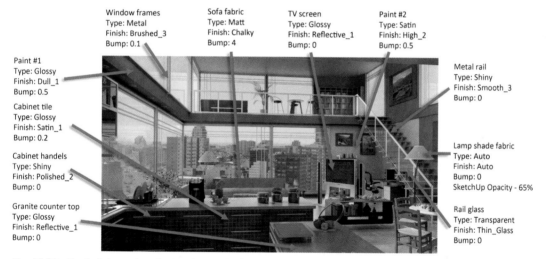

Window frames
Type: Metal
Finish: Brushed_3
Bump: 0.1

Sofa fabric
Type: Matt
Finish: Chalky
Bump: 4

TV screen
Type: Glossy
Finish: Reflective_1
Bump: 0

Paint #2
Type: Satin
Finish: High_2
Bump: 0.5

Paint #1
Type: Glossy
Finish: Dull_1
Bump: 0.5

Metal rail
Type: Shiny
Finish: Smooth_3
Bump: 0

Cabinet tile
Type: Glossy
Finish: Satin_1
Bump: 0.2

Cabinet handels
Type: Shiny
Finish: Polished_2
Bump: 0

Lamp shade fabric
Type: Auto
Finish: Auto
Bump: 0
SketchUp Opacity - 65%

Granite counter top
Type: Glossy
Finish: Reflective_1
Bump: 0

Rail glass
Type: Transparent
Finish: Thin_Glass
Bump: 0

Fig. 27.20: Shaderlight settings for interior render featured in Chapter 2

PV cells
Type: Shiny
Finish: Polished_1
Bump: 0

Stucco and EIFS
Type: Satin
Finish: Low_3
Bump: 0

Window frame
Type: Metal
Finish: Satin_3
Bump: 0

Window glass
Type: Transparent
Finish: Thin_Glass
Bump: 0
HLS - L value = 97

Ceramic tile roof
Type: Satin
Finish: Low_2
Bump: 0.2

Roof overhangs
Type: Satin
Finish: Low_2
Bump: 0.1

Wood column
Type: Satin
Finish: Low_3
Bump: 0

Cobble paving
Type: Satin
Finish: Medium_1
Bump: +1

Soil/groundcover
Type: Matt
Finish: Chalky
Bump: +4

Fig. 27.21: Shaderlight texture values for Clarum home rendering using Shaderlight

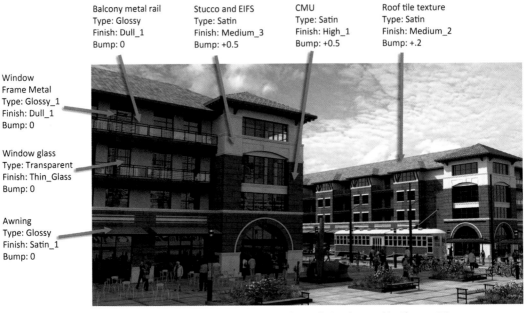

Balcony metal rail
Type: Glossy
Finish: Dull_1
Bump: 0

Stucco and EIFS
Type: Satin
Finish: Medium_3
Bump: +0.5

CMU
Type: Satin
Finish: High_1
Bump: +0.5

Roof tile texture
Type: Satin
Finish: Medium_2
Bump: +.2

Window
Frame Metal
Type: Glossy_1
Finish: Dull_1
Bump: 0

Window glass
Type: Transparent
Finish: Thin_Glass
Bump: 0

Awning
Type: Glossy
Finish: Satin_1
Bump: 0

Fig. 27.22: Shaderlight texture values for exterior plaza and condo rendering featured in Chapter 20

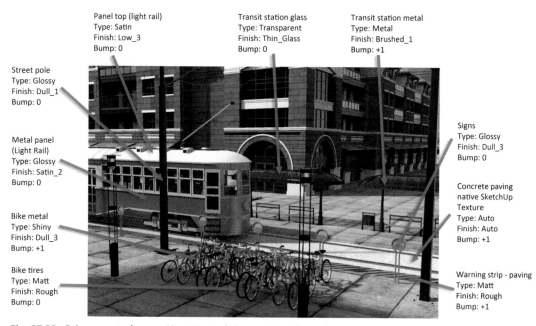

Panel top (light rail)
Type: Satin
Finish: Low_3
Bump: 0

Transit station glass
Type: Transparent
Finish: Thin_Glass
Bump: 0

Transit station metal
Type: Metal
Finish: Brushed_1
Bump: +1

Street pole
Type: Glossy
Finish: Dull_1
Bump: 0

Signs
Type: Glossy
Finish: Dull_3
Bump: 0

Metal panel
(Light Rail)
Type: Glossy
Finish: Satin_2
Bump: 0

Concrete paving
native SketchUp
Texture
Type: Auto
Finish: Auto
Bump: +1

Bike metal
Type: Shiny
Finish: Dull_3
Bump: +1

Bike tires
Type: Matt
Finish: Rough
Bump: 0

Warning strip - paving
Type: Matt
Finish: Rough
Bump: +1

Fig. 27.23: Enlargement of area with settings of plaza and condo rendering

Ped light glass
Type: Translucent
Finish: Thin_Reflective
Bump: 0

Shrub leaf #1
Type: Glossy
Finish: Dull_2
Bump: 0

Shrub leaf #2
Type: Satin
Finish: High_2
Bump: 0

Corrugated metal
Type: Metal
Finish: Satin_1
Bump: +1

Ped light pole
Type: Glossy
Finish: Dull_1
Bump: 0

Planter edge
Type: Satin
Finish: Low_2
Bump: 0

Bench wood
native SketchUp
Texture
Type: Auto
Finish: Auto
Bump: +1

Table and chair wood
Type: Glossy
Finish: Satin_1
Bump: 0

Bench metal
Type: Metal
Finish: Polished_1
Bump: 0

Concrete paving
Type: Satin
Finish: Meidum_3
Bump: 0.6

Fig. 27.24: Enlargement of area with settings of plaza and condo rendering

The Type setting is the key for most materials because it sets the main look and character for the image. The suggested settings use Type for the main setting. You'll need to adjust the range of finishes as needed. You'll quickly realize if a material is rendered too flat or too reflective.

Some surfaces have multiple entries representing the possible range of values. You will have to determine which settings work best for your situation. Adjust them as needed through the iterative rendering process outlined in Chapter 20.

Glass and Water Material Values

Glass and water transparencies are set with the aid of the SketchUp Material menu. Click the Edit Tab and choose Picker HLS (Fig. 27.25). (See Chapter 8 for a refresher.) The SketchUp Opacity settings under the Paint Bucket do not affect a texture's transparency.

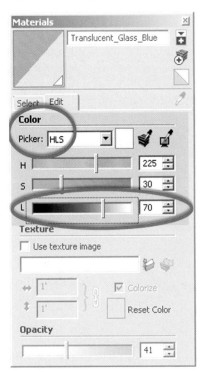

Fig. 27.25: Edit is selected in the SketchUp Paint Bucket menu. HLS is used to control how transparent water and glass materials will appear once rendered in Shaderlight.

The important value in HLS (Hue, Lightness, and Saturation) is the lightness. When the transparency or translucent material presets are used, lightness acts exactly the same as SketchUp opacity does: the higher the values, the greater the transparency. Similar to SketchUp's opacity, lightness ranges from 0 percent (solid) to 100 percent (completely see-through).

SketchUp surfaces have two sides. Typically, this has no bearing on textures and rendering. However, with glass and water, the texture should be applied to both sides of the material (Fig. 27.26).

Glass

Set the glass materials Type to Transparency and set Finish to THIN_GLASS. Adjust the Lightness value (L) in the HLS settings to achieve the following results (Fig. 27.27):

▶ **Reflective Glass**: 30 to 49

▶ **Mostly Reflective** : 50 to 75

▶ **Slightly Reflective**: 76 to 90

▶ **Mostly Transparent**: 91 to 96

▶ **Transparent**: 96 to 100

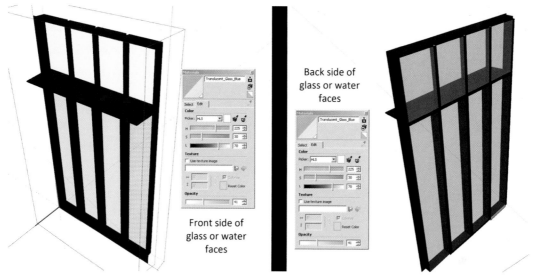

Fig. 27.26: Apply glass and water textures to both sides of SketchUp faces to achieve the best result.

Fig. 27.27: In the HLS settings applied to the windows, the L value is 40 (left), the L value is 75 (middle), and the L value is 100, making the windows almost completely transparent.

There are additional transparency finishes, including Thick_Glass, Frosted_Glass, and Liquid. Experiment with these settings to learn how and when to apply them. Thin_Glass should work for most glass materials.

Water

Rendered water ranges from clear and transparent, to calm but reflective, to turbulent. To achieve those results, practice with these three approaches and settings.

Water Basin

If you want to model water, you'll have to model the container holding the water—be it a pool, a cup, a lake, or a basin (Fig. 27.28). The sides and bottom provide context when you peer through the water. Use lighter colors for the container surfaces. Dark textures might overwhelm the water material. Place the water texture (surface) in the container, elevated above the bottom (Fig. 27.29).

Fig. 27.28: The water basin is modeled and includes a bottom. When the water is rendered and made transparent, the bottom of the basin will become visible.

Fig. 27.29: The water texture/surface is placed above the bottom of the basin.

Transparent Water

These settings are applicable for transparent water. You can achieve two types of results: calm and reflective, and turbulent and reflective. In both situations, the water surface is transparent. The settings for both types are relatively identical. The difference is in the use of a solid, nontextured surface to create a calm and reflective water surface.

Calm, Transparent, and Reflective   The key to this method is using a solid color for the water surface. No texture image is required (Fig. 27.30, Fig. 27.31, Fig. 27.32).

▶ **Type**: Transparency

▶ **Finish**: Liquid

▶ **HLS - Lightness (L)**: 60 to 100. The higher the number, the more transparent (lighter) but less reflective the water will be.

▶ **Bump**: 0

Fig. 27.30: For calm, reflective water, no texture image is required, just a solid surface.

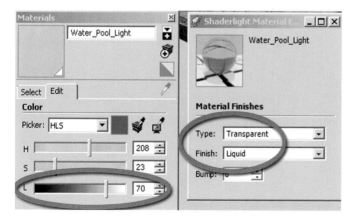

Fig. 27.31: The L value is set to 70, giving the water surface both transparent and reflective qualities (left). The Shaderlight settings for the water surface are (right).

Fig. 27.32: The resulting render of the calm, reflective water

Turbulent, Transparent, and Reflective This method does require the use of water texture. CG Textures.com has a large variety of water surfaces that you can download. In this case, a bump value is provided, which helps enhance the water ripples and create the sense of movement across the top surface of the water (Fig. 27.33, Fig. 27.34).

▶ **Type**: Transparency

▶ **Finish**: Liquid

▶ **HLS - Lightness (L)**: 50 to 70. The higher the number, the more transparent (lighter) but less reflective the water will be.

▶ **BUMP**: +5 to +7

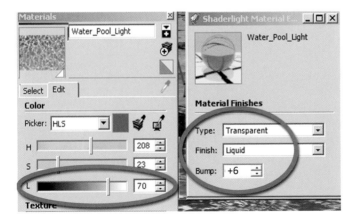

Fig. 27.33: In the SketchUp and Shaderlight settings for turbulent but reflective water, a texture is used for the water (as shown in Fig. 27.29 above).

Fig. 27.34: The resulting render displays turbulent and reflective water.

Turbulent and Reflective Water

The method used for reflective water requires the use of a water texture. Turbulent and reflective water uses a different setting. In this case, the water will not be transparent, so water texture is required. This method uses a Shiny type with a Smooth finish. However, you might need to adjust the finish to be more or less reflective (Fig. 27.35, Fig. 27.36).

- ▶ **Type**: Shiny
- ▶ **Finish**: Smooth_2 (experiment with other finishes under Shiny as needed)
- ▶ **Bump**: 0 to +5
- ▶ **HLS - Lightness (L)**: Range 35 to 55

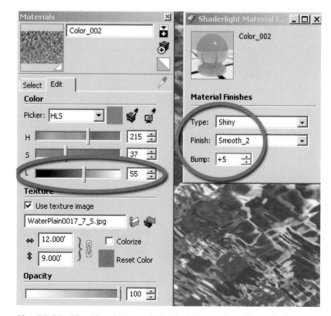

Fig. 27.35: The SketchUp and Shaderlight settings for turbulent water are used when water texture is required.

Fig. 27.36: The resulting rendering of turbulent water.

Shaderlight Exterior Lighting and Backdrops

Shaderlight's diverse exterior lighting options range from Physical Sky, which references the SketchUp Shadow menu settings, to preset and preinstalled HDRI. This chapter explores these options for setting exterior light in Shaderlight (Fig. 28.1).

Fig. 28.1: The alley render

The topics discussed include the following:

- **SketchUp Shadow Menu**: The SketchUp Shadow menu is used to set light strength and direction. Part 4 reviews how to use this menu in detail.

- **SketchUp Dark Slider**: The SketchUp Shadow Menu Dark slider (see Part 4) affects lighting in Shaderlight. The Dark slider acts as a secondary exposure setting. If not properly set, the Dark slider can cause some improper results.

- **Physical Sky/SketchUp Sky**: These two options reference the SketchUp Shadow menu to establish light settings. In order to use the SketchUp Sky option, you must have SketchUp Shadows turned On when rendering. You should not use SketchUp Sky for lighting; focus on Physical Sky and HDRI options.

- **Image-Based Lighting/HDRI:** Shaderlight comes with preinstalled image-based lighting options. These options sample light for photographs and re-create the light in rendered scenes. See Chapter 25, for a general description of image-based lighting.

- **Backgrounds:** Shaderlight provides an easy-to-use option for inserting background images into the render. Once placed, they appear in the backdrop of the rendered image.

- **Auto Exposure/Exposure:** Never use the Auto Exposure setting in Shaderlight. You should always manually set the exposure when you generate renderings.

SketchUp Dark Slider

The Dark slider on the SketchUp menu affects all of the Shaderlight exterior lighting options. In order to generate consistent results, it's imperative that it be set and then left alone. Otherwise, images will appear over- or underexposed. A good practice is to position the Dark slider at 35 (as shown in the various figures) regardless of which lighting option is used (Fig. 28.2).

Fig. 28.2: The SketchUp Shadow Menu Dark slider is set to 35.

The only way that lighting brightness should be adjusted is by using the Exposure option in the Shaderlight Render settings under Lighting. In this chapter, the specific exposure settings are reviewed with each lighting type. The Light slider in the SketchUp Shadow Menu has no effect on rendering lighting or exposure.

Physical Sky

The Physical Sky setting is the quickest way to get exterior lighting results. For most users utilizing Physical Sky will be enough. The following settings yield good, consistent results (Fig. 28.3):

- ▶ **SketchUp Shadow Menu**: Time: Between 10:30 AM and 2:30 PM.
- ▶ **SketchUp Shadow Menu**: Date: Between August and September.
- ▶ **SketchUp Shadow Menu**: Set Dark slider to 35.
- ▶ **Shaderlight Render Settings**: Under Lighting, select Physical Sky.
- ▶ **Shaderlight Render Settings**: Make sure that Auto Exposure under the Shaderlight options is *unchecked* and Exposure is set to zero (0).
- ▶ **SketchUp Solar North**: Adjust SketchUp Solar North for the best lighting results.

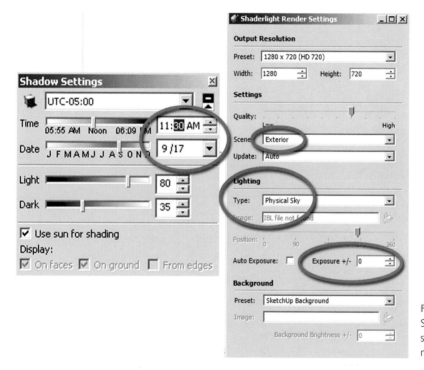

Fig. 28.3: These Physical Sky and SketchUp Shadow settings are useful for many exterior renderings.

You can use different Time settings but with a caveat. Earlier or later times will cause less light to be generated in the rendering, which will cause it to appear somewhat flat. Adjusting the Date (month) yields more or less light, depending on the month. For example, summer months produce more light and greater exposure than winter months, which have less light, longer shadows, and less exposure.

HDRI Lighting

As indicated in Chapter 24, it takes some practice to master HDRI lighting. Start with Physical Sky settings if you are unsure of how to use image-based lighting.

Shaderlight has three options under lighting for IBL: Preset, Moofe, and Custom (Fig. 28.4). Preset and Moofe are sets of preinstalled HDRI images (Fig. 28.5). Once either of them is selected, additional choices will become available under Type → Image, allowing you to select a specific HDRI. Select Custom to insert your own HDRI image into Shaderlight.

The actual photo image of the HDRI can be exposed in the rendering. To do this, use the Background settings at the bottom of the Shaderlight Render Settings menu.

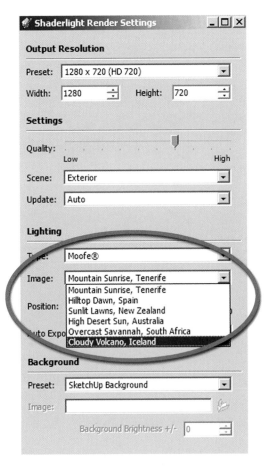

Preset, Moofe, and Custom

The HDRI options under Preset and Moofe include descriptive names indicating the type of light the HDRI will produce. For example, under Preset the option of Business Park Daytime indicates the image content (a photo of a business park) and the lighting type (daytime).

Preset

The Preset image options provide decent lighting. There are four HDRI types (Fig. 28.6). They are

▶ Business Park Daytime

▶ Golf Course

▶ London Morning (Fig. 28.7)

▶ Meeting Room

Fig. 28.4: The HDRI Moofe options in the Shaderlight Lighting menu

Fig. 28.5: An HDRI image that comes with Shaderlight

Lighting

Type:	Preset ▾
Image:	Business Park Daytime ▾
	Business Park Daytime
Position:	Golf Course Evening
	London Morning
	Meeting Room
Auto Exposure: ☐	Exposure +/- 0 ⬍

Lighting

Type:	Moofe® ▾
Image:	Mountain Sunrise, Tenerife ▾
	Mountain Sunrise, Tenerife
Position:	Hilltop Dawn, Spain
	Sunlit Lawns, New Zealand
	High Desert Sun, Australia
Auto Expo	Overcast Savannah, South Africa
	Cloudy Volcano, Iceland

Fig. 28.6: The preset HDRI options (top); Moofe HDRI options (bottom)

Fig. 28.7: Rendering completed using the London Morning Preset HDRI

Moofe

Moofe is a company that specializes in HDRI images (www.moofe.com). Shaderlight purchased the rights from Moofe to include some of these images in the IRP. The Moofe options are excellent alternatives to Physical Sky lighting (Fig. 28.6). Using the Custom options, you can sample additional HDRI images from Moofe and insert them into Shaderlight.

As mentioned, the image name indicates the photo content and lighting type. The HDRI images available under Moofe include:

- ▶ Mountain Sunrise
- ▶ Hilltop Dawn (Fig. 28.8)
- ▶ Sunlit Lawns
- ▶ High Desert Sun
- ▶ Overcast Savannah
- ▶ Cloudy Volcano (Fig. 28.9)

Custom

If you have downloaded any HDRI images, you can insert them into Shaderlight. Select Custom to access a browse option to select and insert the image.

Setting HDRI Values

The HDRI options do not use the same settings as Physical Sky (Fig. 28.10):

Fig. 28.8: Moofe Hilltop Dawn HDRI lighting used in the rendering

Fig. 28.9: Moofe Cloudy Volcano HDRI lighting used in the rendering

The differences between using them include:

▶ The HDRI images do not reference the SketchUp Shadow menu. The direction and position need to be set in Shaderlight.

▶ The exposure settings differ for each HDRI image.

▶ Draft renders must be run to assess the previous factors.

Image Type

Every HDRI image will have a different lighting output and appearance. The only way to assess the lighting is to try the various options. Make sure to spend some time experimenting with multiple HDRI types, be they preset, Moofe, or custom.

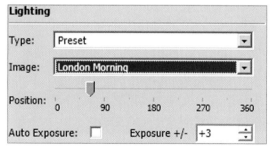

Fig. 28.10: In these typical HDRI settings, the exposure is set to +3, which set the correct lighting from the HDRI.

Exposure

Adjusting the exposure is the key to obtaining the results you want. Exposure values for HDRI images will have different ranges. Your initial values should start at around 3 and range as high as 5.5, and include all values in-between (ex. 3.6, 3.7, 3.8 etc...). At least for now, an exposure setting of +3 works well with the Moofe and presets available as part of Shaderlight. If +3 does not work, adjust the exposure values for the best result.

Rotating

The Position slider, which is part of the Shaderlight Render Settings menu under Lighting, is used to adjust the direction and source light from the HDRI. The slider ranges from 0 to 360 degrees (Fig. 28.11). It functions the same way the SketchUp Solar North tool works (Chapter 17). The slider rotates the light source from the HDRI around the model.

Rotate the HDRI position to get good lighting. For many renders, the light will be flat or dark if you don't adjust the initial rotation (Fig. 28.12). Adjust the rotation angle by 90-degree increments. Once you've achieved good exposure, further adjust the angle by smaller increments to fine-tune the light (Fig. 28.13).

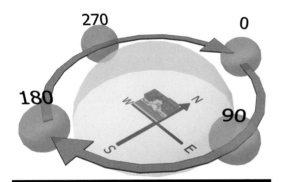

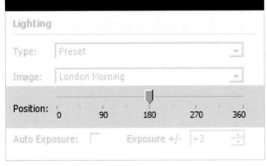

Fig. 28.11: To rotate the HDRI lighting 360 degrees, use the Position slider.

Draft Render Assessment

To assess HDRI lighting, run draft renders and make sure Shaderlight light is set for Dynamic rendering: select Settings → Update → Auto. Run low-quality draft renders with low resolution and with model detail turned off. See Chapter 20 for complete Draft settings and recommendations.

Once the render starts to process and display in the preview window, adjust the HDRI image type, position, and exposure. Any adjustments will cause the render to update and display the new settings. This is an effective way to assess the light settings.

The HDRI content image, the *actual* photo, can be set to display in the rendering using the options outlined in the next section.

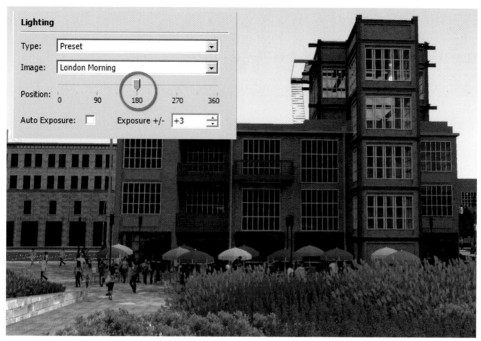

Fig. 28.12: In this London-morning Moofe render, the light from the HDRI originates from an angle that does not provide enough light for the scene. The Position slider needs to be adjusted to obtain a better result.

Fig. 28.13: Once the Position slider is adjusted, the HDRI provides good lighting for the scene.

Background and Backdrops

The Shaderlight Render settings include an option to insert backgrounds and backdrops. Three options are available under Background. Inserting custom backgrounds can be useful, but mastering the technique takes practice and the right image. If you're new to rendering and Shaderlight, use the default setting of SketchUp Background to add background during postprocessing (see Part 7).

SketchUp Background

This is the default option. The rendering will reference the SketchUp Style menu (Window → Styles → Edit → Background Settings), causing the SketchUp Sky color to display in the rendering (Fig. 28.14). If no sky is set in the background, the sky will render white.

Lighting Environment

The rendering will display the image of the specified HDRI option (Fig. 28.15). You can determine this using the Preset, Moofe, or custom settings as discussed. For example, if Preset → London Morning is selected, the actual HDRI photo will display. However, this might not always yield the results you want, as shown in the example (Fig. 28.16). In these cases, use the Custom feature as outlined next.

Custom

The Custom option allows you to insert images with various image formats (Fig. 28.17). These images will appear in the background of the rendering. Exterior renderings benefit from sky and cloud, city backdrops, and similar photos.

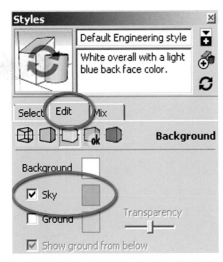

Fig. 28.14: The Sky option is checked in the SketchUp Style menu, causing the sky to render in blue.

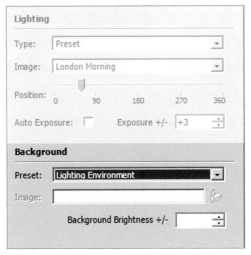

Fig. 28.15: Setting Lighting Environment will cause the HDRI image to be exposed in the background of the render.

Fig. 28.16: The London Morning HDRI is exposed in the background. However, that is not the desired result.

Fig. 28.17: Using the Background → Custom option, you can insert your own image background that will appear when the model is rendered.

Background Brightness

Once a background is inserted or revealed, the Background Brightness needs to be set (Fig. 28.18). This value exposes the image. The goal is to match the exposure of the background to the rendering itself (Fig. 28.19). The value will usually start at a base of 1 and range to 3.5. The type of image being used determines the brightness value.

Background Brightness can be adjusted during the draft-rendering process. This allows the brightness to be assessed dynamically, similarly to the way HDRI settings are assessed.

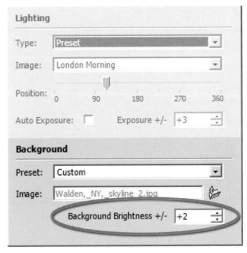

Fig. 28.18: The inserted custom background will need to use a Brightness value set to match the overall lighting of the rendering.

Fig. 28.19: The inserted custom background renders with the scene.

Shaderlight Simulated Lighting

Shaderlight offers a variety of options that include unique lighting elements not found in other IRPs. Shaderlight's simulated light settings are a bit more complex than most but not hard to master. This chapter describes the different lighting types and specific settings used to establish lighting for rendering (Fig. 29.1).

This chapter is designed to be used in conjunction with Chapter 20 and Chapter 24, which provide overviews and strategies for using simulated lighting. The material in these chapters is key to working with Shaderlight (and other IRP) simulated lighting options.

Fig. 29.1: Shaderlight simulated lighting rendering

Many of the rendered images in this chapter were completed in a test model. The model consisted of a floor, walls, associated textures, furnishings, and various lights. Using a test model is an ideal way to learn how to use a specific IRP's lighting system. The results are easily transferable to other models and allow users to quickly test light placement and settings.

Shaderlight Lighting Options

Shaderlight uses the same basic lighting system outlined in Chapter 24. This includes using point, spot, IES lighting profiles, and light-emitting materials (LEM) (Fig. 29.2, Fig. 29.3). The placement and use of those lights follows the universal method outlined in that chapter. Shaderlight also included two unique options:

- ▶ Skylight portal
- ▶ Area lights

Skylight Portals

This unique feature offers an exciting way to light a scene. The skylight is a square surface light placed over windows and open portals. It samples exterior lighting and streams it into the scene, just as with a real skylight or window (Fig. 29.6, Fig. 29.7).

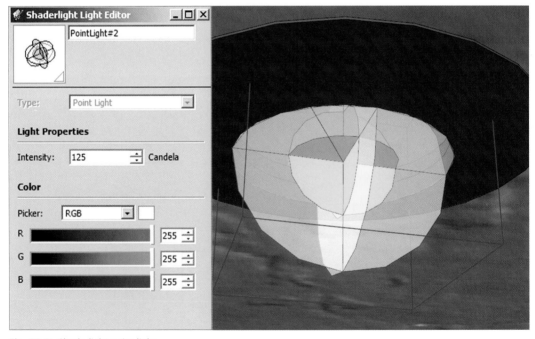

Fig. 29.2: Shaderlight point light

Fig. 29.3: Rendering of point light

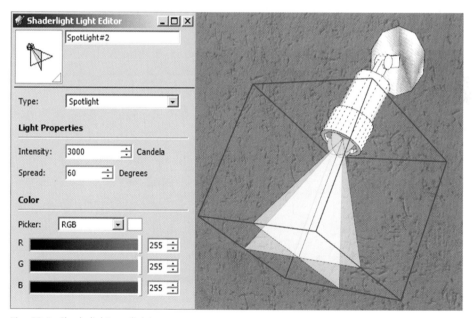

Fig. 29.4: Shaderlight spotlight

Fig. 29.5: Rendering of spotlight

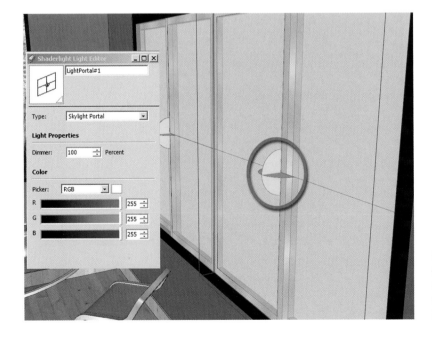

Fig. 29.6: The red circle over the geometry of the portal indicates the direction the light will emit.

Fig. 29.7: Skylight Portal rendering

Unlike all of the other lighting in the model, the Skylight Portal option actually uses the SketchUp Shadow menu to set the lighting. In essence, it conveys and focuses exterior lighting.

When you're positioning the Skylight portal into the model, you should consider the following points:

- ▶ The Skylight Portal square *must* be placed onto a surface that contains a transparent material such as window glass or an unobstructed opening; otherwise, it won't be able to sample the light and stream it into the scene (Fig. 29.6). Place the Skylight portal to cover the entire window or portal opening.

- ▶ The Skylight portal must be oriented in the right direction. The Skylight portal has two directions: one side emits light that needs to face into the scene, and the other side, which samples light and faces away from the scene. The Skylight Portal geometry indicates which side is which by including emitter geometry on the side that should face the scene (Fig. 29.6). You might need to rotate the Skylight portal to face the right direction. Use the Move tool's crosshairs to rotate the light (Fig. 29.8).

Area Lights

Not to be confused with a point light, the Shaderlight *area light* is a square surface light similar to the skylight. Whereas point lights mimic lightbulbs, producing light from a single point, area lights produce a light across the entire surface. Area lights for Shaderlight do what LEMs accomplish in other IRP programs (Fig. 29.9, Fig. 29.10). These lights are great to use for ceiling lights, acting like fluorescent tube lighting and strip lighting.

Fig. 29.8: Use the Move tool's Rotate option to rotate the Skylight portal into the correct position facing into the scene after it's placed.

Fig. 29.9: The Shaderlight area light is placed inside the fixture.

Fig. 29.10: Shaderlight area light rendering

Light Skylight Portals, area lights have an emitting side that needs to be placed facing the right direction. Placing area lights can be tricky because they need reference geometry (see Chapter 24) to be accurately placed.

Shaderlight does provide the option to use LEMs. However, they do not actually give off light but act as glowing surfaces. Use area lights instead.

Light Editor

The Shaderlight Light Editor is activated from the Shaderlight main menu (Fig. 29.11). You can select the various lighting options from the Type pull-down menu. Once you've picked a lighting option, the SketchUp cursor turns into a lightbulb, allowing you place the light emitter.

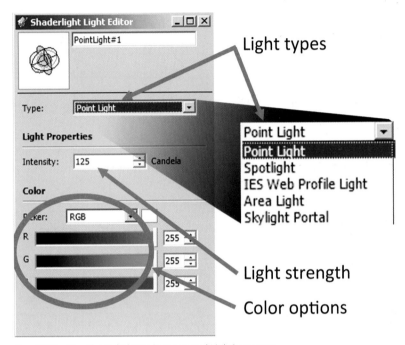

Fig. 29.11: The Shaderlight main menu and Lighting menu

The Light Editor has three functions:

- ▶ To select and place a lighting option
- ▶ To set light strength
- ▶ To set light color

Light Strength

The strength of an emitter is measured by Shaderlight in *candelas* (Fig. 29.12). Candelas represent units of luminous intensity. For example, a single Shaderlight candle is equal to one real-world candela (hence the name). One candela is equivalent to 1.2 watts. In Shaderlight, the default Candela setting for lights is 125. This is equivalent to a 100-watt lightbulb. However, exposure plays a big part in lighting up a scene, working in tandem with the Candela setting. Some specific candela strengths and Exposure settings are provided in the following sections to help you get started with lighting.

Before you place an emitter, and after you select a light Type, enter the desired candela value to set the light strength. The settings provided are initial baseline candela values for the different light types.

Once an emitter is placed in the model, its candela strength can be adjusted. Simply select the emitter (with the SketchUp Select tool) and open the Shaderlight Lighting menu. With the emitter selected, change the candela value; you can edit only one emitter at a time.

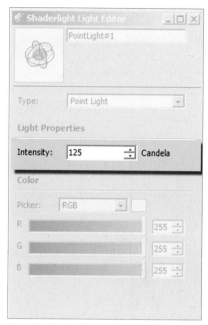

Color

Two color options are available for lighting. The first option sets the light's color. The second option allows you to edit the color using RGB or HSB settings. You can edit a light's color and its Candela setting after the light has been placed. Most settings retain the default color of white. Experiment with Color settings once you are comfortable working with simulated lights.

Fig. 29.12: The Shaderlight Candela menu option

Shaderlight Render Settings

To render simulated lighting, you'll need to set specific options in the Shaderlight Render Settings menu (Fig. 29.13).

Use the settings as described here:

1. Under the Scene options, set the option to Interior (GI).

2. Under Update, keep Auto. The Update option will be changed to Tile based on the quality level of the rendering.

3. Under the Lighting section, from the pull-down menu, select Artificial Lights Only. Skylight Portals will use different settings.

4. From the pull-down menu under Background Preset, select Lighting Environment.

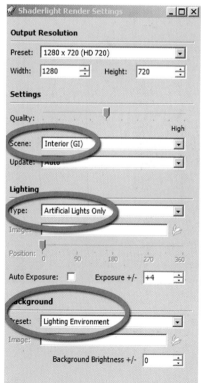

Fig. 29.13: The Shaderlight Render Settings menu used to render simulated lighting

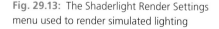

Quality Settings

The specific Quality settings you'll need depend on where you are in the iterative rendering process, as outlined in Chapter 20 and Chapter 26. When you're running drafts, do not set Quality above 60 percent, because this will automatically set Shaderlight to rendering in Tiled mode (Fig. 29.14). This can take a considerable amount of time when you're rendering with lights.

However, for final renderings, you'll need 70 to 100 percent Quality in order for the lighting scenes to render correctly. In most cases, for final renderings, you'll set the Quality to 100 percent (Fig. 29.15).

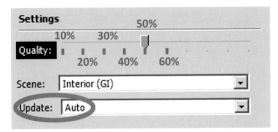

Fig. 29.14: Quality Settings under 60 percent   Fig. 29.15: Quality Settings over 70 percent

Lighting Settings

The following section details settings for different light types. It focuses on Candela strengths and Exposure settings. These settings work in tandem to achieve the desired output image.

Exposure

In order to achieve good rendering results for simulated lighting, you'll need to adjust the Exposure setting (under Lighting). For *most* simulated lighting renderings, Exposure will range from +1 to +7. Determining the value is one of your most important tasks during the draft-to-final iterative process.

However, the Exposure setting is easy to work with: you can adjust it up or down and it will update the image automatically *without* restarting the rendering process. You can do this even

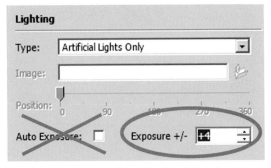

Fig. 29.16: Exposure setting in the Shaderlight Render Settings menu

after the render is complete. This makes it easy to assess the amount of exposure needed for an image prior to setting the final render.

The exposure dynamic update works only if Update is set to Auto. Once Quality is set between 70 and 100 percent (typical for final renderings), Update will change to Tile mode and prevent all dynamic rendering/updating, including exposure.

As with Physical Sky renderings, do not use Auto Exposure. You will need to set the exposure manually (Fig. 29.16).

Candela Strength and Exposure

You'll need to perform a balancing act with the values between Candela and Exposure. Each light type will have a set Candela value; however, even with high Candela values, your scenes might render dark. Therefore, the approach outlined here provides baseline Candela values for lights in tandem with a range of exposures.

Setting a baseline for all of the lighting allows the exposure to be adjusted in a way that takes into account all of the light types. This allows you to have a combination of lighting types, each using a baseline value while the exposure can be quickly adjusted for best result. Although your final goal might be to represent lighting in a scene as accurately to real-world conditions as possible, the method used here provides settings to create clear renderings.

Point Lights

For point lights, use the base setting of 125 Candelas. Candela can be increased in increments ranging upward as needed to allow brighter emitters. The baseline works well when Exposure is set between +3 and +7 (Fig. 29.17, Fig. 29.18, Fig. 29.19, Fig. 29.20). Fig. 29.19 and Fig. 29.20 show how setting a high exposure brings out the desired lighting. Fig. 29.18 and Fig. 29.19 show that even with higher exposure settings, the light appears too dark. Part of the reason is that more lights are needed. Ceiling lights are added, each with a Candela strength of 200. The resulting renderings are assigned Exposure settings of 5 (Fig. 29.21) and 7 (Fig. 29.22).

Fig. 29.17: Each point light was set to 125 candelas.

Fig. 29.18: In this rendering, Exposure is set to +3.

Fig. 29.19: In the rendering, Exposure is set to +5.

Three ceiling lights are added at 200 candelas each.

Fig. 29.20: Additional point lights are placed.

Fig. 29.21: In this rendering, Exposure is set to +5.

Fig. 29.22: In this rendering, Exposure is set to +7.

Spotlights

In comparison to point lights, spotlights need to have a high Candela value. A good baseline value is 3000 and can range even higher. These high values will ensure that the spotlights function well with Point Light Candela values and overall exposures ranging from +2 to +7. Spotlights have a second value called Spread. *Spread* defines the radius of the cone of light as it emits from the spotlight. The default value is 60 degrees (Fig. 29.23, Fig. 29.24, Fig. 29.25, Fig. 29.26).

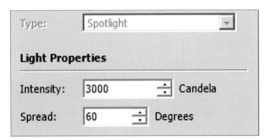

Fig. 29.23: Spotlight In the Shaderlight Lighting menu. A Candela of 3000 is a good baseline for spotlights.

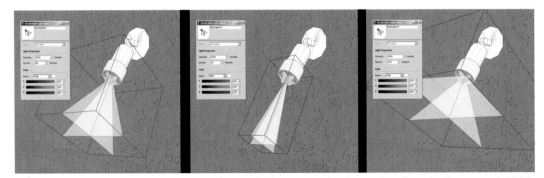

Fig. 29.24: The Spotlight Spread starts at 60 degrees (left). The spread radius can be adjusted to be narrow (middle) or wide (right) by adjusting the Spread value.

Part 6: Shaderlight by ArtVPS

Fig. 29.25: Each spotlight has a value of 3000 but varying degrees of spread.

Fig. 29.26: The resulting rendering with the Exposure level set to 5

Area Lights

Area lights have high Candela settings to ensure they render properly. As with spotlights, a baseline of 3000 is a good place to start. In Fig. 29.27 the area lights are placed into the fixture (Fig. 29.9). The rendered scene uses an Exposure setting of +5 to achieve good lighting results (Fig. 29.28)

Fig. 29.27: Area lights highlighted in blue (left); area lights placed in SketchUp (right)

Fig. 29.28: Rendering of area lights

Combined Lighting

By using the point-light and spotlight baseline values and setting the exposure range between +5 and +7, you can combine the lights in a single render (Fig. 29.29, Fig. 29.30). Area lighting could have been easily inserted and would also have fit within the settings.

Fig. 29.29: The red circles indicate point lights; the blue circles represent spotlights.

Fig. 29.30: Rendering of the combined point and spotlights

Postproduction

Performing the postproduction process in a photo-editing program will do much to enhance your final images and you should include it as an essential part of your rendering process (see Chapter 31). Using the Photoshop → Levels tool, you can expose and adjust the simulated lighting for better effects. In addition, during postproduction, you can use the Lens Flare filter to create the illusion of light sources.

Skylight Portal

Skylight Portal uses specific settings to achieve lighting. First, lighting must be set using the SketchUp Shadow menu (see Part 4). Light should be directed to stream through openings and portals, especially the portals that have a Skylight portal placed over them (Fig 29.31). The Shadow menu does not have to cast light into the scene because the Skylight portal will sample the ambient light established by SketchUp. However, it does provide a nice, if not unique, effect that most other IRPs do not currently have.

Next, you should set the Shaderlight Render Setting menu to Interior (GI) under Scene and then set Physical Sky to Lighting. You could also use the native Shaderlight HDRI images (Moofe and Preset). Set Exposure to 0. Increasing the exposure will dramatically brighten the scene. In the rendered scene, a background was included because the scene is visible through the portals/windows (Fig. 29.32, Fig. 29.33).

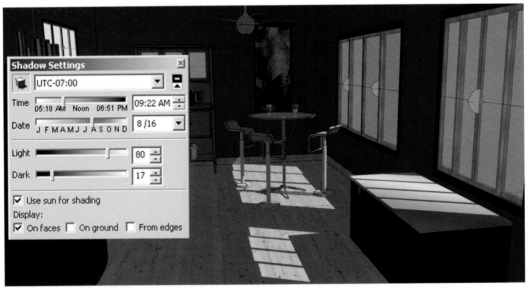

Fig. 29.31: Using the SketchUp Shadow Menu, the lighting is set to stream through the window. This enhances the quality of lighting brought into the scene by the Skylight portal.

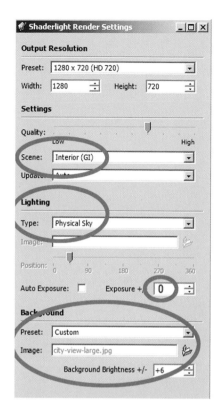

Fig. 29.32: The Shaderlight Render Settings menu must be set to Interior (GI) Physical Sky for lighting, and 0 for Exposure. You should use a background or include one during postproduction.

Fig. 29.33: The resulting rendering matches the light settings established in Fig. 29.31.

Dimmer

Instead of using a Candela setting, Skylight Portal has a Dimmer setting. Keeping it at default of a 100 should suffice for most needs (Fig. 29.34). However, if not enough light is entering the scene through the portal, increase the dimmer by increments of 50 or conversely increase the Exposure to +1.

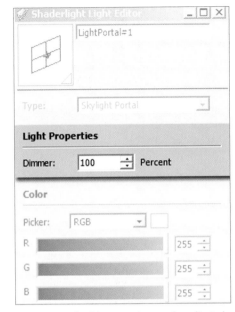

Fig. 29.34: The Dimmer value can be adjusted to decrease or increase the amount of light brought into the scene with the skylight.

Shaderlight Special Features

S haderlight has several unique features (including batch rendering, proxy components, and creating clay renders) that affect the rendering process. This chapter explores the various features outlined here:

- ▶ **Dynamic Preview**: Shaderlight allows users to adjust the camera view, textures, lighting, and resolution while the render is being processed. This feature can be leveraged for batch rendering.

- ▶ **Animation**: Using the Animation menu, Shaderlight can generate animated fly-throughs. Rendered animations are a separate topic not reviewed in this book. However, the Shaderlight Animation tools are ideal for batch rendering.

- ▶ **Batch Rendering**: Dynamic preview and the Animation tools provide the ability to *batch render* (create multiple images quickly).

- ▶ **ReplaceMe**: ReplaceMe is a proxy render feature. Any existing component in a model can be linked to an external component model file. During rendering, the object in the model is swapped with the linked file, rendering the linked object instead of the one in the model.

- ▶ **Chalk Renders**: The Chalk Render options are Shaderlight's version of clay renderings.

Batch Rendering

Batch rendering refers to the ability for Shaderlight to generate multiple renderings in a single render session (Fig. 30.1). The batch rendering process leverages Shaderlight's dynamic preview and Animation tools. You can take two different approaches to batch rendering. The first approach is to do it manually. The second approach automates the process, leading to a leave-it-and-render system. Approach 2 builds on the approach 1, so make sure you understand both.

Fig. 30.1: All six images were created in a single rendering session.

The key to batch rendering is to use preexisting SketchUp scenes (Fig. 30.2). If you click on a new scene during the rendering process, Shaderlight will update the dynamic preview based on the scene's camera view. Cycling through multiple scenes and saving them as they complete is at the heart of the batch render process.

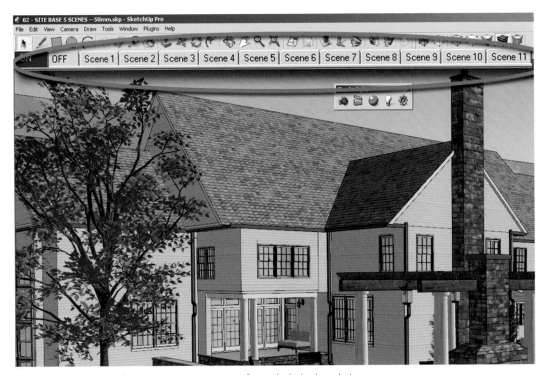

Fig. 30.2: Use the SketchUp menu to create scenes for each desired rendering.

The batch process skips two time-consuming aspects of rendering: uploading the model and processing it for display. Instead, Shaderlight simply renders whatever camera view is set in SketchUp without having to reprocess the model for every scene. For large models, this can save you a great deal of time.

Manual Scenes

If you use the manual approach, you'll have to cycle through the scenes and save the renders when they process. Here are the steps to the manual approach:

1. Create a series of scenes with saved camera views in SketchUp. Create as many scenes as desired.

2. Make sure the Shaderlight Render setting under Update is set to Auto (Fig. 30.3).

3. Make sure all of the lighting and other rendering options (Texture Value, Resolution) are set.

4. Click the Render button.

5. Wait for the render to display and finish processing the first scene. At any time during the process, you can click File in the preview window and select Save As to save the scene (Fig. 30.4).

6. Once the initial render is complete, go back to SketchUp and click the next scene. SketchUp will adjust the camera to the saved view. Do not close the Shaderlight window. That would halt the rendering process.

7. Shaderlight will immediately start to render the new camera position. Wait for it to complete and save the scene (Fig. 30.5).

8. Repeat the process with other scenes.

Fig. 30.3: In Shaderlight's Render Settings menu, Update must be set to Auto.

Consider the following points when you use the manual approach:

▶ **Save Anytime**: As mentioned, a render can be saved at any time during the process. You don't always need to let a render complete before you move on to the next scene. This is especially true when you're doing draft renders for assessment.

▶ **Sixty-Percent Quality**: Shaderlight Quality cannot be set greater than 60 percent (six notches to the right). If it is, dynamic preview will be turned off (Fig. 30.6).

Fig. 30.4: When the first render in finished, save the completed image.

Fig. 30.5: In SketchUp, click on the next scene you want to render. SketchUp will reposition the view, and Shaderlight will immediately start to process the rendering.

- **Simulated Lighting**: Many simulated lighting renders need to have the Quality set between 70 percent and 100 percent, especially final renders. In such cases, use the automated approach instead. The manual process is still useful for simulated lighting draft renders to assess the scenes.

- **No Dynamic Preview**: At times, dynamic preview won't update the camera view of a new scene. If this happens, start the process over.

- **Layer Visibility**: You will not be able to toggle on or off components on layers and let them update in the render. What is visible when the process is started will be visible through all of the batch scene renders.

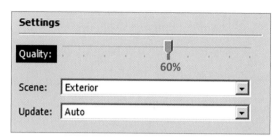

Fig. 30.6: The process will not work if you set the render quality above 60 percent.

Automated Batch Rendering

The second approach utilizes Shaderlight's Animation menu to automate the process. This is an ideal way to generate final renderings that take longer to produce at higher quality for both exterior and simulated lighting models. The process requires three set-up steps.

1. Adjust the SketchUp settings (Fig. 30.7).

   a. Create the desired scenes with saved camera views
   b. Go to View → Animations → Settings. This will open Model Info under the Animation tab.
   c. Enable Scene Transitions and set it to 1 second.
   d. Set Scene Delay to 0.
   e. Close the menu.

2. Adjust the Render settings.

   These settings are subjective and depend on what you are trying to render. If you're doing this for draft renders, set the quality and resolution lower. Here are some setting suggestions to demonstrate the process:

   - Open the Shaderlight Render Settings menu.
   - Set the resolution, lighting, and quality as done for typical rendering.

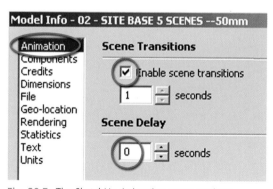

Fig. 30.7: The SketchUp Animation menu settings

▶ If you are doing final exterior renders, set the quality between 60 and 100 percent.

▶ For final simulated lighting, set the quality between 70 and 100 percent.

3. Use the Shaderlight Animation menu (Fig. 30.8).

   a. Set the Shaderlight Animation menu for automated batch rendering.

   b. Click and open the Shaderlight Animation menu.

   c. Under Settings → Save To, click on the Browse button (Fig. 30.8, no. 1)

   d. Navigate to where you want the images saved.

   e. Select a File type. Choose one of three options (PNG, JPEG, or TIFF) (Fig. 30.8, no. 2).

   f. Go to Frame Rate and select 1 from the pull-down menu (Fig. 30.8, no. 3).

   g. Check Duration (the number of frames should equal the number of SketchUp scenes).

   h. Leave all of the other settings as is.

   i. Click Render. Shaderlight will start to process the model and automate the renderings (Fig. 30.8, no. 4).

   j. The renders will appear in the designated folder.

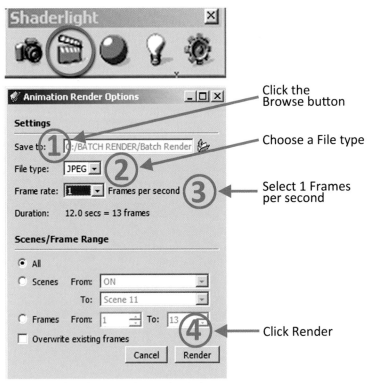

Fig. 30.8: Select the Animation Render Options in the Shaderlight menu.

ReplaceMe

The ReplaceMe feature allows you to perform *proxy rendering,* which uses the render engine to swap a version of a component in the model with an external component file. For example, a 2D tree, copied and placed in the model, could be linked to a 3D detail tree component located on the computer hard drive. When the render is started, Shaderlight will swap the 2D tree and render the linked 3D tree in its place. It won't swap out the objects in the model, only in the generated graphic.

This feature is useful for vegetation models. You can populate your model with simple, low-face-count components that won't impede SketchUp's performance when visible. For example, you could place a swath of 2D plants in a model with all of them linked to 3D detailed counter-parts. SketchUp computer performance would be maintained and the rendering would contain high-quality vegetation models.

Any type of component can be linked to another. You just need to know the location of component models to be linked. Once a component in the model is linked to an external component, all versions of that component in the model will be linked and replaced.

The linking process is as follows (Fig. 30.9):

1. In the mode, select the component to be replaced.
2. Go to Plugins and select Shaderlight for SketchUp → ReplaceMe Creator (Fig. 30.10).
3. The Replace Me Creator menu will appear. The name of the selected component will be listed (Fig. 30.11).

Fig. 30.9: The 2D trees and shrubs (SketchUp)

4. Check the ReplaceMe box.

5. Next to Source, click on the Browse button and navigate to the replacement component (Fig. 30.12).

6. Complete this process for all of the components to be replaced.

7. Return to Plugins → Shaderlight For SketchUp and select Enable ReplaceMe (Fig. 30.13). This will activate the Replace Me feature when you render.

8. Close the menu and start the render (Fig. 30.14).

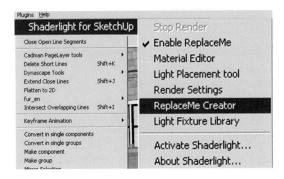

Fig. 30.10: From the Shaderlight secondary menu, select ReplaceMe Creator.

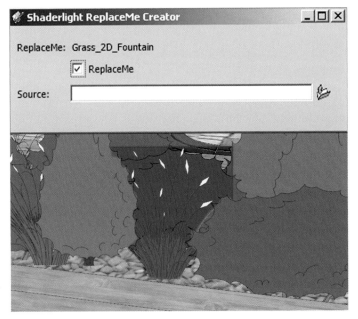

Fig. 30.11: Select the 2D plant to be replaced.

Fig. 30.12: Select the Browse button from ReplaceMe Creator, navigate to the location of the 3D plant, select the plant component, and click Open.

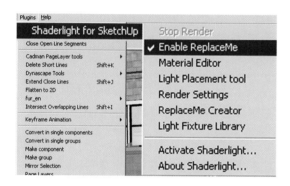

Fig. 30.13: Go back to the Shaderlight secondary menu and make sure Enable Replace Me is checked.

The size and number of faces of linked components will still affect the rendering process. For example, placing one hundred 2D trees in SketchUp and linking them with a 3D high poly-count tree with many faces will impact the rendering times. Shaderlight will still need to process all the geometry in the detailed 3D trees.

Use layers with vegetation and keep your models organized, as discussed in Chapter 14.

Fig. 30.14: Shaderlight will replace all vegetation linked to a 3D plant as shown in the rendering.

Chalk Rendering

A *chalk rendering*, sometimes called clay rendering in other rendering programs, produces an image without any texture. A chalk render highlights the light and dark values on surfaces and cast shadows, creating *ambient occlusion* (Fig. 30.15). Chalk renders can be used to display the space, structure, and form of a rendering without the distraction of other details.

Fig. 30.15: A chalk rendering in Shaderlight

Chalk renders make ideal overlays to enhance a rendering during the post-production process. Overlaying a chalk render over a normal rendered view will help enhance shadows and contrast to provide greater depth. This method is reviewed in Chapter 31.

To create a clay render, follow these steps:

1. Select Chalk Render from the Lighting menu in the Shaderlight Render Settings menu (Fig. 30.16).

2. Set the resolution. If you are going to use the chalk render as an overlay, make sure the settings match the resolution and camera view of the full rendered graphic (Fig. 30.17).

3. Set Update to Auto and Quality to 60 percent. This enables the dynamic preview so alterations can be made as needed (Fig. 30.17).

4. Set the Shadow Range as needed (Fig. 30.17).

5. The Background should be set to SketchUp Background. If SketchUp Sky is toggled On (under the SketchUp Styles menu), the specified sky color will render in the scene.

6. Run the render.

Chalk Render includes a value called Shadow Range. The lower the number, the lighter the Chalk Render will be. The higher the number, the deeper and darker the Chalk Render will be.

The Shadow Range can vary depending on the size of the render and camera view. A good place to start is with the value of 50. Lower values might be too light, and higher values greater than 200 tend to be too dark (Fig. 30.18, Fig. 30.19, Fig. 30.20).

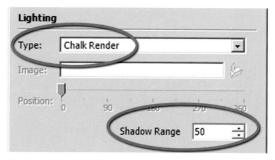

Fig. 30.16: Select Chalk Render from the Shaderlight Render Settings menu under Lighting and then select a Shadow Range.

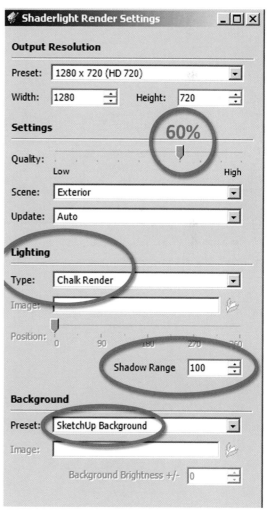

Fig. 30.17: Complete Chalk Render settings

Adjust the Shadow Range dynamically while the image is rendering and assess for best results.

Fig. 30.18: Chalk Render with Shadow Range set at 20

Fig. 30.19: Chalk Render with Shadow Range set at 100

Fig. 30.20: Chalk Render with Shadow Range set at 200

The Photoshop Postproduction Process

Postproduction Effects

The postproduction process in photo-editing software is used to enhance the quality and content of rendered images (Fig. 31.1, Fig. 31.2). This chapter discusses some quick and frequently used modifications that affect light, color, and contrast; and it includes effects such as atmospheric haze. Chapter 32 reviews some additional alterations you can make, including entourage elements and realistic detailing.

Many professional rendering artists consider post processing the key to generating high-quality, hyper-realistic images. In fact, they often spend more time photo-editing an image than they do modeling or rendering it (Fig. 31.3, Fig. 31.4). These artists use endless editing variations and effects.

Fig. 31.1: Final rendered image before postproduction editing

Fig. 31.2: Image after postproduction

Fig. 31.3: Controlling Nature (rendering by Ryan Knope)

Fig. 31.4: Exterior night (rendering by Akiko Okabe)

With that in mind, these chapters are meant to provide a starting point for commonly made modifications. They are not a comprehensive postproduction guide. Several online and published resources that provide additional methods are available: Check out *Digital Drawing for Landscape Architecture* by Bradley Cantrell and Wes Michaels (Wiley, 2010) and *Photoshop for 3D Artists, Vol. 1* by Andrzej Sykut, Fabio Rahonha, Zoltan Korcsko, and Richard Tilbury (3DTotal Publishing, 2011).

Fig. 31.5: Photoshop is used for the examples in Part 7.

Part 7 uses Photoshop CS 5.5 to demonstrate modifications (Fig. 31.5). The content assumes that you are familiar with the program (or similar software such as Gimp).

Methods

Three general types of post-processing methods are used to modify images:

▶ **Light and Color Adjustments**: Modifying color, contrast, and lighting levels.

▶ **Effects**: Adding atmospheric effects such as haze, blurred objects, and photo grain.

▶ **Entourage Modification**: Placing realistic grass, enhancing water, and including backgrounds, skies, and objects. You'll learn more about these methods in Chapter 32.

▶ Combined Methods.

For best results, you can combine methods when it is appropriate. For example, haze, grain, and clay overlays will enhance the realism in exterior renders. Similarly, interior renders will benefit from adjusting the lighting levels, fixing hotspots, and altering color hue/saturation (Fig. 31.6).

Fig. 31.6: Multiple effects and alterations were made to the image used for the cover of this book: the original render (1), a background image in the process of being added (2), a clay render overlay enhances shadows and contrast (3), interior scene rendered separately and combined into the overall image (4)

Using Original Images and Layers

Before altering the image, make a copy of the original image by saving a copy of the file or duplicating the original image layer. A copied or duplicate layer of the graphic will allow you to compare or undo any modifications.

The typical Photoshop process uses layers. Using layers will allow you to mask specific parts of the image, apply effects, and make adjustments. To make some of the suggested alterations, you'll need to use layers (Fig. 31.7).

Masking

Masking is used to isolate or select specific areas of a photograph. There are several ways to mask objects in Photoshop. Common masking tools include: Magic Wand, Paths, Pen, and Lassos. You can also select by color range and create a masking layer (Fig. 31.8).

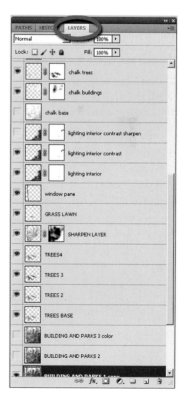

Fig. 31.7: Layers are just as useful in Photoshop as they were in SketchUp.

Fig. 31.8: Masking parts of the image is an important part of the postproduction process. The image shows two types of Photoshop masks being applied.

Light and Color

The following modifications affect light, contrast, and image color. These tools are meant to be used with the various effects and methods outlined in the rest of this chapter and in Chapter 33.

Adjusting Lighting Levels

Use Edit → Adjustment → Levels to alter the lighting exposure of an image (Fig. 31.9) and brighten or darken an image to affect its overall look and feel (Fig. 31.10, Fig. 31.11). Similarly, parts of an image can be masked and used with Levels to expose (lighten) or hide (darken) detail. Lighting a dark region can reveal parts of the image previously hidden (Fig. 31.12, Fig. 31.13). Darkening specific areas can create greater contrast and depth.

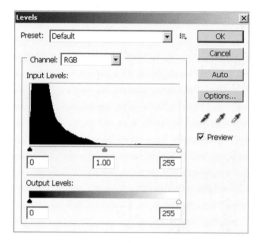

Fig. 31.9: The Photoshop Levels menu

Fig. 31.10: The interior scene rendered somewhat dark, which is not uncommon

Fig. 31.11: Using the Levels tools, the scene is brightened and contrast is balanced.

Fig. 31.12: The exterior scene landscape rendered dark.

Fig. 31.13: Using the Levels tool, the scene is brightened and contrast is enhanced.

Using levels may sometimes increase or decrease color saturation. This can be easily fixed with the Hue/Saturation tool.

Altering Hue/Saturation

Adjusting saturation is usually one of the first alterations you'll make to an image. It's not uncommon for renderings to be over- or undersaturated in relationship to overall or specific colors. The Hue/Saturation tool (Edit → Adjustment → Hue/Saturation) can decrease/increase the saturation of all or specific colors (Fig. 31.14, Fig. 31.15, Fig. 31.16, Fig. 31.17, Fig. 31.18).

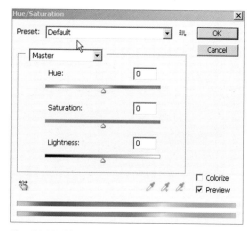

Fig. 31.14: The Hue Saturation menu from Photoshop

Fig. 31.15: The interior render can use more color.

Fig. 31.16: Use the Hue Saturation tool to saturate color in the render.

Fig. 31.17: The riverwalk render is overly gray.

Fig. 31.18: Cranking up the color helps make the image look more vibrant with more realistic color tones.

Increasing the saturation of a specific color is an excellent way to create focus or to balance an area obscured by or competing with other colors (Fig. 31.19, Fig. 31.20). Similarly, the Hue/Saturation tool is useful in altering a color to a different hue.

Fig. 31.19: The trees do not have enough color and appear dark gray-green. The trees (and other green vegetation) will be adjusted using Hue/Saturation's ability to isolate and affect a single color.

Fig. 31.20: Increasing the green saturation helps provide greater color contrast to the scene.

Clay Render Overlay and Graphics

Clay renderings can be leveraged to achieve a number of results. There are two ways to approach them (Fig. 31.21). The first approach helps increase the depth of a rendering by overlaying the clay render over the original. The second approach is used to create focused nonphotorealistic graphic images.

Fig. 31.21: At top is a normal render. Below it is the clay render of the same scene. These two images will be combined to produce varying results.

Clay Render Overlay

The rendering Clay preset is an excellent way to increase the contrast of light, dark, and shadow values to create more depth and realism. Although they require additional rendering time, clay renders are quick to generate. Use this method when the render looks flat or does not have enough contrast or shadow depth.

1. Create a clay (chalk in Shaderlight) render of the exact camera view of the rendered graphic.

2. Insert/import/place the clay render over the rendered image in Photoshop.

3. Under the Layer options, select Multiply. This will cause the darker values of the clay render to merge with the image, resulting in greater depth and contrast (Fig. 31.22).

4. If needed, tone down the clay render by lowering the layer opacity.

5. Consider masking out parts of the clay render that are too dark. This will allow you to give depth to specific parts of the image (Fig. 31.23).

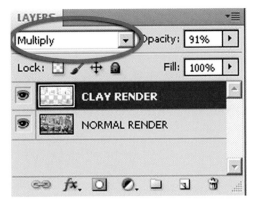

Fig. 31.22: The Photoshop Layer menu shows the Clay Render layer over the Normal Render layer. The Layer Effects box (circled) is set to Multiply, causing the Clay Render layer to provide more contrast to the Normal Render layer.

Fig. 31.23: The resulting combined render

Clay Render Hybrid Graphics

This approach combines a clay render with a normal final render. Parts of the final render are merged with the black-and-white context of the clay render. The results are images where the colored portions of the graphic become the focus of the image while the black-and-white clay portions serve as context, backdrops, and setting.

The process is simple:

1. Generate the final normal rendering of the model.

2. Generate a clay render of the model. Make sure the camera view is identical to the final normal render.

3. Open both images and place them in the same file. Place the clay render over the final render.

4. Cut out the clay render portions that obscure the final render. Remove areas of the clay render that are obscuring the portions of the final render you want visible (Fig. 31.24, Fig. 31.25, Fig. 31.26).

Fig. 31.24: The part of the image that will be replaced with the clay render is masked and deleted.

Fig. 31.25: The resulting image is a combination of the clay render and normal render, creating a graphic with a more direct focus.

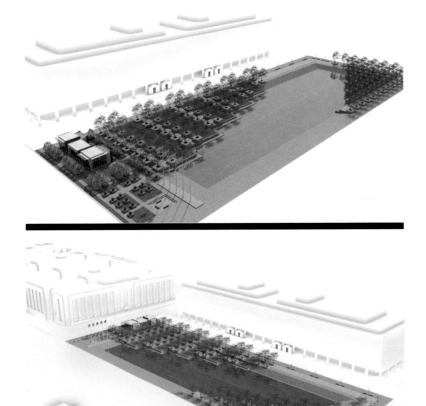

Fig. 31.26: The hybrid method is used to provide context and focus for the Eisenhower Memorial (student project by Scott Preston).

Effects

By representing atmospheric properties, enhancing textures, and creating focus, *effects* are used to add another layer of realism to renderings.

Haze

Haze is an excellent addition to exterior renders. You should include or add a sky to the background of a render prior to adding haze. Creating haze requires masking an additional layer to create a mist/fog/vapor effect over the image (Fig. 31.27).

Fig. 31.27: The completed preproduction rendering (top); haze added to soften up the image and create more depth (bottom)

To create haze, follow these steps:

1. Create a new layer at the top of the layer list and name it **Haze**. Make sure the layer is active (Fig. 31.28, Fig. 31.29).

2. Select the entire image (Ctrl+A for Windows, Option+A for Mac).

3. Go to Edit → Fill. Fill this new layer with a white color (Fig. 31.30).

4. Lower the white layer's opacity to between 10 percent and 20 percent (Fig. 31.31).

5. Create a Mask option in the haze layer. Use the Paint Brush (set to Black) and lower the opacity to 45 percent (Fig. 31.31).

6. Start to mask out the selected color from the image. Focus on the foreground and midground. Remember to expose the sky and background underneath the haze layer (Fig. 31.32). Objects in the distance and tall objects (buildings) should possess more haze. When working, occasionally turn off the haze layer for comparison (Fig. 31.33).

Fig. 31.28: Original render

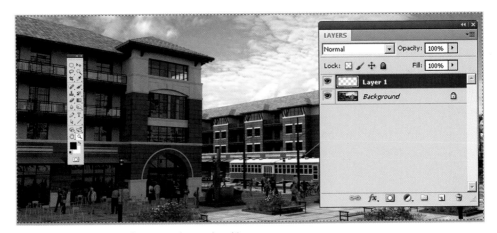

Fig. 31.29: Create a new layer over the rendered image.

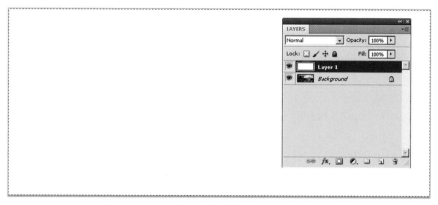

Fig. 31.30: Fill the entire new layer with a solid white color.

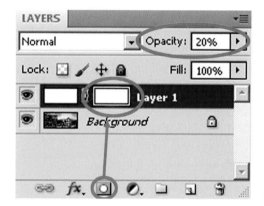

Fig. 31.31: Set the new layer with white fill to between 10 and 20 percent opacity. Create a new mask for this layer (circled portion of image with arrow showing the created mask).

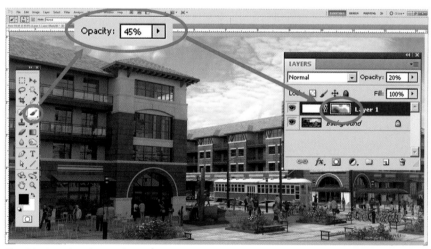

Fig. 31.32: Using the Brush tool, set to 45 percent opacity. With the mask selected, begin to mask out the haze from the rendering.

Fig. 31.33: The completed effect provides depth and focus while softening the tones in the image.

Motion Blur

The Blur filter provides useful options for creating motion and focus. One of those is the motion blur. A *motion blur* is useful for objects associated with movement like vehicles and people. The affect adds the impression of action to the image.

1. Mask the vehicle or person. Include a small area behind the vehicle or person (Fig. 31.34).

2. Go to Filers → Blur → Motion Blur (Fig. 31.35).

3. Apply a light blur (between 5 and 10) and adjust the angle to parallel the direction of travel (Fig. 31.36).

Fig. 31.34: The car is masked in the image. The mask includes an area behind the car to help create the sense of direction and movement.

Fig. 31.35: The Motion Blur tool in Photoshop

Fig. 31.36: Resulting motion blur added to the cars and some of the people in the rendering

Simulated Light Lens Flares

Using the Lens Flare filter, you can enhance or even create sources of light that are absent in many simulated lighting renders (Fig. 31.37).

In this example, the track lights have a point light generating light for the scene. However, they do look as if they have lightbulbs (sources). You can easily fix the problem with the Lens Flare tool (Fig. 31.38).

Fig. 31.37: Interior rendering with lens flares added to the track lighting

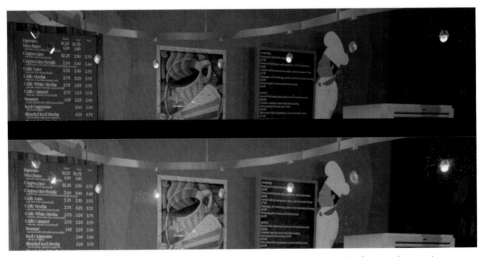

Fig. 31.38: The track lighting without lens flares (top); lens flares added to the fixtures (bottom)

The Lens Flare options work best when small areas of image are cropped out. This ensures that when the Lens Flare filter is activated, you can easily place the flare.

1. Using the Marquee tool, create an outline around one of the track lights in the image (Fig. 31.39).

2. Copy and paste the track light onto its own layer (Fig. 31.39).

3. Go to Filter → Render → Lens Flare.

4. Select any one of the flare options; 50 to 300 mm Zoom is recommended.

5. Position the flare directly over what would be the source of light for the fixture (Fig. 31.40).

6. Set the flare strength. A common mistake is to make the flare strength strong. This can be distracting. A subtle lens flare is useful.

7. Repeat this process for each light.

Fig. 31.39: One of the fixtures is selected with the Marquee tool and then copied and pasted onto its own layer. This will ensure that the Lens Flare filter can be used with accuracy, and, if needed, you can delete the layer with lens flare.

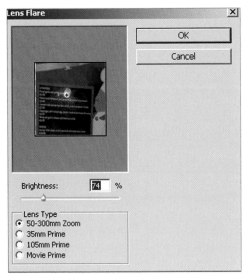

Fig. 31.40: In the Lens Flare menu, the lens flare (the X) is placed on the light.

Detailed Postproduction

This chapter reviews additional postproduction modifications that are more time-intensive than the modifications discussed in Chapter 31. These modifications add realistic detail and features to enhance realism and context.

Realistic Vegetation

Making lawns appear real, with strands of grass, is not feasible in SketchUp. Similarly, while shrubs and large swaths of ground cover can, in theory, be added, the time required to do it can be very prohibitive. Instead, during the postproduction process, you can fit an image of realistic grass and vegetation into the open spaces of the rendering to create the illusion of a complete landscape.

This method requires that you have specific images available. Collect images of grasses and vegetation that match the perspective and angles of the rendering. You can find them online using an image search engine or by taking your own photos, which is recommended. Collecting multiple lawn images is useful: eye-level, bird's-eye, close-ups, etc. Having a range of images will make it easier to match the camera view of the rendering.

The following steps add vegetation, lawns, and grasses to the original rendering (Fig. 32.5, Fig. 32.6, Fig. 32.7, Fig. 32.8, Fig. 32.9).

1. Insert the desired vegetation image into the rendering in Photoshop. Hide the layer (Fig. 32.1, Fig. 32.2).

2. Select the areas in the render that will include the vegetation. Use Select → Color Range for the quickest result.

3. Once the area is selected, use the Add Layer Mask option and mask out the area for future use.

4. Turn on the vegetation image and position/scale it over the appropriate location in the render (Fig. 32.3).

5. Activate the Layer Mask.

6. Go to Select → Modify and choose Expand. Set the option to 2 pixels. This will allow a greater area of the vegetation image to remain, overlapping edges like paved or similar surfaces in the rendering.

7. Make the vegetation image active. Go to Select, click Inverse, and press Delete. What should remain is the lawn image filled in over the solid grass areas (Fig. 32.4).

Fig. 32.1: In this rendered image, the vegetation needs to be added to the green areas on the terrain.

Fig. 32.2: The vegetation image is inserted into the Photoshop file. Then the layer is turned off.

Fig. 32.3: The open/green areas in the render are masked.

Fig. 32.4: The vegetation image is placed into position. The mask is activated.

8. Adjust and tweak the color, scale, and position of the vegetation. Dither the edges of the lawn where they overlap or extend over edges (delete or mask these edges). Try to make the grass edge look as natural as possible. This is the time-consuming part of the method.

9. You will need to match the inserted vegetation to the hue, contrast, and color of the rendering. There are several options. Use Levels, Hue Saturation, and Layer options. The Burn tool is useful in darkening the vegetation to match any shadows (Fig. 32.5).

Fig. 32.5: The vegetation layer is color and contrast adjusted. (Levels, Hue Saturation, and Layer properties are all adjusted.)

Fig. 32.6: In the completed render, a lawn will be placed in the image foreground.

Fig. 32.7: The lawn image is inserted into the render graphic. Marquees can be seen in the figure, outlining the portion of the lawn that will remain and placed in the foreground.

Fig. 32.8: The lawn image is cut out. It needs to be color and contrast adjusted to fit the image.

Fig. 32.9: The completed image with lawn

Architecture Photo Placement

Inserting a rendered building into a photo is an excellent method for creating a realistic graphic. To implement this technique, you'll need a photo or photos of the site or area where the building is to be placed.

1. Start with the destination image into which the rendered building will be edited (Fig. 32.10).

2. Render the building without any site context, backdrops, or backgrounds. Set the lighting to match the direction and shadows of the image into which the building will be inserted (Fig. 32.11).

3. Make sure the camera view matches, as best possible, the angle and perspective of the image in which the building will be placed.

4. Insert the cut-out building into the context (site) photo (Fig. 32.12).

5. In Photoshop, mask and cut out the building render (Fig. 32.13).

6. Use the Transform and Distort tool and fit the Building into the photo. Erase/hide parts of the building to allow site objects and terrain to appear in front and/or behind (Fig. 32.14).

7. Adjust the building layer color and levels to match the photo and vice versa.

Fig. 32.10: The destination image is a panoramic of the hills in Kauai, the proposed house's location.

Fig. 32.11: The house is rendered in SketchUp (using Twilight Render in this instance). Only the building needs to be rendered. No site context or details are needed.

Fig. 32.12: The building rendering is inserted into the destination image file.

Fig. 32.13: The building render is cleaned up. The excess edges are deleted, leaving a tight outline of the building.

Fig. 32.14: The building is scaled and then, using the Mask tools, fitted into the image.

Backgrounds/Backdrops

Using the IRP settings to insert backgrounds or render HDRIs is useful, but does not always provide an accurate appearance. Adding custom backgrounds during postproduction will give you greater control over the backdrop look.

To execute this method, you'll need background and backdrop images. A search for panoramic, backgrounds, and skies on CG Textures.com will yield some results. Many IRP websites include background image downloads.

There are two approaches to including backdrops, depending on whether the scene is exterior or interior.

Exteriors

Exteriors benefit from skies, cities, and neighborhood backgrounds. The biggest challenge can be masking out the original sky of rendering. Rendered trees inevitably are in the selection causing the tree edges (where they meet the sky) to overly dither when masked, distorting their appearance once a background is inserted. In those cases, use a path (Pen tool) and take the time to remove the sky with precession while considering the effect on tree edges.

1. Create a duplicate layer of the rendering. Turn the original render off.
2. Mask/select the sky/background on the duplicate render layer and delete it (Fig. 32.15).
3. Insert the background image behind the layer (Fig. 32.16).
4. Scale and move the image to fit.
5. Match and color-correct the background. For many sky images, adjust the Hue/Saturation; desaturating and lightening the image usually works well (Fig. 32.17).
6. Add haze to the image (Fig. 32.18).

Fig. 32.15: The rendered image without a sky background

Fig. 32.16: The background image is inserted into the render graphic file in Photoshop.

Fig. 32.17: The background image is scaled and placed behind the main image layers.

Fig. 32.18: The completed image with lawn, hillside, and sky are Photoshopped in place. The lawn and hillside were Photoshopped using the methods for realistic vegetation.

Interiors

Interior views that include portals and openings such as doors and windows benefit from exterior backgrounds. Effective background use requires you to carefully mask and select openings, which will display the background. Background images must match the perspective of the drawing and are usually an eye-level view of a street, neighborhood, or city.

1. Create a duplicate layer of the rendering. Turn the original render off (Fig. 32.19).

2. Carefully select glass and similar openings that look out from the scene where the backdrop would appear (Fig. 32.20).

3. Copy and place the selection onto a new layer. Adjust the opacity of the layer to 50 percent. Skip this step if the opening does not include glass or other transparent surface.

4. Insert the background image between the rendering copy and the copied portal's window layers (Fig. 32.21).

5. Scale and move the background image to fit.

6. Adjust the opacity of the portal window layer. The goal is to make the openings slightly opaque to appear as if viewing out a window. Typical opacity is 10 to 15 percent.

7. Match and color-correct the background (Fig. 32.22).

Fig. 32.19: The interior rendering without background

Fig. 32.20: The windows in the back of the rendering are carefully masked. The background image will be placed in the magenta area.

Fig. 32.21: The background skyline is inserted into the rendering image file in Photoshop.

Fig. 32.22: The background skyline is placed behind the interior render, scaled, and color-corrected to fit the rendered context.

Water Fountains and Pools

When you're using an IRP, reflecting and transparent water can be difficult to get just right. The goal is to get the right balance of water texture, reflection, and transparency through the water. The following simple approach achieves that goal. It requires creating three renderings, all of the same camera view. The three renderings will be combined in Photoshop. They are:

▶ **Reflective Water:** The first render is set with the water being highly reflective (Fig. 32.23).

▶ **Nonreflective Water**: The second render is set with the water surface being flat/nonreflective (Fig. 32.24).

▶ **No Water**: The third render is set without the water surface. Only the water container (pool, fountain walls, and bottom) is visible (Fig. 32.25).

Fig. 32.23: Rendering of water that is 100-percent reflective

Fig. 32.24: Rendering of water that is solid without reflection

Fig. 32.25: Rendering of pool steps and basin

To hide the water, in SketchUp, double-click on the water surface to select it, right-click over the selection, and choose Group. Then select the Group, right-click, and select Hide. If you are using scenes, ensure that the water is not visible again when creating the rendering. To turn the water surface back on, go to View → Hidden Geometry. You will see an outline of water surface. Select it, right-click, and choose Unhide.

Make sure you turn off all the detail in the model (vegetation, furnishings, and similar) for the nonreflective water and no-water renders. This will speed up the render process. The details should be visible in the reflective water render to ensure that they reflect in the water.

Open and place the three renderings into a single Photoshop file. Place them in the following layer order from top to bottom:

- ▶ Nonreflective water
- ▶ No-water surface
- ▶ Reflective water

Mask and cut out the water surface areas from the nonreflective water and no-water render: the only thing that should remain is the reflective water surface and the container (pool, fountain, etc.), bottom, and sides. Leave the reflective water layer as is.

Adjust the opacity of the nonreflective and no-water surface to control what is visible and to merge the three layers of water and fountain surfaces. The goal is to get a subtle mixture of container surfaces, water texture, and reflection (Fig. 32.26).

Fig. 32.26: The combined images

Anatomy of a Rendering

Building the Base Model

Part 8 demonstrates the modeling and rendering process outlined in Part 2. The goal is to provide you with a specific context to view how the various tools and settings are used from start to finish (Fig. 33.1, Fig. 33.2). This chapter includes some important things to note about the content found in this part. The remainder of the chapter details modeling and texturing the base model.

Fig. 33.1: Final render of Exterior example model

Fig. 33.2: Final render of Interior example model

Chapter Relationships

The chapters in Part 8 can be referenced to other portions of the book. When you're reviewing the chapters, refer to the cross-referenced parts of the book for explanations of how the various tools and processes work.

- ▶ **Chapter 33 corresponds to Part 2:** This chapter includes building the base model and adding textures.

- ▶ **Chapters 34, 35, 36, and 37 relate to Part 3:** These chapters cover placing and organizing model detail and creating scenes to help control model performance and content. Chapter 34 focuses on architecture, Chapter 35 on interior detailing, and Chapter 36 on site components. Chapter 37 reviews the creation of On/Off and additional scenes.

- ▶ **Chapter 38 relates to Part 4:** This chapter demonstrates how to set up lighting using the SketchUp Shadow menu.

- ▶ **Chapter 39 relates to the processes and concepts outlined Part 5 and Part 6:** Chapter 39 provides a detailed, step-by-step demonstration of the iterative rendering process for the exterior portions of the model leading to draft and final renderings.

- ▶ **Chapter 40 relates to the processes and concepts outlined in Part 5 and Part 6:** Chapter 40 provides a detailed, step-by-step demonstration of the iterative rendering process for the interior portions of the model leading to draft and final renderings. This includes how to place and set the model for rendering with simulated lighting. Shaderlight is used for these examples including specific settings.

- ▶ **Chapter 41 references Part 7:** Chapter 41 provides a quick demonstration of postprocessing in Photoshop for exterior renderings.

The Example Model

The example models correspond to the three disciplines reviewed in this book: architecture, site, and interior design. The model itself can be downloaded from the book's resources webpage (www.ambit-3d.com). More than one version of the model is available for you to download. The various models correspond to the different stages of the model's development—from base model, to adding textures, the placement and organization of component detail, setting light, and providing render values.

General Approach

As mentioned throughout the book, the process from modeling to rendering is not always linear. These chapters detail how the process can jump around to tweak the model.

To reference how tools and methods work, go back to the specific part and chapter that describe them. The examples provide some exacting approaches and settings, but the purpose is to show a holistic approach instead of delving into specific how-to processes for the tools.

The Base Model

The following figures illustrate how the base model is created (Fig. 33.3, Fig. 33.4, Fig. 33.5, Fig. 33.6).

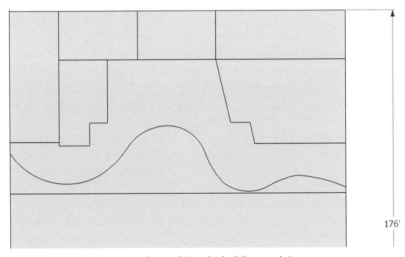

176'

Fig. 33.3: 2D SketchUp base plan outlining the buildings and site

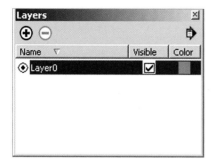

Fig. 33.4: All base modeling is done with Layer 0 as the active layer. Layer 0 is always set to the default when you first start a SketchUp model. If you're working with imported information from CAD programs or an image, make sure that Layer 0 is active when you draft SketchUp edges and faces.

Fig. 33.5: Additional edges and faces are added to the base plan.

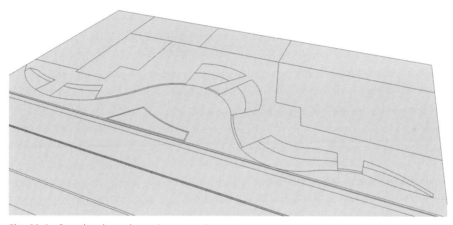

Fig. 33.6: Complete base shown in perspective

Solid Color to Surfaces

The following figures illustrate the process of adding solid colors to the model 2D faces prior to extruding forms (Fig. 33.7, Fig. 33.8, Fig. 33.9). The solid colors will coat the extruded faces, allowing an efficient workflow.

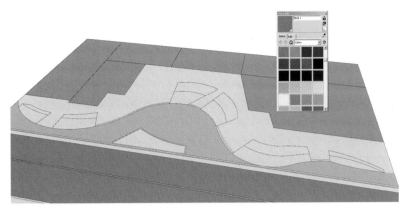

Fig. 33.7: A solid color texture is added to the building footprints of the site base. Add solid colors to all surfaces. Solid colors should correspond to materials and textures that will be added to the model. For every texture intended for the model, add a corresponding solid color to the surfaces that will possess that texture. The solid colors will be swapped with texture images.

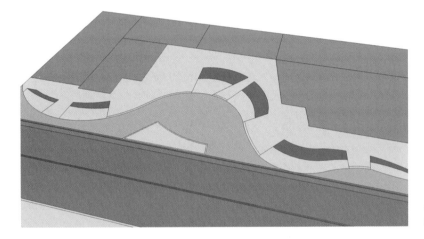

Fig. 33.8: Add solid colors to the ground plane surfaces.

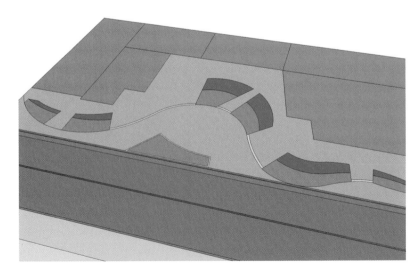

Fig. 33.9: Solid colors have been added to all surfaces.

Base Model Extrusion

The following figures show how the model base is extruded (Fig. 33.10, Fig. 33.11, Fig. 33.12). The applied solid colors will coat the extruded faces.

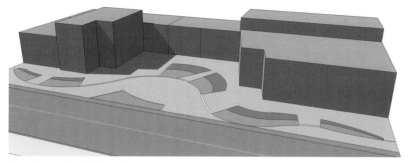

Fig. 33.10: The building footprints are extruded to various heights.

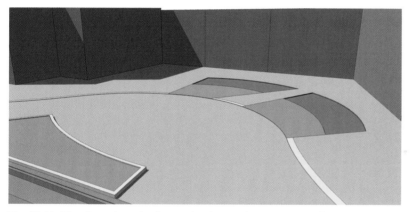

Fig. 33.11: The site paving, planting, and curbs are given some extrusion.

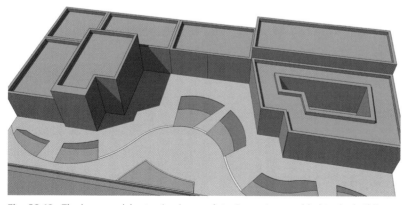

Fig. 33.12: The base model extrusion is complete. Parapets are added to the building.

Solid Colors Swapped with Textures

The solid colors placed on surfaces will be swapped with image textures. These textures correspond to the surface and material intent of the model (Fig. 33.13, Fig. 33.14, Fig. 33.15, Fig. 33.16, Fig. 33.17, Fig. 33.18, Fig. 33.19). You'll need to get the textures from third-party websites and then place them into an organized Texture Library for easy access and use. This last set of steps will complete the base model.

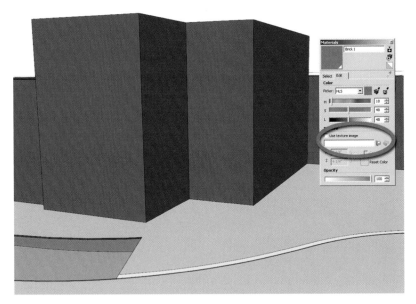

Fig. 33.13: The building's solid color will be swapped with a brick texture. The Browse button, under Texture in the Paint Bucket menu, is selected to access the Texture Library (which must be linked between SketchUp and the Texture Library folder).

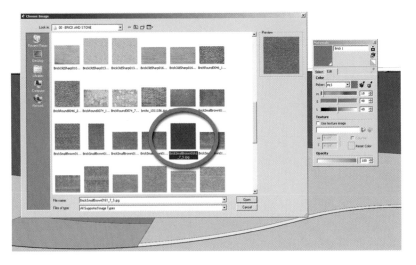

Fig. 33.14: The Texture Library has many folders. The Brick and Stone folder of the Texture Library is shown. The desired brick texture is selected to replace the solid color on the building.

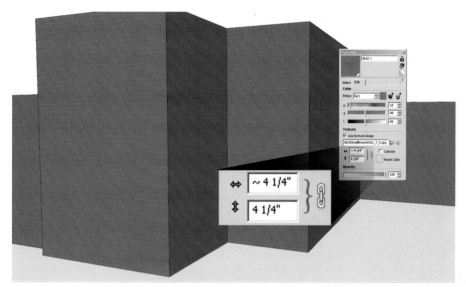

Fig. 33.15: As with many inserted/swapped textures, the scale of the texture image is incorrect (it's usually too small) and needs to be adjusted. The enlarged area of the Paint Bucket tool shows the Texture scale option.

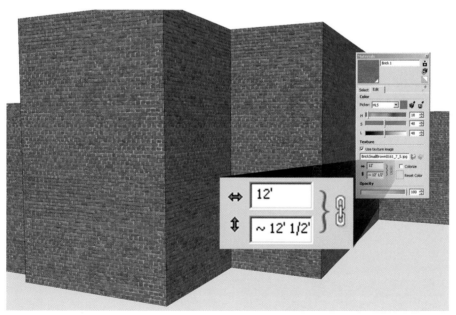

Fig. 33.16: The Texture scale is adjusted (increased), allowing it to achieve an appropriate look on the building facade.

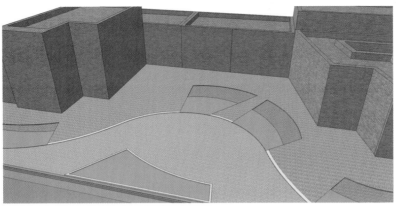

Fig. 33.17: The solid colors of the paving and planting beds are swapped with texture images. They are at the wrong scale and need to be adjusted.

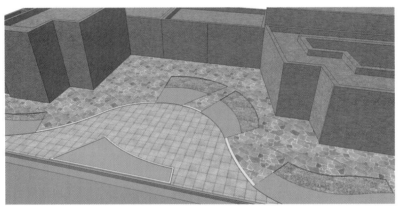

Fig. 33.18: The paving and planting bed textures are scaled upward, taking on the correct appearance.

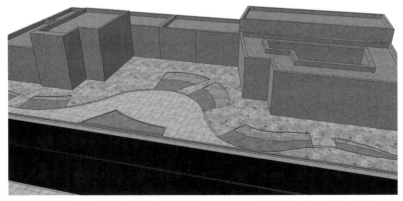

Fig. 33.19: The remainder of the solid colors are swapped with textures. The textures are correctly scaled to a realistic size and appearance.

Building Detail

This chapter demonstrates how to detail the building mass with various features ranging from windows and doors to gutters and ornamentation (Fig. 34.1 through Fig. 34.15). The additional details bring the building to life, providing scale, context, and design intent. The figures and images correspond to Part 3. Please take note of how layers are used to organize the building and building detail. The layer-naming convention that is used ensures that the added detail is identifiable with the buildings.

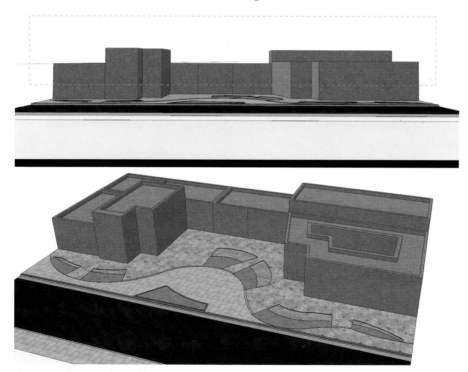

Fig. 34.1: The extruded building is selected in its entirety.

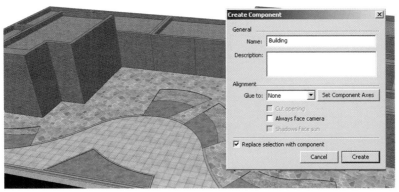

Fig. 34.2: The selected building is converted into a component by right-clicking over the selected faces and choosing Make Component.

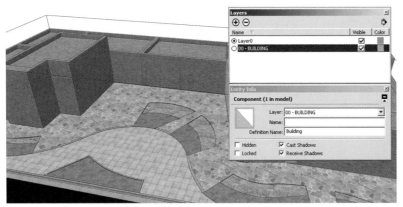

Fig. 34.3: A new layer called 00 - Building is created. Using Entity Info, the newly created building component is placed on the Building layer. The building can now be toggled off and on as needed.

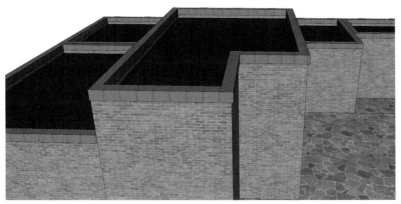

Fig. 34.4: The parapet is further detailed. The faces of the parapet are slightly extruded and have a new texture material.

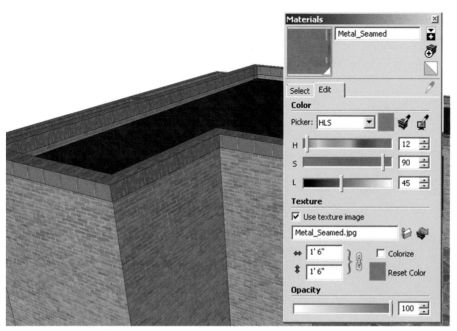

Fig. 34.5: The color of the parapet is adjusted using the Paint Bucket tool. The HLS sliders are used to adjust the color from gray to red. However, the result causes the color to become multihued and illegible.

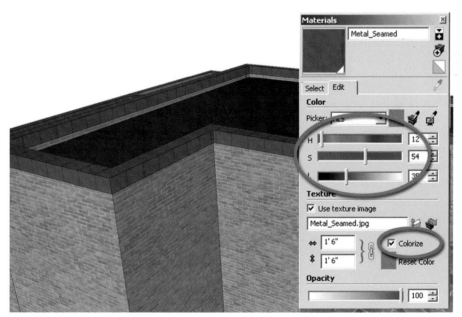

Fig. 34.6: Selecting the Colorize option fixes the texture hue problem. The color is then further tweaked.

Fig. 34.7: Window and door components are constructed and placed on the building vertical faces. The components are placed inside the building component instance so they will cut openings on the building walls, providing views into the interior. For specific instructions on constructing building and door components, see *Google SketchUp for Dummies* (Wiley, 2007) or *Google SketchUp for Site Design* (Wiley, 2009).

Fig. 34.8: The window and door components are placed around the building facade, adding an important level of articulation to the architecture.

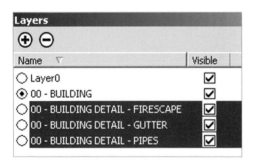

Fig. 34.9: New layers are created. These layers correspond to the type of component detail that will be added to the building. The added component detail will be placed on these layers so they can be easily toggled on or off.

Fig. 34.10: Architectural detail can be downloaded from the FormFonts webpage and included in the model. This example shows a fire escape that will be integrated into the building model. The fire escape was downloaded from FormFonts and placed into the Component Library.

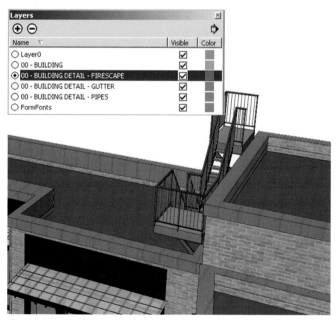

Fig. 34.11: The FormFonts fire escape is placed onto the building. The 00 - Building Fire Escape layer is the active layer when the component is inserted, placing it on that layer.

Fig. 34.12: A building gutter is available for use from Trimble 3D Warehouse.

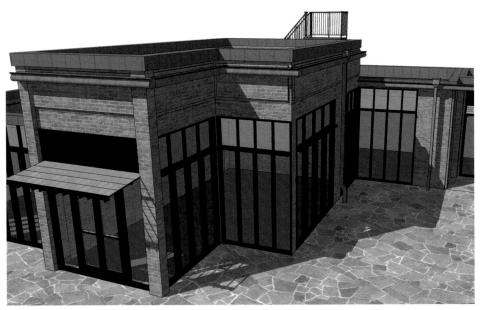

Fig. 34.13: The gutter is added to the building. The gutter's color is adjusted and placed on its own layer that was created prior to its insertion (00 - Building Gutter).

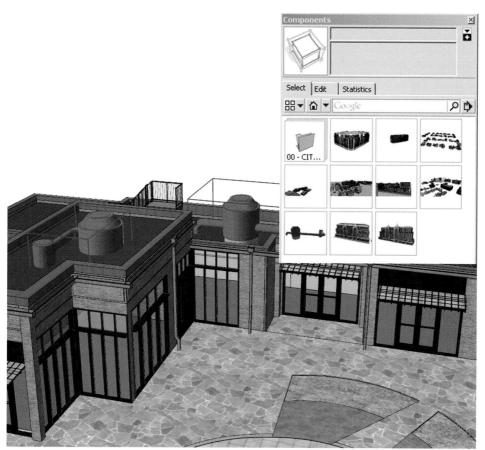

Fig. 34.14: The Component Library is accessed using the SketchUp browser. Additional building detail is placed into the model.

Fig. 34.15: The completed building as viewed in SketchUp with Shadows turned on

Interior Detail

This chapter illustrates how to add detail to the interior of the model. It demonstrates how to place various aspects of the building, such as the roof, on its own layers to better access the model interior. This makes it easier to incorporate interior component detail and to add and adjust interior textures.

The process includes adding floor and wall colors and textures, creating component detail layers that correspond to the interior, and placing two types of interior detail.

Interior Base Model

Before detail is added, the interior of the building needs to be made accessible. Components and layers are used to do this (Fig. 35.1 through Fig. 35.11).

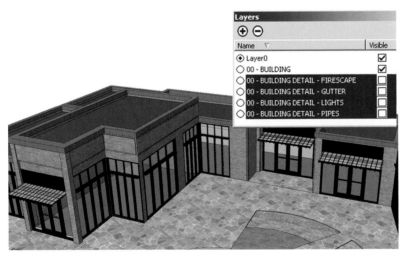

Fig. 35.1: The building detail layers are turned off. The component detail on the layers added in the previous chapter are toggled off, making it easier to access the building structure and interior.

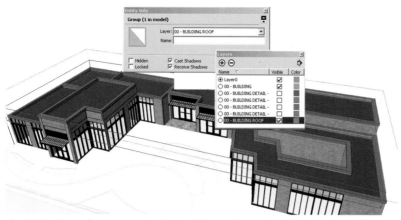

Fig. 35.2: The surfaces composing the building roof are selected and converted into a component. The roof component is then placed on its own layer, 00 - Building Roof. The roof can then be turned off, allowing access into the model interior.

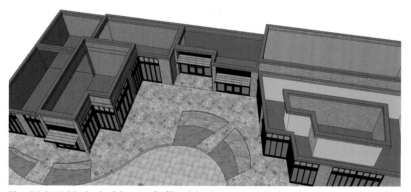

Fig. 35.3: With the building roof off, solid colors are applied to the interior walls and floors. Several different colors are applied, differentiating the wall and floor materials to be added to the interior scenes.

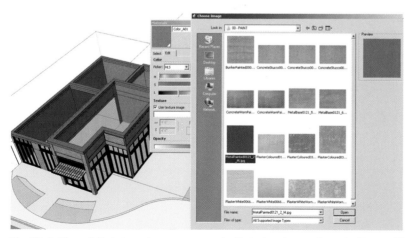

Fig. 35.4: The solid interior colors are swapped with texture images from the Texture Library.

Fig. 35.5: View of the model with the solid colors replaced with texture images

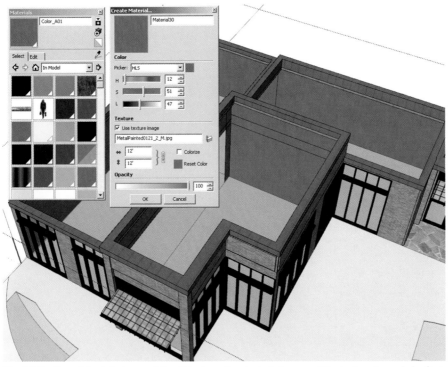

Fig. 35.6: One of the interior model wall textures is selected. A copy of the texture is made by first selecting the texture and then clicking on the Create Material button on the Paint Bucket. A new window opens, showing a duplicate of the material.

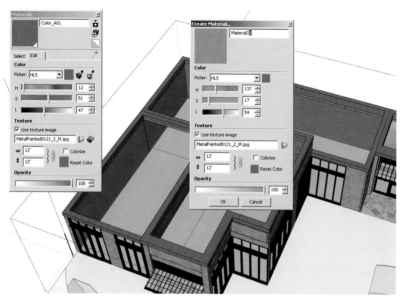

Fig. 35.7: Using the HLS sliders (HSB on a Mac), the duplicate wall texture is adjusted from orange to green. The texture character remains the same, the only difference being the color of the material. The new material is then applied to various interior wall surfaces.

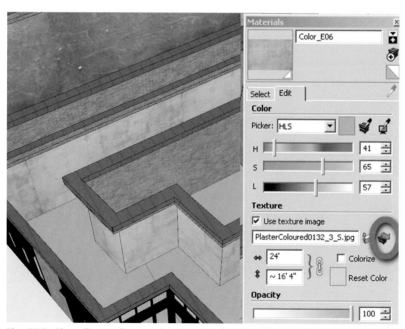

Fig. 35.8: The yellow wall texture is selected to be edited in Photoshop. With the texture selected, the Edit in External Texture Button is clicked in the Paint Bucket menu.

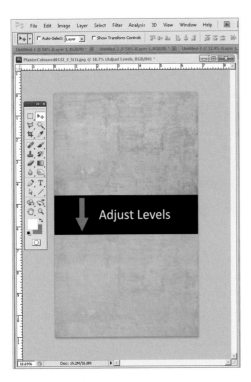

Fig. 35.9: The yellow texture is edited in Photoshop. In this case, the color levels are adjusted, altering the texture appearance to a more muted, softer color. With the alteration complete, the material is saved.

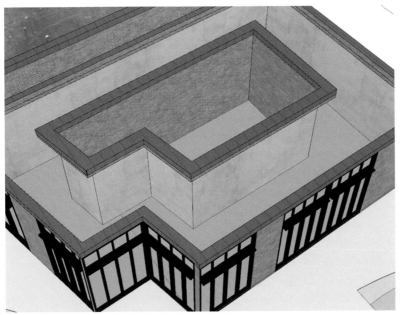

Fig. 35.10: Once the material is saved in Photoshop, it automatically updates in the SketchUp model and on all of the surfaces to which the texture is applied.

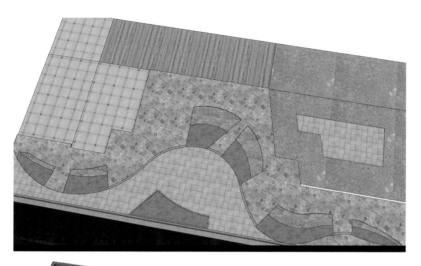

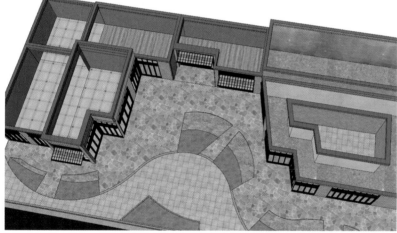

Fig. 35.11: The building layer and all its details are toggled off. The site and interior ground plane and their associated textures remain visible. Different flooring textures are added to the interior model, delineating the different surfaces.

Interior Detailing

Two types of interior component details will be added. The first is contextual detail for the building exterior. When the building is viewed from an exterior view, the windows will allow a view into the interior. Adding a minimal amount of component detail provides an important backdrop and context for the building.

The second type is detailing relative to a given interior scene, in this case, a cafe bar. The goal is to create a specific interior design scene for rendering. The context interior detail is leveraged and built upon to create a realistic interior scene for rendering.

After the interior of the building is accessible, the contextual interior detailing can be added (Fig. 35.12 through Fig. 35.16).

Fig. 35.12: FormFonts and 3D Warehouse component details (table with chairs and seating) to be used for creating contextual and detailed interior settings

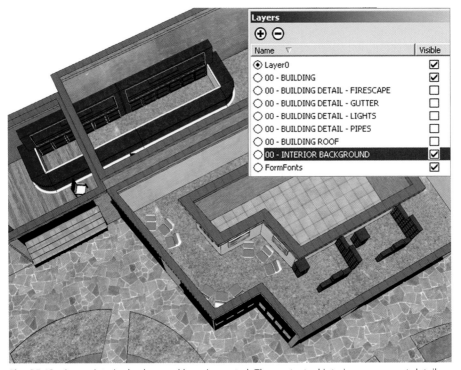

Fig. 35.13: A new interior background layer is created. The contextual interior component details will be inserted onto this layer.

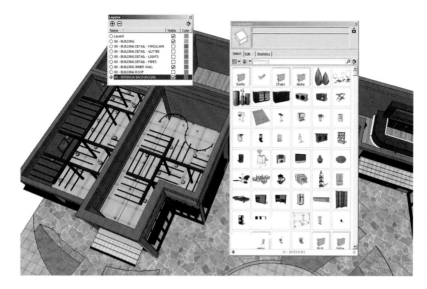

Fig. 35.14: The Component Library is accessed using the SketchUp browser. Additional building detailed is placed into the model.

Fig. 35.15: The interior context detail is visible through the building windows. Once rendered, both the interior walls and furnishings will help provide context to enhance the overall building and site exterior renders.

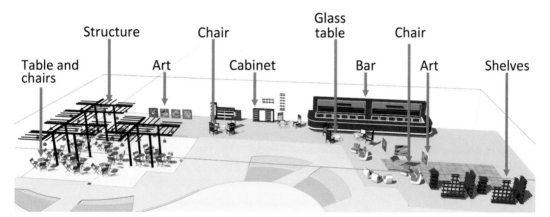

Fig. 35.16: Interior context details added to the model

The next set of component details to be added defines a specific scene, in this case, a café (Fig. 35.17 through Fig. 35.27). The entire scene is constructed from various components obtained from FormFonts and 3D Warehouse. Although many if not most interior design scenes include custom elements, forms, and objects, the goal of these illustrations is to highlight how a complete interior scene can be constructed using components for these two sources.

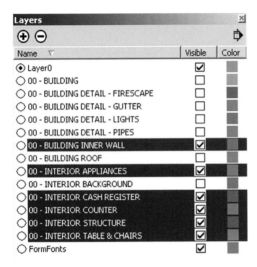

Fig. 35.17: New layers are added to the model. These layers will contain the various interior details to be used. One of the layers is called 00 - Building Inner Walls.

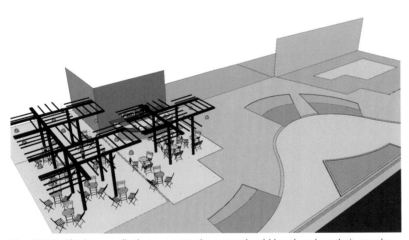

Fig. 35.18: The inner walls that compose the scene should be placed on their own layers, separate from the exterior building walls. Separating the interior walls provides better control for evaluation and object placement. In addition, the interior context details added in the previous steps should be shunted onto their own layers that correspond to the detailed interior cafe scene.

Fig. 35.19: A view of some of the component details added to define the cafe scene

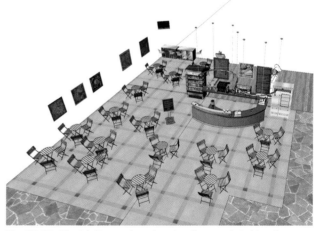

Layers

Name ▽	Visible
⦿ Layer0	☑
○ 00 - BUILDING	☑
○ 00 - BUILDING DETAIL - FIRESCAPE	☑
○ 00 - BUILDING DETAIL - GUTTER	☑
○ 00 - BUILDING DETAIL - LIGHTS	☑
○ 00 - BUILDING DETAIL - PIPES	☑
○ 00 - BUILDING INNER WALL	☑
○ 00 - BUILDING ROOF	☑
○ 00 - COUNTERS	☑
○ 00 - INTERIOR APPLIANCES	☑
○ 00 - INTERIOR ART	☑
○ 00 - INTERIOR BACKGROUND	☐
○ 00 - INTERIOR CASH REGISTER	☑
○ 00 - INTERIOR COUNTER	☑
○ 00 - INTERIOR CROCKERY	☑
○ 00 - INTERIOR FURNITURE	☑
○ 00 - INTERIOR MENU BOARD	☑
○ 00 - INTERIOR STRUCTURE	☑
○ 00 - INTERIOR TABLE & CHAIRS	☑
○ 00 - INTERIOR VENDING FRIDGE	☑
○ A - counter pendant lights	☑
○ A - front spot lights	☑
○ FormFonts	☑
○ Google Earth Snapshot	☑
○ Google Earth Terrain	☑

Fig. 35.20: More layers are added to give more detail to the model.

Fig. 35.21: The bird's-eye view showing the completed interior scene with added detail components

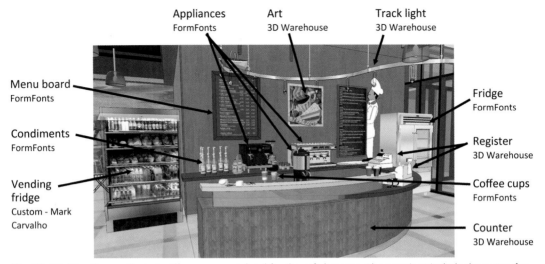

Appliances FormFonts   **Art** 3D Warehouse   **Track light** 3D Warehouse

Menu board FormFonts

Condiments FormFonts

Vending fridge Custom - Mark Carvalho

Fridge FormFonts

Register 3D Warehouse

Coffee cups FormFonts

Counter 3D Warehouse

Fig. 35. 22: The diagram illustrates the component detail for the cafe bar area. The notations include the source for the component: FormFonts or 3D Warehouse.

Furniture FormFonts   **Flatscreen** 3D Warehouse   **Stools** FormFonts   **Mural texture** 3D Warehouse

Art FormFonts

Menu sign FormFonts

Table and chairs 3D Warehouse

Fig. 35.23: The diagram shows the remainder of the component detail added to the scene. The notations include the source for the component: FormFonts or 3D Warehouse.

Fig. 35.24: Image showing the completed interior scene and associated detail

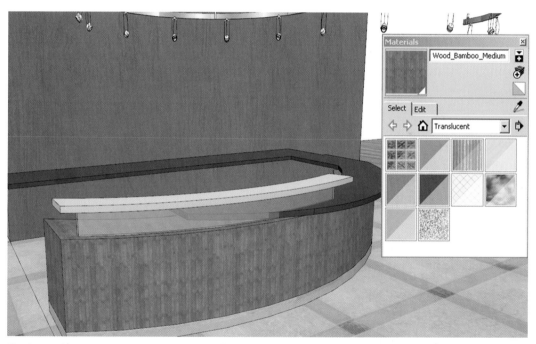

Fig. 35.25: The customer counter textures (the front facade and the countertop) need to be adjusted.

Fig. 35.26: The countertop and front facade of the customer counter are given new textures. The Browse button option on the Paint Bucket Editor is used to swap out the old textures with new ones.

Fig. 35.27: The final interior scene with Shadows turned on, providing a preview of the rendering

CHAPTER 36

Site Detail

The last aspect to the model is adding exterior site detailing to provide context for the site design and architecture (Fig. 36.1 through Fig. 36.18). High face-count vegetation models (trees and shrubs) need to be added to the scene, which makes using layers paramount. To maintain SketchUp performance, vegetation layers will be toggled off right after the vegetation is added to the model.

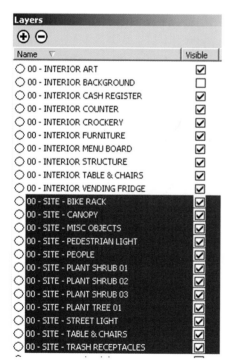

Fig. 36.1: New layers are created to contain the site component details that will be added to the model.

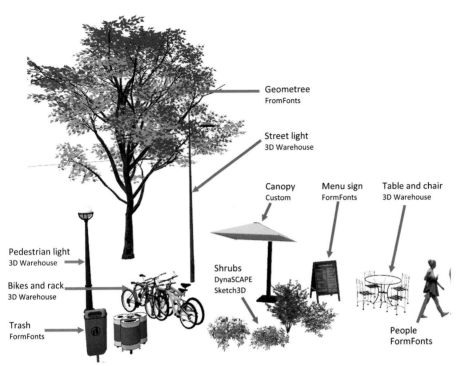

Fig. 36.2: The various site details to be added to the model, and their source: FormFonts, 3D Warehouse and Sketch3D

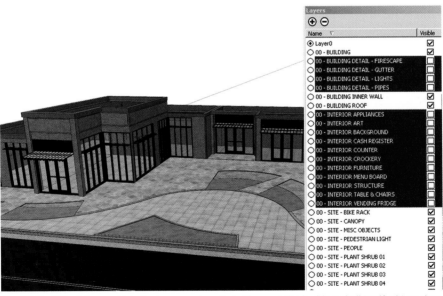

Fig. 36.3: All building and interior layers are toggled off except the building shell itself. This makes it easier to maintain computer performance while inserting site component details into the model.

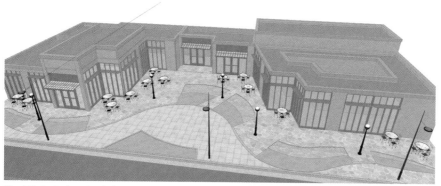

Fig. 36.4: Pedestrian lights, street lights, and tables and chairs are copied and arranged around the model site.

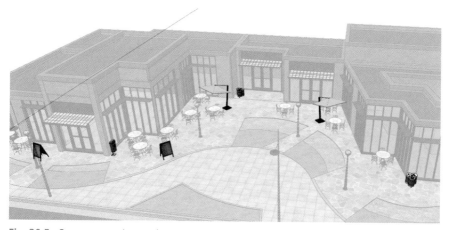

Fig. 36.5: Custom canopies, trash receptacles, and signage are placed into the site model.

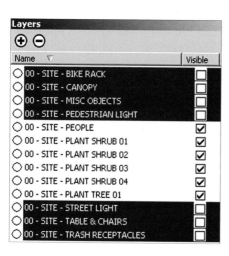

Fig. 36.6: Additional layers are added for the various vegetation components.

Fig. 36.7: Detailed trees are placed into the site.

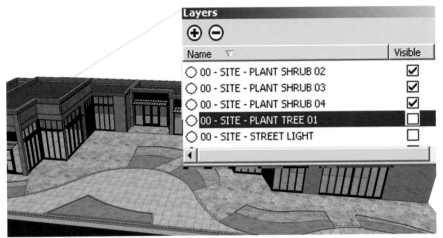

Fig. 36.8: The detailed tree layers are turned off immediately after the trees are placed into the site plan. This ensures the model maintains good computer performance and functionality.

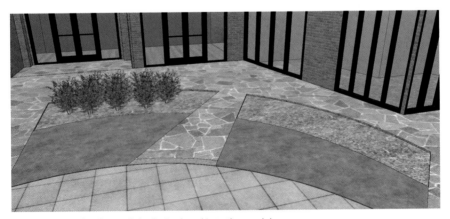

Fig. 36.9: The first layer of shrubs is placed into the model.

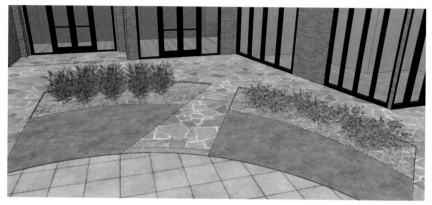

Fig. 36.10: Additional shrubs are inserted, copied, and placed into the planting areas.

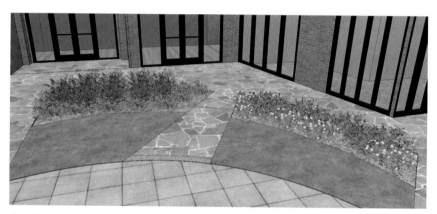

Fig. 36.11: More shrubs are inserted, copied, and placed into the planting areas.

Fig. 36.12: All the vegetation is visible and placed into the site plan.

Fig. 36.13: All of the site plan details are included, completing the detailed model.

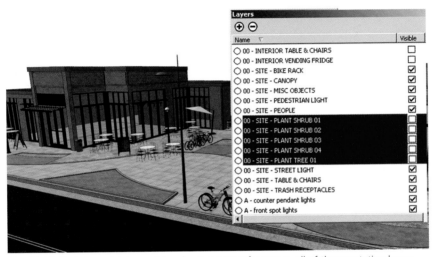

Fig. 36.14: To help maintain model and computer performance, all of the vegetation layers are turned off.

Fig. 36.15: FormFonts Fotofigure component people are added to the model site to provide scale, context, and activity.

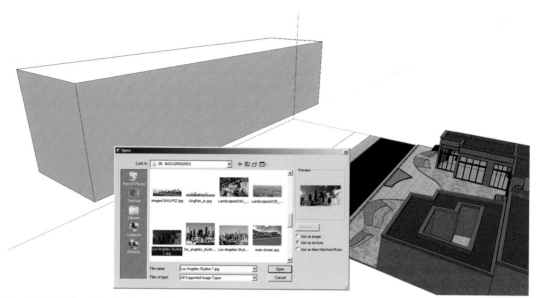

Fig. 36.16: A backdrop/background is created away from the main model, but parallel to the model building windows. Once rendered, the backdrop will provide reflections for the windows even though the backdrop itself will not be visible. In this figure, the rectangular cube to hold the backdrop image is created.

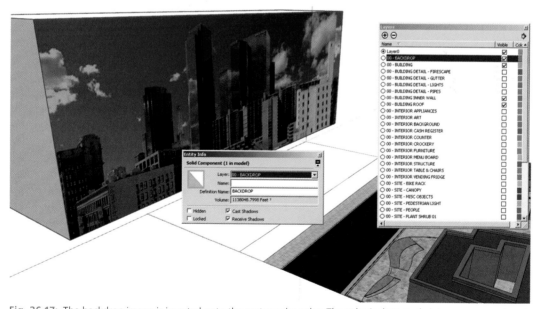

Fig. 36.17: The backdrop image is inserted onto the rectangular cube. The cube is then made into a component and placed onto the newly created 00 - Backdrop layer.

Fig. 36.18: The backdrop and site are shown in context, relative to each other. Again, the backdrop will be offscreen and not visible in any renders. However, the windows on the building will reflect the content image placed on the backdrop cube.

CHAPTER

37

Scenes

S cenes are used to save camera views, control the visibility of component objects, and maintain SketchUp performance. Several types of scenes can be created—for example, On/Off scenes that allow model detail to be toggled on and off quickly.

Before you create a scene, always check to see which scene properties are checked and unchecked in the Scene menu. Click on the newly created Scene tab to make sure the scene and its options were correctly created.

Cleaning Up the Layer List

Before you create any scenes, you need to review and clean up the layer list (Fig. 37.1, Fig. 37.2).

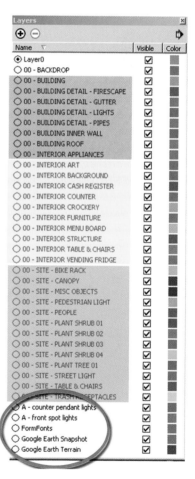

Fig. 37.1: The diagram displays the various layers present in the model: blue for architecture, yellow for interior, and green for the site. At bottom are the extra layers that were generated when components were imported into the model.

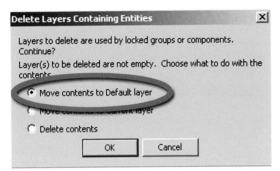

Fig. 37.2: The extra layers (ones not associated with a specific part of the model) are selected. The Delete button is clicked at the top of the layer list. The extra layers are moved to the default Layer 0, making a clean layer list.

Off/On Scenes

Fig. 37.3 shows how to create the Off scene.

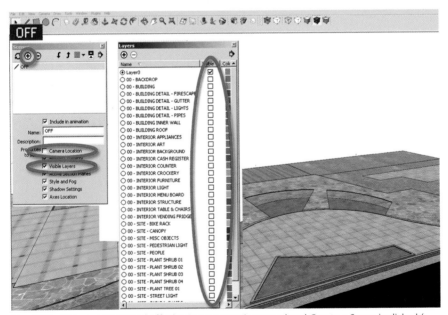

Fig. 37.3: All layers are turned off. The Scene menu is opened and Create a Scene is clicked (+ button at the top). The scene is then renamed and called OFF.

The Camera Location option in the Scene Manager is unchecked. This allows all of the component details to be turned off without reorienting the model to a specific view.

The On scene is created in Fig. 37.4.

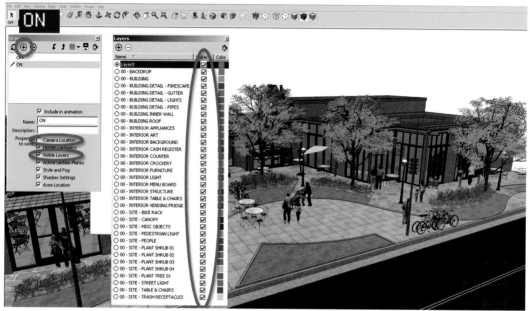

Fig. 37.4: All layers are turned on. The Camera Location button is unchecked, allowing all the layers to be made visible from any vantage or view point.

Specific Control Scenes

Specially designed control scenes are useful when you want to view specific model details and aspects. For example, you could create a building scene to highlight the architecture while turning off all other details such as the interior and site components (Fig. 37.5, Fig. 37.6, Fig. 37.7, Fig. 37.8).

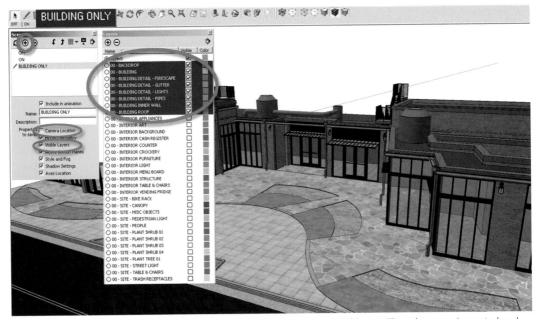

Fig. 37.5: A building scene is created by turning off all interior and site detail layers. Then the scene is created and renamed Building Only. The Camera Location option is unchecked.

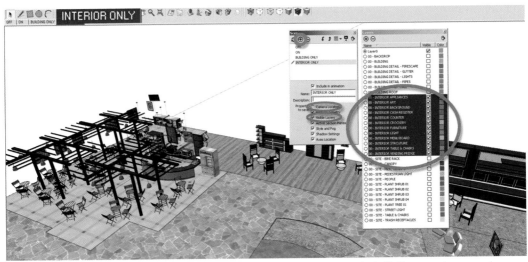

Fig. 37.6: The interior scene is created after the building and site layers are toggled off. The scene is renamed Interior Only. The Camera Location option is unchecked.

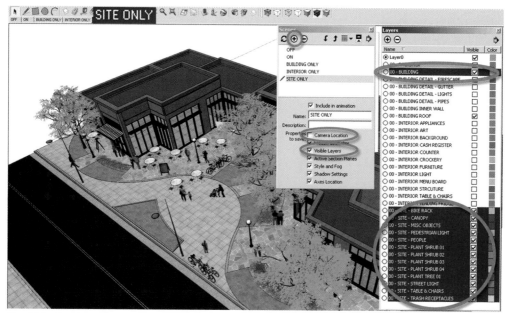

Fig. 37.7: The site-only scene is created when the interior layers are toggled off. All of the building detail is turned off except for the building shell. The building itself provides important context for the site. The scene is renamed Site Only. The Camera Location option is unchecked.

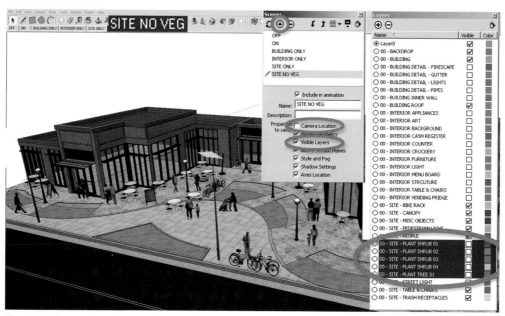

Fig. 37.8: A secondary site scene is created. This is the same as the scene generated in Fig. 37.7 except the vegetation layers are toggled off.

Camera View Scenes

You can also create specific camera view scenes. They are used to set lighting, camera, and views for the renderings. In all cases, the Camera Location option in the Scene menu must be checked. To do this, you create the first camera view scene: move the camera view of the model to the desired location, create the scene, check the Camera View Location box, and update the scene. If you don't do this, SketchUp won't remember the specific camera view (a minor bug in SketchUp). One strategy is to toggle off all the detail using Off or Building Only, position the camera, turn on the detail layers using On, and then save/create the new scene (Fig. 37.9, Fig. 37.10, Fig. 37.11, Fig. 37.12, Fig. 37.13).

Fig. 37.9: Position the camera and view to focus on the building. Turn on all relevant detail. In this case, the site layers and the interior details layers will be off. The interior context layers will be on. When the camera is in position, the scene is created and renamed Building Scene 1.

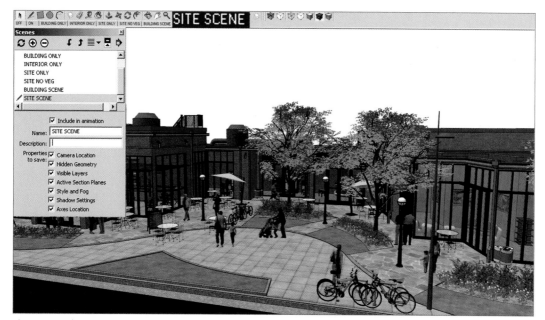

Fig. 37.10: The camera is positioned to focus on the site. The site detail, including the building and the interior context layers, is toggled on. The scene is then saved and renamed as Site Scene.

Fig. 37.11: Position the view inside the interior of the model. The site and building detail layers are toggled off, and then the scene is created and renamed Interior Scene.

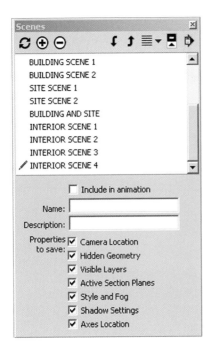

Fig. 37.12: Many additional camera view scenes can be created for both exterior and interior views.

Fig. 37.13: The camera is positioned and the various layers are toggled on and off as needed.

Setting Light with Shadows

I n this chapter, the SketchUp Shadow menu will be used to set lighting in the model (Fig. 38.1 through Fig. 38.11). The IRPs rely on the SketchUp Shadow menu to determine exterior light. The various scenes created in the previous chapter will be used to help assess and save light settings in the model.

Fig. 38.1: One of the building scenes with a saved camera view is selected from the Scene tabs (1). SketchUp will swing the camera view to the saved position. The detailed layers are toggled to visible. Next, the Building Only scene (2) is clicked, turning off all the detail but preserving the camera view. Shadows can be turned on and adjusted for best result. Turning off the detail associated with the camera views makes it easier to turn on and assess the shadows.

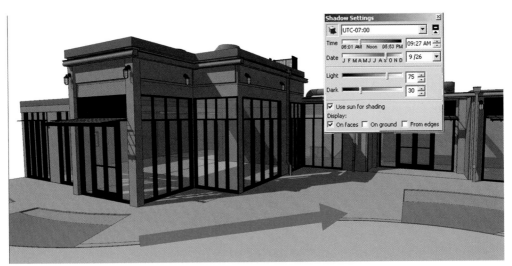

Fig. 38.2: The Shadows are turned on and adjusted. The Shadows are set to produce a good amount of contrast between the various building surfaces. Although the shadow direction is good for rendering, there is not enough contrast in the scene.

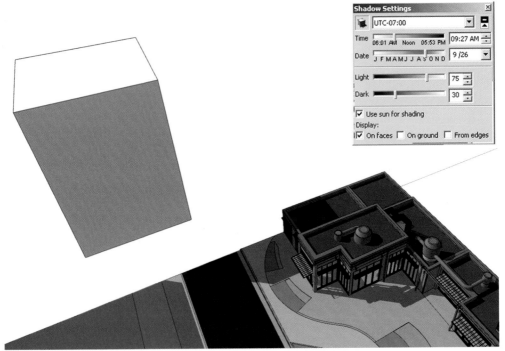

Fig. 38.3: A shadow box is created, placed on its own layer, and positioned in the model. Turning on the Shadows shows where the shadow box shade is directed into the model. The type of shadow that is cast is based on the camera view. In this instance, the shadow box is casting shadow onto a part of the building that is visible in the building scene.

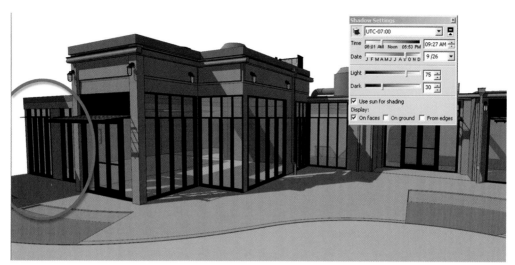

Fig. 38.4: With the shadow box in position and the Shadows turned on, the shadow cast becomes visible in the saved building scene. Keep a record of the settings in the Shadow menu. They will be used to update the detailed building scene when the layers are turned on.

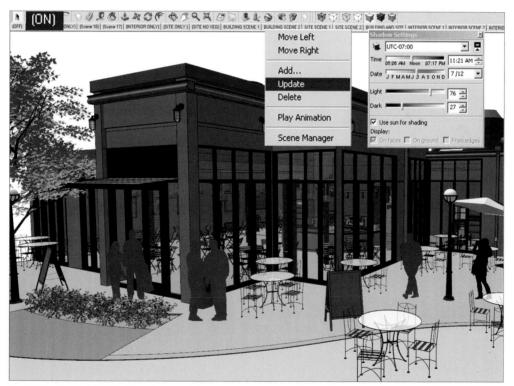

Fig. 38.5: The detailed Building Scene tab is selected, turning on all the relevant details. The Shadow menu is manually adjusted to reflect the new shadow settings as determined in the previous steps. The scene is updated by right-clicking on the Scene tab and selecting Update, saving the new Shadow settings into the scene.

Fig. 38.6: To determine lighting, the detailed Site Scene tab is selected, causing SketchUp to move to the specific camera position and turn on all the site detail (1). Then, the Site No Veg scene is selected (2), turning off all the site vegetation and making it easier to turn on and play with the Shadow settings.

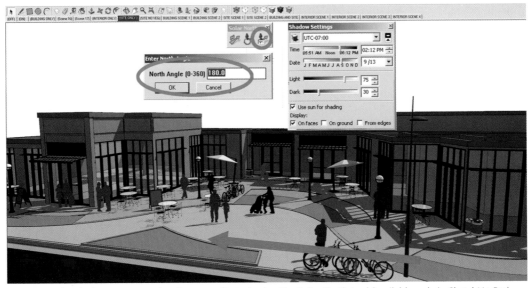

Fig. 38.7: The shadows are turned on but are adjusted using the Solar North tool (available only in SketchUp Pro). The sun angle is adjusted 180 degrees to optimize the light direction for the scene. (Note the specific Shadow settings in the Shadow menu. They will be needed to manually adjust the shadows and update the site scene.)

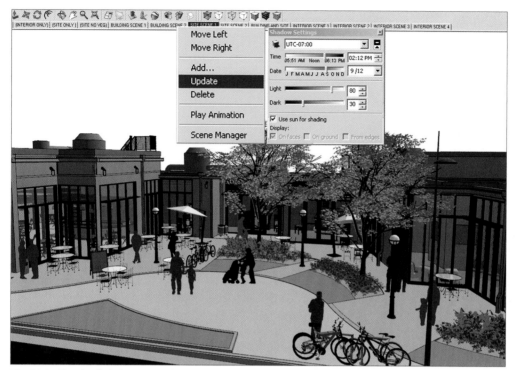

Fig. 38.8: The detailed Site Scene tab is selected again. Next, the Shadow Setting sliders and Solar North values are manually adjusted to match the shadows used in the previous scene. The scene is then updated to reflect the changes.

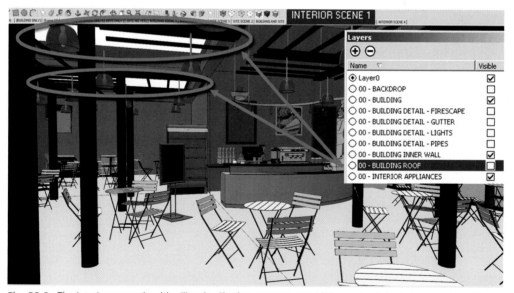

Fig. 38.9: The interior scene should utilize the Shadow menu to establish exterior light. Exterior Light settings are used in the draft rendering process to help assess the textures prior to adding interior simulated lighting. The building roof layer is turned off to allow SketchUp sunlight into the scene.

Fig. 38.10: The Shadows are turned on in the scene. The Shadow settings will be used to update the scene.

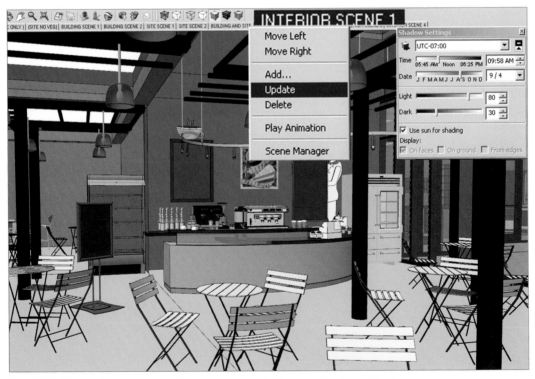

Fig. 38.11: The Shadows are turned off to manually update the scene Shadow settings.

The model exterior is now ready to be rendered. In this example (Fig. 35.1 through Fig. 39.35), Shaderlight is used for the rendering process. The texture and lighting values are set in Shaderlight. The various options and settings are reviewed in Part 5 and Part 6.

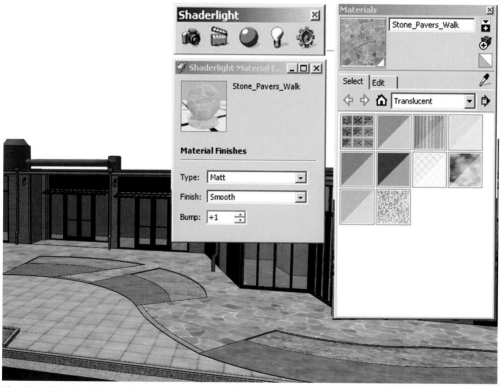

Fig. 39.1: The Shaderlight Material menu is opened from the Shaderlight main menu. The Shaderlight Material menu will be used to provide rendering values to the model textures. The SketchUp Paint Bucket is opened, and the SketchUp Paint Bucket Eye Dropper is used to select the materials in the model.

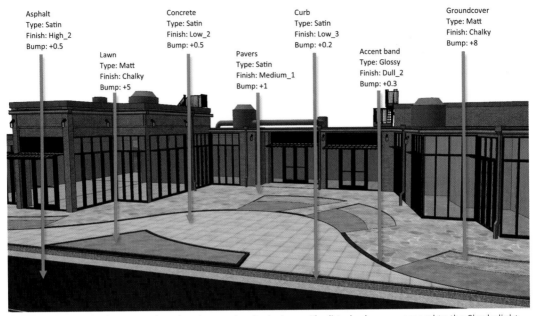

Asphalt
Type: Satin
Finish: High_2
Bump: +0.5

Lawn
Type: Matt
Finish: Chalky
Bump: +5

Concrete
Type: Satin
Finish: Low_2
Bump: +0.5

Pavers
Type: Satin
Finish: Medium_1
Bump: +1

Curb
Type: Satin
Finish: Low_3
Bump: +0.2

Accent band
Type: Glossy
Finish: Dull_2
Bump: +0.3

Groundcover
Type: Matt
Finish: Chalky
Bump: +8

Fig. 39.2: Material values are assigned to the exterior site textures. The listed values correspond to the Shaderlight Material menu. Each texture is selected and the values are applied.

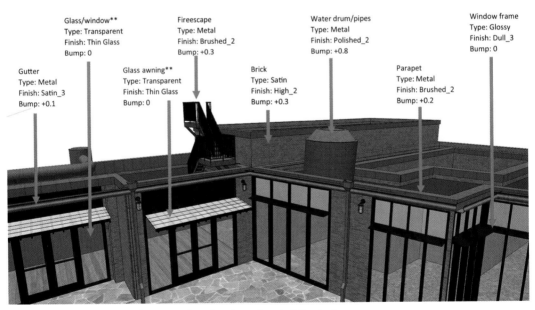

Glass/window**
Type: Transparent
Finish: Thin Glass
Bump: 0

Fireescape
Type: Metal
Finish: Brushed_2
Bump: +0.3

Water drum/pipes
Type: Metal
Finish: Polished_2
Bump: +0.8

Window frame
Type: Glossy
Finish: Dull_3
Bump: 0

Gutter
Type: Metal
Finish: Satin_3
Bump: +0.1

Glass awning**
Type: Transparent
Finish: Thin Glass
Bump: 0

Brick
Type: Satin
Finish: High_2
Bump: +0.3

Parapet
Type: Metal
Finish: Brushed_2
Bump: +0.2

Fig. 39.3: The Shaderlight values are assigned to the various building textures.

Fig. 39.4: In the SketchUp Paint Bucket, the glass texture's L values for the awning and window glass need to be adjusted.

Bikes tires
Type: Matt
Finish: Rough
Bump: 0

Bikes frames
Type: Shiny
Finish: Polished_1
Bump: 0

Bikes rims
Type: Metal
Finish: Chrome
Bump: 0

Bikes handle
Type: Satin
Finish: Medium_1
Bump: 0

Bikes rack
Type: Metal
Finish: Satin_3
Bump: 0

Fig. 39.5: The Shaderlight values are assigned to the bikes and bike racks in the model.

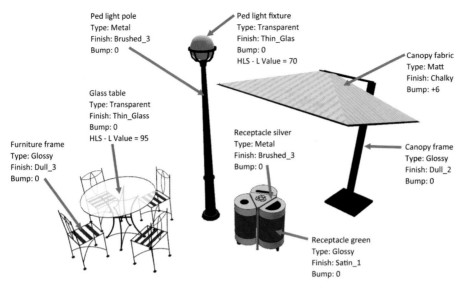

Ped light pole
Type: Metal
Finish: Brushed_3
Bump: 0

Ped light fixture
Type: Transparent
Finish: Thin_Glas
Bump: 0
HLS - L Value = 70

Canopy fabric
Type: Matt
Finish: Chalky
Bump: +6

Glass table
Type: Transparent
Finish: Thin_Glass
Bump: 0
HLS - L Value = 95

Receptacle silver
Type: Metal
Finish: Brushed_3
Bump: 0

Canopy frame
Type: Glossy
Finish: Dull_2
Bump: 0

Furniture frame
Type: Glossy
Finish: Dull_3
Bump: 0

Receptacle green
Type: Glossy
Finish: Satin_1
Bump: 0

Fig. 39.6: The Shaderlight values are assigned to the materials composing the table and chairs, pedestrian light, custom canopy, and trash receptacle.

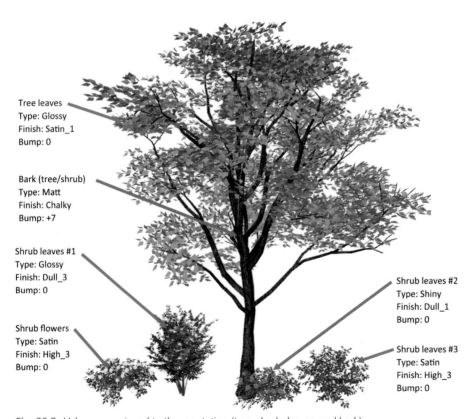

Tree leaves
Type: Glossy
Finish: Satin_1
Bump: 0

Bark (tree/shrub)
Type: Matt
Finish: Chalky
Bump: +7

Shrub leaves #1
Type: Glossy
Finish: Dull_3
Bump: 0

Shrub leaves #2
Type: Shiny
Finish: Dull_1
Bump: 0

Shrub flowers
Type: Satin
Finish: High_3
Bump: 0

Shrub leaves #3
Type: Satin
Finish: High_3
Bump: 0

Fig. 39.7: Values are assigned to the vegetation (tree, shrub, leaves, and bark).

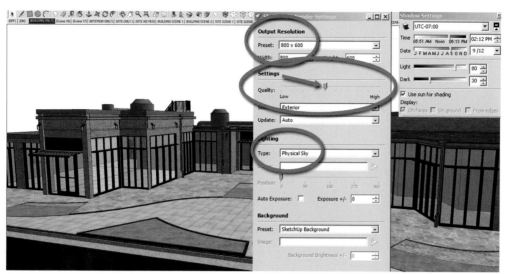

Fig. 39.8: The initial draft settings are shown. The camera view for the scene is selected but the various details are turned off. No interior or detailed site layers are on. The Output resolution is set to a low value and Shaderlight Quality is placed at 50 percent. Physical Sky is selected from the Lighting menu, which tells Shaderlight to reference the SketchUp Shadow menu for light.

Fig. 39.9: The first draft render is completed, but some changes need to be made. The windows do not reflect correctly. The Shaderlight setting (Transparent/Thin Reflective) was not correctly applied to the windows (1). The water tower and pipes are too reflective. They are adjusted by lowering the amount of reflection (2). The paving textures are too bright and colorful. The textures are selected and the Paint Bucket menu is used to adjust the hue, desaturating the texture to be grayer (3).

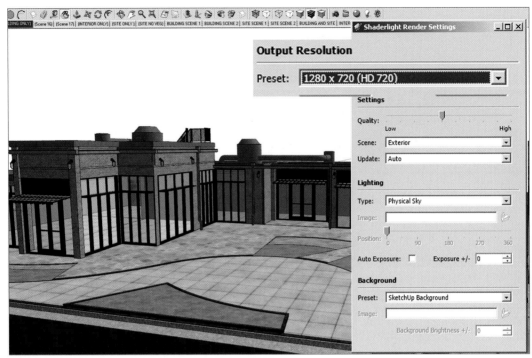

Fig. 39.10: The output resolution is increased to 1280 × 720. This resolution will be used for the remainder of the drafts leading to the final. The second draft render is ready to be run.

Fig. 39.11: The second render is completed. The base textures look fine. The image is ready to move to the next steps and run more detailed renderings.

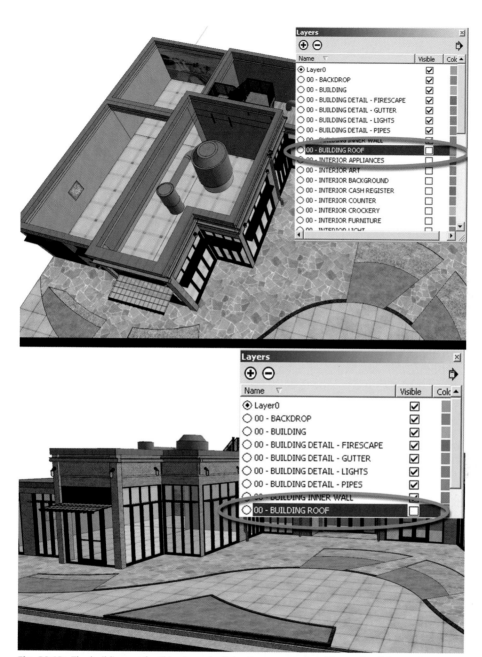

Fig. 39.12: The building roof will be turned off for the next renders. The angle of the rendering will not show that the roof is off. Turning the roof off will allow light to stream into the building, lighting up the interior and providing greater context and detail for the rendering. The top image shows the building roof off. The roof layer will have to be turned off when the specific scene tab is selected, and the scene needs to be updated to remember the setting.

Fig. 39.13: Using the Shaderlight Background option, an image background will be inserted to render with the scene.

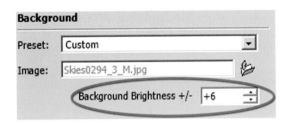

Fig. 39.14: The Background Brightness needs to be set so the selected background image renders with the correct exposure. This setting affects only the background image inserted into the rendering in the previous step.

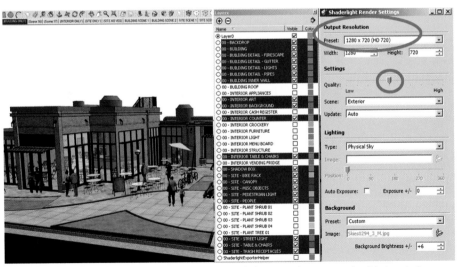

Fig. 39.15: The site details except vegetation are toggled on. Interior context detail is toggled on as well. The render settings for resolution and quality are unchanged from the previous draft.

Fig. 39.16: The third draft is complete. The inserted sky background did not render well, looks out of place, and needs to be adjusted (1). The paving texture doesn't look right, and the Bump settings need to be adjusted (2). The shadows, which look good in the previous render, do not work well in this version and need to be adjusted (3). The asphalt texture looks flat and unrealistic (4).

Fig. 39.17: The background image inserted in Fig. 39.13 is replaced with a new image.

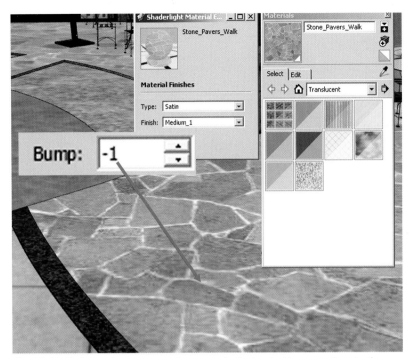

Fig. 39.18: To invert the texture so the pavers look elevated in comparison to the adjacent joints when rendered, the Bump value for the stone pavers is reversed to –1 (from +1).

Fig. 39.19: The shadows are adjusted in the opposite direction, making the contrast more balanced.

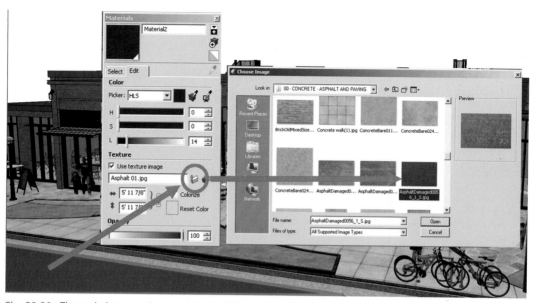

Fig. 39.20: The asphalt texture is swapped out with a new version that is irregular in character.

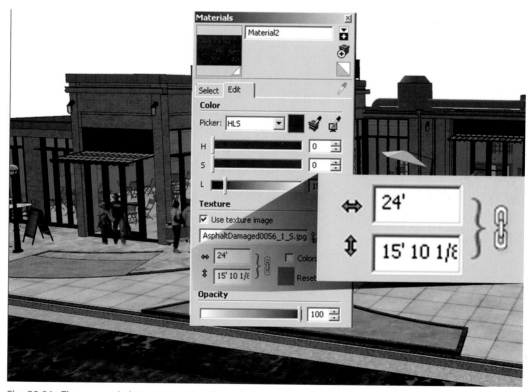

Fig. 39.21: The new asphalt texture needs to be scaled upward.

Fig. 39.22: The fourth draft render is complete. The asphalt texture has a notable seam that needs to be adjusted (1). There is too much contrast from the building shadows (2).

Fig. 39.23: The asphalt texture is selected. The right-click Texture tool will be used to move and scale it so the seam does not appear visible in the scene.

Fig. 39.24: The asphalt texture is scaled slightly upward, and the seam is moved out of the camera view.

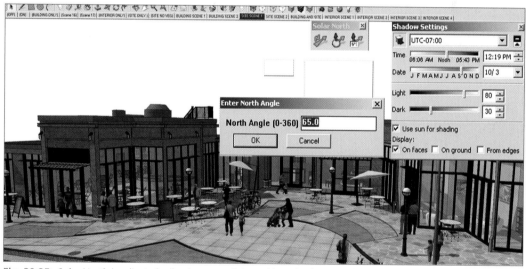

Fig. 39.25: Solar North is adjusted, allowing more light and less shadow into the scene. The building now has good contrast between surfaces.

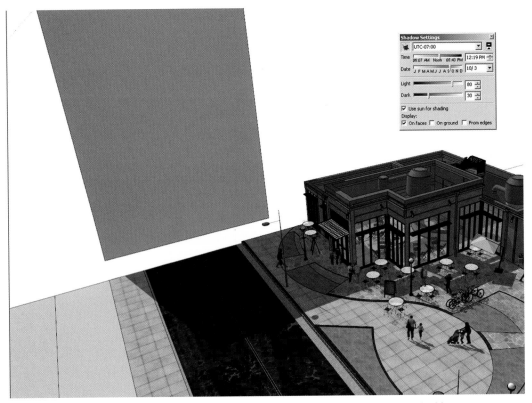

Fig. 39.26: The shadow box is relocated to provide more contrast into the site and onto the building.

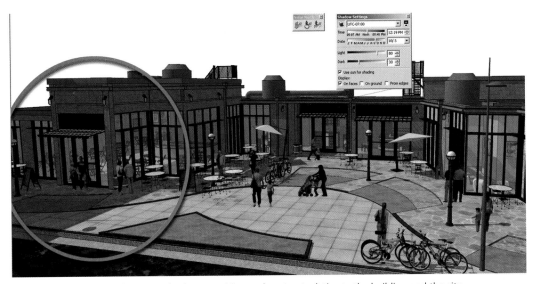

Fig. 39.27: The shadow box casts shade to provide good contrast relative to the building and the site.

Part 8: Anatomy of a Rendering

Fig. 39.28: Because they are distracting, some people components are removed from the scene. Additional table and chairs are copied and placed around the site.

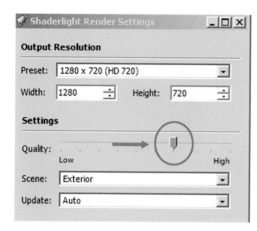

Fig. 39.29: With everything in place, the Quality setting is increased for the next render. The rendering is ready to be taken to the next level.

Fig. 39.30: The fifth draft rendering is completed. The lighting, textures, and sky background look finished.

Fig. 39.31: The vegetation layers are turned on for the final rendering.

Fig. 39.32: The Resolution is increased to final (1920 x 1080) and the Quality set to maximum.

Fig. 39.33: The final render is generated.

Fig. 39.34: Additional scenes can be rendered to completion.

Fig. 39.35: The final scene

The Iterative Rendering Process for Interior Scenes

The model interior will be rendered next (Fig. 40.1 through Fig. 40.27). The example uses Shaderlight for rendering and to set the texture and lighting values. Draft renders will be run using exterior lighting to assess texture values. Then, simulated point lights will be added and rendered.

The Shaderlight Material Editor and SketchUp Paint Bucket are used to select and apply values to texture in the model. The Shaderlight Lighting menu will be used to insert point lights into lighting components for rendering.

The site and building detail layers are turned off for all the interior renderings. This will speed up the rendering process because Shaderlight won't need to process the component details on those layers (they are not going to be visible).

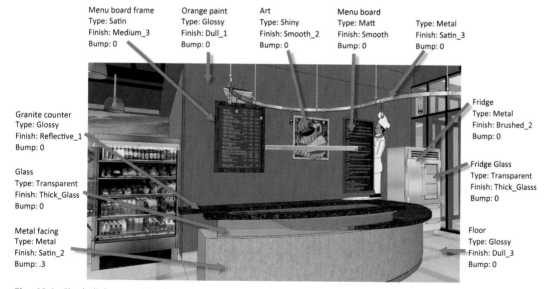

Menu board frame
Type: Satin
Finish: Medium_3
Bump: 0

Orange paint
Type: Glossy
Finish: Dull_1
Bump: 0

Art
Type: Shiny
Finish: Smooth_2
Bump: 0

Menu board
Type: Matt
Finish: Smooth
Bump: 0

Type: Metal
Finish: Satin_3
Bump: 0

Fridge
Type: Metal
Finish: Brushed_2
Bump: 0

Granite counter
Type: Glossy
Finish: Reflective_1
Bump: 0

Glass
Type: Transparent
Finish: Thick_Glass
Bump: 0

Fridge Glass
Type: Transparent
Finish: Thick_Glasss
Bump: 0

Metal facing
Type: Metal
Finish: Satin_2
Bump: .3

Floor
Type: Glossy
Finish: Dull_3
Bump: 0

Fig. 40.1: Shaderlight material values are applied to the cafe bar's menu boards, walls, and counter areas.

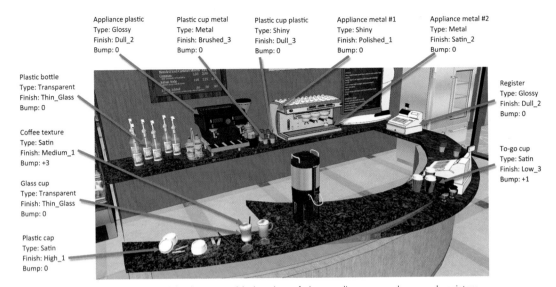

Appliance plastic
Type: Glossy
Finish: Dull_2
Bump: 0

Plastic cup metal
Type: Metal
Finish: Brushed_3
Bump: 0

Plastic cup plastic
Type: Shiny
Finish: Dull_3
Bump: 0

Appliance metal #1
Type: Shiny
Finish: Polished_1
Bump: 0

Appliance metal #2
Type: Metal
Finish: Satin_2
Bump: 0

Plastic bottle
Type: Transparent
Finish: Thin_Glass
Bump: 0

Register
Type: Glossy
Finish: Dull_2
Bump: 0

Coffee texture
Type: Satin
Finish: Medium_1
Bump: +3

To-go cup
Type: Satin
Finish: Low_3
Bump: +1

Glass cup
Type: Transparent
Finish: Thin_Glass
Bump: 0

Plastic cap
Type: Satin
Finish: High_1
Bump: 0

Fig. 40.2: The Shaderlight material values are added to the cafe bar appliances, crockery, and registers.

Green paint
Type: Satin
Finish: Medium-2
Bump: 0

Fixture glass
Type: Thin
Finish: Transparent
Bump: 0
HLS - L value = 50

Fixture metal
Type: Metal
Finish: Polished_3
Bump: 0

Post
Type: Glossy
Finish: Dull_1
Bump: 0

Mural
Type: Satin
Finish: Medium_3
Bump: 0

Chair wood
Type: Glossy
Finish: Dull_2
Bump: 0

Menu board
Type: Matt
Finish: Smooth
Bump: 0

Chair metal
Type: Metal
Finish: Polished_2
Bump: 0

Menu board metal
Type: Metal
Finish: Satin_1
Bump: 0

Fig. 40.3: The values are applied to the rest of the coffee shop interior, including the table and chairs, lights, and structure.

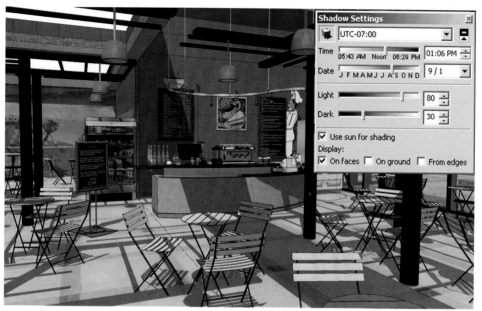

Fig. 40.4: The roof layer is turned off so that exterior lighting can be cast into the scene. The SketchUp Shadow menu is set, and the first draft is ready to be run.

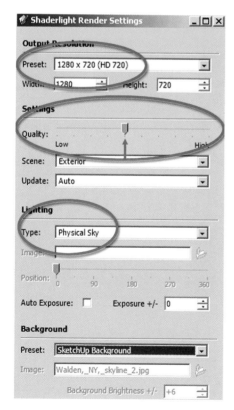

Fig. 40.5: The Shaderlight Render settings are displayed. These settings are identical to the values set for the second exterior render draft.

Fig. 40.6: The first draft render is complete. The flooring color needs to be adjusted for greater contrast relative to the rest of the model. Also, the flooring does not have enough reflection value (1). The table-and-chair texture is too light, making the tables and chairs hard to see (2). The counter facade could use some more reflection (value) (3).

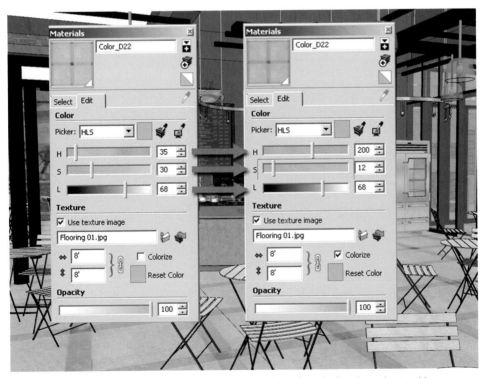

Fig. 40.7: The SketchUp Paint Bucket HLS settings are used to adjust the flooring color to a blue-gray.

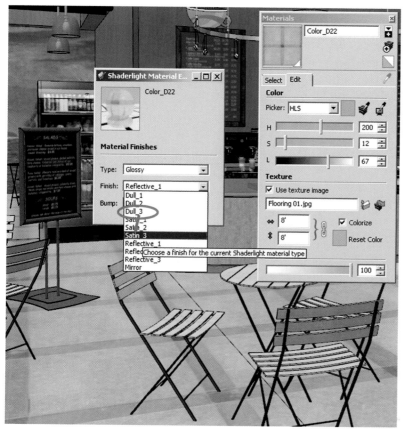

Fig. 40.8: The Shaderlight Material Editor is used to adjust the flooring from a Dull to a higher Satin reflection.

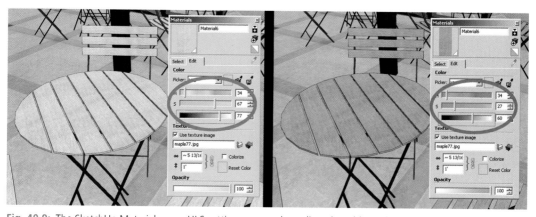

Fig. 40.9: The SketchUp Material menu HLS settings are used to adjust the table-and-chair texture to appear darker.

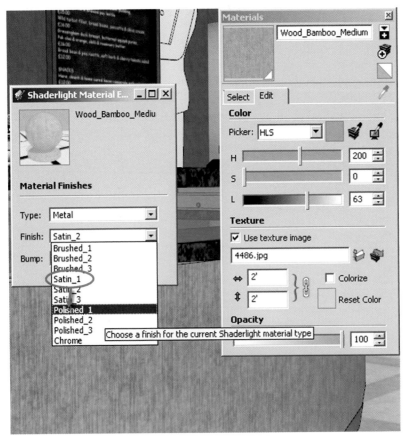

Fig. 40.10: The counter-facade render value is adjusted to be more reflective.

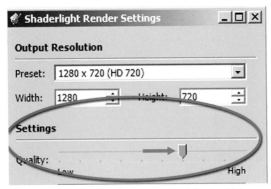

Fig. 40.11: The texture changes were minimal, which allowed the Quality setting to be increased for the next render.

Fig. 40.12: The second draft render is complete. The textures need no further adjustment. The model is ready for simulated lighting.

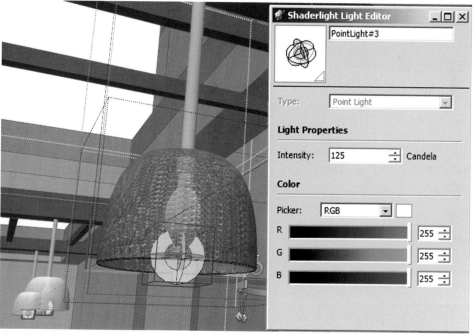

Fig. 40.13: The Shaderlight Simulated Lighting menu is opened. A point light is selected and inserted into the lighting component. The point light intensity and color are left at their default settings.

Fig. 40.14: Because the point light was inserted into the light fixture component, all copies of the component now have a point light. This is an effective way to quickly populate a model with simulated lighting.

Fig. 40.15: All detail interior (and exterior) detail layers are turned off. Only the base interior model will be visible for the first simulated light draft render.

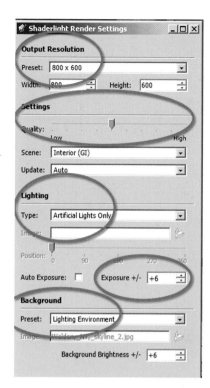

Fig. 40.16: The Shaderlight Render settings are adjusted for simulated lighting. The resolution is lowered to 800 × 600 and quality is at 50 percent. Interior (GI) is selected for scene, Artificial Lights Only is selected under Lighting, and Exposure is set to +6. The Background is set to Lighting Environment. These settings allow the point lights to render the scene.

Fig. 40.17: The first simulated light draft render is complete. Although the simulated lights are in the fixtures, the fixtures themselves did not glow. This makes the source of light ambiguous and unrealistic.

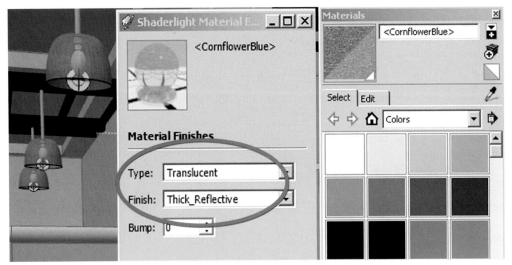

Fig. 40.18: The glass light fixtures are selected and given a Translucent/Thin Reflective texture value. The light sources inside the fixture will simulate real light sources by causing light to reflect off the fixture interior.

Fig. 40.19: The second simulated lighting draft is run. The fixtures now glow, providing a visible light source.

Fig. 40.20: The third simulated light draft is run. The detail interior layers were turned on and the resolution was increased to 1280 × 720.

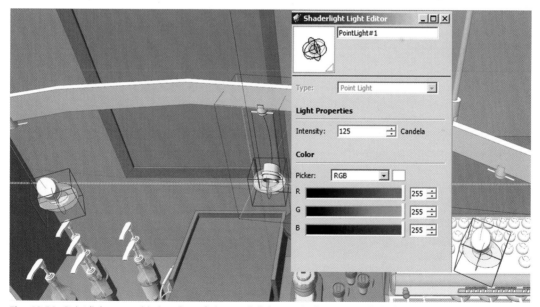

Fig. 40.21: Point lights are added to the cafe bar track lights. As in the previous light fixtures, these are components. Inserting a point light into one fixture will update all like versions with a point light.

Fig. 40.22: The fourth draft render is complete.

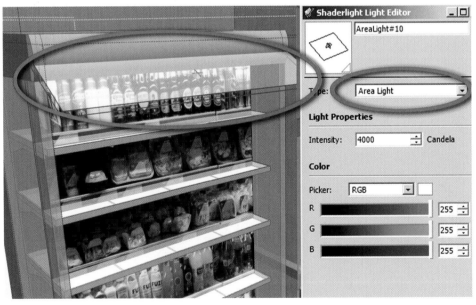

Fig. 40.23: An area light is added to the product fridge to the left of the counter.

Fig. 40.24: A draft render of the fridge is run. The light is too bright and over-exposes the texture image.

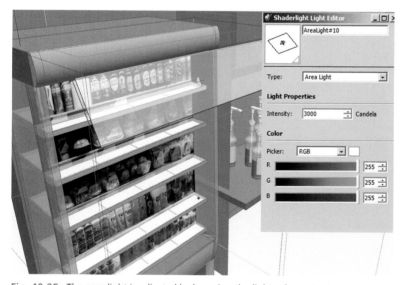

Fig. 40.25: The area light is adjusted by lowering the light value output.

Fig. 40.26: The final interior render is run.

Fig. 40.27: Additional interior scenes are generated.

Fig. 40.28: The final scene

Postproduction of Exterior Scene

The last step is to complete some quick postproduction to one of the exterior renderings. The quick edits will include cropping the image to create better focus, add realistic lawn to the foreground, fix blemishes in textures, and adjust the overall hue and cast of the image.

Fig 41.1: The Photoshop Crop tool is used to create a better proportioned image by cutting out some of the sky. This allows for a better focus on the relevant content of the rendering, namely the building and foreground.

Fig 41.2: An image of lawn in perspective is inserted into the rendering Photoshop file. The lawn areas in the image are masked. The masks (dashed lines) are aligned with the lawn areas of the image. The outlined lawn areas in the image will be cut out and placed into the render.

Fig41.3: The cut out lawn as seen in the context of the render. The remainder of the original lawn image is deleted.

Fig 41.4: The cut out lawn (on its own layer) is color adjusted using the Hue/Saturation menu.

Fig 41.5: The asphalt texture at the bottom of the image is lightened and toned down to bring it in line with the overall lighting and mood of the image.

Fig 41.6: The overall levels of the image are adjusted, adding a bit more haze and grey.

Fig 41.7: Final render with postproduction complete

Index